Talking Back
to Shakespeare

Talking Back
to Shakespeare

Martha Tuck Rozett

DELAWARE

Newark: University of Delaware Press
London and Toronto: Associated University Presses

Associated University Presses
440 Forsgate Drive
Cranbury, NJ 08512

Associated University Presses
25 Sicilian Avenue
London WC1A 2QH, England

Associated University Presses
P.O.Box 338, Port Credit
Mississauga, Ontario
Canada L5G 4L8

The paper used in this publication meets the requirements
of the American National Standard for Permanence of Paper
for Printed Library Materials Z39.48–1984.

Library of Congress Cataloging-in-Publication Data

Rozett, Martha Tuck, 1946-
    Talking back to Shakespeare / Martha Tuck Rozett.
        p.   cm.
    Includes bibliographical references and index.
    IBSN 0-87413-529-X (alk. paper)
    1. Shakespeare, William, 1564–1616—Criticism and interpretation—
History.   2. Shakespeare, William, 1564–1616—Adaptations—History
and criticism.   3 . Shakespeare, William, 1564–1616—Study and
teaching (Higher)   4 . English drama—Adaptations—History and
criticism.   5. Reader-response criticism.   I . Title
PR2965.R69   1994
822.3'3—dc 20   93-45821
                                                                              CIP

PRINTED IN THE UNITED STATES OF AMERICA

For John, Josh, and Alex,
who also talk back

Contents

Acknowledgments

Parts of Chapter 1 originally appeared as "Holding Mirrors Up to Nature," in *Shakespeare Quarterly* 41 (Summer, 1990) and as "Talking Back to Shakespeare: Student Reader Responses to *Othello*," in *Othello: New Perspectives*, edited by Virginia Vaughan and Kent Cartwright (Fairleigh Dickinson University Press, 1991). Part of Chapter 3 appeared as "Gertrude's Ghost Tells Her Story" in *Cross Cultural Performances: More Women's Re-visions of Shakespeare*, edited by Marianne Novy (University of Illinois Press, 1993), and a short excerpt from Chapter 2 appeared in "Getting to Know a Play Five Ways," in *Teaching Shakespeare Today*, edited by James E. Davis and Ronald E. Salamone (NCTE, 1992). I would like to thank Virginia Vaughan, Kent Cartwright, Marianne Novy and Edward Pechter for generously reading and commenting on parts or all of the manuscript; also, my brother Jonathan Tuck and my good friend Judith Barlow for their suggestions, editing, and moral support. Thanks are also due to the many students who have contributed to this project over the years, and especially to the students in the 1987 and 1988 graduate seminars who introduced me to Shakespeare re-visions I had not yet discovered. In the early stages of this project, two of my colleagues, Kathleen Thornton and Elizabeth Wilson, kindly allowed me to use their students' responses to *Othello* and *Hamlet*, and Albert Asermely invited me to serve as literary consultant for his productions of *Twelfth Night* and *Measure for Measure*. I am also grateful to the Shakespeare Association of America for giving me the opportunity to present earlier versions of parts of Chapters 1 and 5 at the 1988, 1992, and 1993 meetings, and to the Folger Library, where I stumbled upon *Gertrude of Denmark* on a Saturday in 1988. Finally, I wish to thank Carey Cummings for technical assistance of all kinds, and my husband John Rozett, for many long hours at the computer, and much more.

Introduction

Talking Back to Shakespeare grows out of my experiences as a teacher. In the mid–1980s, after a dozen years of college teaching, I became interested in the fact that my students were taking Shakespeare's comic characters very seriously; they were trying to make sense of what they read and saw, and they did this by criticizing, offering advice, and "talking back" to the characters and the author. The theoretical and pedagogical developments in English studies since the mid-1980s have enabled me to see these student readings as part of a larger cultural phenomenon. By questioning the assumption that a published text is finished or "stable," postmodernism invites a re-visioning of canonical texts that acknowledges their status as culturally determined verbal constructs capable of acquiring new meanings and, indeed, new forms. Viewed from this perspective, my students belong to a long and lively tradition of editors, bowdlerizers, stage directors, parodists, playwrights, libretticists, novelists, and film makers, all of whom are appropriating Shakespeare and are influenced, whether they realize it or not, by prior appropriations and transformations of what we call Shakespeare.

I also came to this study via an interest in Shakespeare's use of his sources. Shakespeare's transformations of his sources belong to an ongoing process of reworking old stories, and to treat his versions as the "end" of that process is at best an arbitrary imposition of closure, particularly in this era of canon revision. In 1987 I started teaching Shakespeare to graduate students by juxtaposing the plays with their sources and transformations. We read Plautus's *Menaechmi* and *The*

Comedy of Errors, Belleforest and *Hamlet* and Tom Stoppard's *Rosen-crantz and Guildenstern Are Dead*; we juxtaposed *King Lear* with Kuro-sawa's magnificent film *Ran.* This graduate course led to another one, called Writing and Revision. Meanwhile, I had discovered Lillie Buf-fum Chase Wyman's *Gertrude of Denmark: An Interpretive Romance* in the Folger Library and had started actively seeking out other Shake-speare transformations.

As the book evolved, so did my undergraduate teaching. In some classes, I invited students to come to terms with a play by writing a transformation; in others, I assigned a contemporary transformation, Arnold Wesker's *The Merchant,* for them to respond to. Students also kept reading journals in which they described their initial responses, or first readings. I returned to certain plays again and again: *Twelfth Night, The Merchant of Venice, Hamlet, Measure for Measure, Macbeth, Othello, All's Well That Ends Well, The Tempest.* The student-generated "talking back" in this book comes out of those undergraduate classes. It constitutes the dominant voice in Chapter 1, and returns in Chapters 2 and 5, and briefly in Chapter 3, mostly in discussions of women char-acters. The responses I discuss are not always the most sophisticated or articulate ones I have received from the many fine students who have passed through my classes. Rather, I deliberately chose to dwell on those moments when student readers debated with Shakespeare rather than celebrated or interpreted him, when they questioned what they saw as the plays' assumptions and offered alternative possibilities. To dis-miss student comments as "too jejune to be significant" as a reader of an earlier draft of this book suggested to me, says something, I believe, about the great distance between our roles as teachers and as scholars in the current academic climate. I offer these student 'texts' as legiti-mate contributions to the plays' aggregate reception, not as a set of con-clusions about student attitudes or behavior, but as a series of impres-sions, or snapshots, gathered over several years.

During these years, Shakespeare Studies has been changing in sig-nificant ways, as more and more attention is being given to perfor-mance-as-interpretation, the instability of the Shakespeare text, and the cultural histories of the plays. These histories embrace the adapta-tions, performances, appropriations, and allusions that constitute the ongoing life of a literary artifact. By 1991, R. S. White's survey of "The Year's Contributions to Shakespeare Studies" in *Shakespeare Sur-vey* 43 was beginning with a section entitled "Intertextuality and Recep-tion"; White notes that "studies of sources and influences, allusions and imitations are back with us, reshaped as intertextuality and recep-tion." He goes on to say that the ways in which Shakespeare has been received and used are becoming as much subjects for scrutiny as the texts themselves.[1] Such matters tell us as much about the preoccupations and historical limitations of the borrower as about the apparently infinite potential of the Shakespearean text for being reshaped and reinterpreted from generation to generation. Volume 45 of *Shakespeare Survey*, in preparation as White's survey went to press, contains seven essays about aspects of the afterlife of *Hamlet* in production, adaptation and influence.

As I continued to teach and write about Shakespeare, I began to see a kinship, a kind of temperamental and critical affinity, between the talking back that occurred in the classroom and the published transformations I was reading. When writers transform Shakespeare's plays, they challenge the author's perceived intent, or perhaps more precisely, the cultural and critical baggage the text has acquired over time. They talk back to the cultural authority that has been invested in the plays, even as they appropriate that cultural authority as the originating premise for a new imaginative construct. Out of this challenge comes a new text, recognizably descended from the parent text (which is not a text exactly; rather, it is a collection of texts, performances, and associations), but like an assertive adolescent, visibly and volubly talking back to the parent in iconclastic, outrageous, yet intensely serious ways. Much of this talking back comes from marginalized groups: women, like Lillie Wyman and the nineteenth-century women critics discussed in Chapter 3; Jewish writers, like Arnold Wesker, Ludwig Lewisohn, and others in Chapter 2; or the oppositional voices of the 1960s in Chapter 5, such as Charles Marowitz or Aimé Césaire, who are rebelling against what they perceive as an oppressive dominant culture. One of the ironies of cultural change is that rebellions of this kind can acquire canonical status in their own right; the best known Shakespeare transformation of the sixties, *Rosencrantz and Guildenstern Are Dead*, exemplifies this process. The writers I have chosen to include challenge the Shakespeare "establishment" in a variety of ways. For example, Percy MacKaye, whom I have paired with Wyman in Chapter 3, is a little-known theatrical idealist whose attempts to reform the American theatre into a truly populist undertaking led him to create a virtually unactable tetralogy, one that talks back both to the commercial business of play production and to a critical tradition that privileges Hamlet as a tragic character.

This book is not a survey of Shakespeare appropriations; rather, it explores a diverse collection of texts that interact with and transform Shakespeare in the ways I have been describing; many are plays, some are novels, and some are texts that resist categorization by genre, such as Mary Cowden Clarke's nineteenth-century portrait-narratives in *The Girlhood of Shakespeare's Heroines*. Cowden Clarke's fictions are examples of diachronous transformations, supplements to the Shakespeare-an text, in the form of prequels (a term invented by Hollywood); other writers I include have invented sequels that extend the characters' lives beyond Shakespeare's imposed closures into imagined futures. Both forms challenge the logic of Shakespeare's beginnings and endings: sequels attempt closure in much the same way that prequels insist on origins, although these new endings often contest or reject convention-al sixteenth- and seventeenth-century notions about closure. Other appropriations set out to retell or revise one of Shakespeare's plays, not with the Restoration's naive and self-regarding intent to improve on Shakespeare's rough genius, but as an ideologically inspired engage-ment with the text's narrative assumptions, implicit values, and accu-mulated critical reputation. In the introduction to *The Marowitz Shake-speare*, Charles Marowitz proposes a biological metaphor to justify his collage technique, which involves a radical restructuring of Shake-speare's phrases and speeches: "Just as the human organism is under-stood differently when its metabolism is scrutinized in isolation, so cer-tain 'classical' works are understood differently when their components are re-formed." Marowitz continues, "A collage version of a known play assumes a pre-knowledge of the original and although it tends to cover familiar ground (refers to characters, alludes to situations, comments on themes), it is more concerned with the application of all these things in order to foster another concept." This concept, he explains, "must have a purpose as coherent and provable as any conventional work of art."[2] The concepts and purposes that motivate transformations are frequent-ly closer to the surface than they are in other "conventional" works of art. Transformations are, after all, dialogues with another work, dia-logues driven by an impulse to say something to and about the preexist-ing text and its complex social or reception history. Marowitz's collages, Ionesco's *Macbett*, and many of the other transformations I discuss are, in varying ways, acts of rebellion against texts that have been elevated above all others in the conservative literary canon. Talking back to *Hamlet* or *Macbeth*, talking back through *Hamlet* or *Macbeth*, thus become ways of turning the establishment's most sacred cultural icons against themselves.

Still other transformations, some diachronous, some synchronous, some a mixture, starting before Shakespeare's play begins and ending after it ends, arise from the irresistible impulse to fill in gaps. The pur-pose of these authors is less political than psychological, the conse-quence of a set of expectations about characters and their prior and inner lives that did not exist when the plays were originally created. The novelist's tendency to surround the action with visual and histori-cal details, the introspective insights and musings of one or more characters, and the narrator's commentary, are variously evident in *The Girlhood of Shakespeare's Heroines*, Wyman's *Gertrude of Denmark*, Lewisohn's *The Last Days of Shylock*, and most recently, Jane Smiley's *A Thousand Acres*.

Transformations are thus a form of interpretation, but interpretation of a particular kind; their main objective is not so much to explain or elucidate as it is to stretch the texts in new directions, testing the resiliency of their characters and structures, and trying out alternative scenarios. Such scenarios might entail entirely different endings, or radical shifts in perspective so that a character the audience once viewed from a detached and unsympathetic distance moves to the foreground and acquires an expanded inner life that overflows the play's original boundaries. Writers who appropriate Shakespeare's characters may frequently feel, as Alden and Virginia Vaughan observe in their cultural history of Caliban, that a play is "not finished; its characters live on, their problems unresolved."[3] So, for example, Gabriel Josipovici's short story "A Changeable Report" talks back to the happy ending of *Twelfth Night* by reviewing the events of the play from Malvolio's point of view. The story consists of an extended monologue by Malvolio, beginning with the sentence "I have been dead for five years." Josipovici's character study pursues the banished scapegoat once he has left the stage in order to explore the aftereffects of his victimization. Malvolio's anger toward Sir Toby and the Fool continues to torture him:

> They have taken away my life, though no court of law would convict them for it. When I think about that time, what they did to me, my insides get knotted up in anger and despair and I hate them not so much for what they did to me then as for what they are doing to me now, knotting me up with anguish and hatred at the memory.

He tries to write, hoping it will bring understanding and drive away the darkness that surrounds him. One moment he calls himself a "survivor"; in the next, he says "I no longer know who I am." The story ends where it began. Malvolio is "still in the dark and calling out for pen and paper." He hopes that by writing it all down he will be able to "live again," that by enduring he will have his revenge.[4] By extending Malvolio's story and leaving it open-ended, Josipovici invites his readers to reject impositions of closure that focus exclusively on love, marriage, and reconciliation.

A number of critics have devised terms for the kinds of texts Shakespeare's plays have inspired. The plays, to use Paul D'Andrea's "postromantic metaphor," provide the essential "DNA" that gives life to new

works of art.[5] Jonathan Bate proposes the term "afterlife," derived
from the Nachleben tradition of scholarship associated with the Warburg Institute but also popularized by the director Jonathan Miller,
for the echoes, adaptations and transformations Shakespeare has
spawned.[6] Ruby Cohn uses an organic word, "offshoots," to include
adaptations, additions, and transformations. Michael Scott adapts
Cohn's term, speaking of "feed offs" in his discussion of "the intertextual life of the play."[7] Marowitz describes "The Quantum Leap
Approach to Shakespeare," by which "an idea, inspired by the text, but
not necessarily verifiable in relation to it, creates a work of art that
intellectually relocates the original play and bears only the faintest
resemblance to its progenitor." He uses the word "transmutations" for
works like *Kiss Me Kate* and *West Side Story* but finds it more difficult
to categorize *Rosencrantz and Guildenstern Are Dead*, which "operates
within the orbit of the original work," or *The Resistible Rise of Arturo
Ui*, in which "*Richard III* is knocking around somewhere in the back-
ground."[8]

I prefer the term "transformations," which I think of as a recognizable class of inventions located within the larger category of appropriations and intertextual traces, to use the vocabulary of intertextuality.
Alan Sinfield's term "reconstitutions" points to an important distinction between transformations and other forms of re-vision. The author
of a transformation is engaged in dismantling, rearranging, sometimes
fracturing the text, sometimes adding to or updating it, sometimes parodying or inverting it, and then reassembling it into a recognizable
re–imagining of the play as we know it.[9] The transformations I have
chosen to include in this book proceed from the assumption that a work
of art is not a closed system, limited by the words once inscribed by the
"author," an assumption particularly appropriate for the study of
Shakespeare, given the extensive disagreement among textual critics
about variants and multiple versions of plays. The premise behind
these transformations is something like this: If a work can grow as it
is performed and revised during its author's lifetime, why not after his
death, as conventions and tastes and notions about meaning change?
Even readers who recognize that a transformation is less a violation of
Shakespeare's text than it is a testimony to the characters' "realness"
and adaptability, may feel inclined to question the value of such talking back: What constitutes a "good" transformation? Are some
designed mainly to disrupt or shock in ways that seems utterly, even
perversely, contrary to the "intent" of the "original"? Do others senti-
mentalize the text and avoid its "complexity," and if so, of what "value"
are they? As these works question Shakespeare's timebound assumptions about race, gender, politics, or psychologically probable behav-

ior, are they, in Michael Dobson's words, "every bit as historically contingent and socially invested" as the Shakespeare they seek to unsettle?[10] Many of these words and ideas, as I have indicated, are highly contested ones, and their presence here calls attention to some of the most important issues being discussed in Shakespeare studies today.

Offshoots, I would argue, differ somewhat from transformations, in that they are more peripherally related to the plays that inspire them. An offshoot frequently makes no attempt to employ or rework the structure of events in the Shakespeare play; rather, it spins off in new directions, taking along one or more of Shakespeare's characters (often from more than one play) and fragments of text with it. I will discuss a few offshoots in this book, notably Brecht's *Roundheads and Peakheads* and Ann-Marie MacDonald's *Goodnight Desdemona (Good Morning Juliet)*, an offshoot that explores the issue of rewriting Shakespeare's endings, but for the most part I have chosen not to include the many, many texts that contain allusions or that could be considered offshoots. Admittedly, the lines of demarcation among transformations, adaptations, and offshoots are not always clear. There is a similar blurring of the distinctions among transformations, interpretations, and performances. The history of Shakespeare productions, as David Willbern has remarked, "like the history of Shakespeare criticism, traces a trajectory of cultural values: particular stagings mirror their historical circumstances."[11] It is not always obvious when a performance becomes a transformation, or for that matter, when a translation does, since a translation has already taken the necessary step of changing Shakespeare's language. Presumably, a significant element of talking back to standard, conventional performances and "literal" translations of the text would be a determining factor; a surface change of costumes, scenery, and stage business is not enough to make a stylish performance into a transformation. An example of a performance that was, arguably, a transformation when it appeared is Orson Welles's celebrated 1936 all-black "voodoo" *Macbeth*. Although it changed the text much less than the transformations I will be discussing, Welles's production talked back to Shakespeare both as an intertextual appropriation that played upon the audience's familiarity with O'Neill's *Emperor Jones* and popular images of Africa and as an outspoken statement about the accessibility and relevance of Shakespeare to a black audience.[12]

Film and performance criticism are the fastest-growing areas in Shakespeare studies at present, and scholars are more and more inclined to move freely between performances and transformations. Barbara Hodgdon, for example, speaks of performances on and performances of Shakespeare, as a way of drawing attention to the kinship between transformations and what we conventionally think of as performances. In an essay on *Othello* appropriations that ranges from Verdi's *Otello* to Orson Welles's film to Marowitz's *An Othello*, along with films that echo or borrow from *Othello* in more oblique ways, she argues that "the very existence of so many different *Othellos* proves the plurality of that (infinitely desirable) text by demonstrating its ability to be reproduced in another form."[13] The mingling of discourses that characterizes the current state of Shakespeare studies has given us performance studies, reception studies, and books based on interviews like Carol Rutter's *Clamorous Voices*, which, interestingly, invokes actresses as "authorities" on the plays. It has also inspired texts that elude categorizing, like Steven Berkoff's *I Am Hamlet*, which walks the reader through his performance of Hamlet in a narrative interspersed with fragments of Shakespeare's text, with Berkoff/Hamlet as the narrating "I" explaining and describing his feelings, motives, and reactions.[14]

I could easily have begun this book with America's favorite Shakespeare transformation, *West Side Story*. I have always felt that the decision to leave Maria alive and racked with grief at the end of *West Side Story* constituted a very direct rebuttal of the Christian-romantic premise that the lovers, united in death, somehow transcend the tragic events that led to their suicides. Set as it is in New York City in the 1950s, *West Side Story* could not have ended as *Romeo and Juliet* did, with the families joining together to erect statues of the lovers in the town square. *West Side Story* transforms *Romeo and Juliet* so as to dramatize the conditions of modern urban immigrant culture and in doing so talks back to a residual nostalgia for the family structures, authority figures, and imposed resolutions of another era, a nostalgia that one can imagine being validated and encouraged by a "conventional" staging of *Romeo and Juliet*. Such talking back raises questions about our traditional expectations regarding genre, a subject I will return to throughout this book. Comedy and tragedy are slippery and problematic categories, possibly no longer very useful as ways of organizing events and marking outcomes. Much of the talking back I've encountered, both as a teacher and as a reader of transformations, calls into question long-accepted conventions regarding comic and tragic closure and characterization. In many of the texts included here, comedies take on tragic overtones and tragedies become wildly, sarcastically comic; comic characters are taken very seriously and tragic ones are stripped of the nobility and dignity traditionally associated with them.

Revisions that challenge accepted comic and tragic conventions often challenge sexual stereotypes as well, and several recent studies and collections have drawn attention to the gender issues that arise when Shakespeare's plays are transformed. Feminist critics have begun looking at the way women writers appropriate fragments or characters from Shakespeare's plays in order, as Carol Thomas Neely remarks, "subversively to authorize and validate virtues perceived as womanly and crucial." Such appropriations draw on the power and legitimacy that Shakespeare, by virtue of his cultural authority, can confer. Many of the writers discussed in Marianne Novy's two collections of essays about women's re-visions of Shakespeare and Peter Erickson's *Rewriting Shakespeare, Rewriting Ourselves* are, in Neely's words, "defending" Shakespeare by directing their anger "against the male culture which has misread him on behalf of its own values"[15] instead of attacking Shakespeare directly, as other writers, male and female, do. The rapidly increasing numbers of women playwrights and directors are creating and will continue to create feminist re-visions of Shakespeare's plays for the stage. Susan Bennett's *Theatre Audiences: A Theory of Production and Reception* mentions in passing three feminist Shakespeare transformations performed during the seventies and eighties, Melissa Murray's *Ophelia*, Elaine Fienstein's *Lear's Daughters*, and Avon Touring's *Measure for Measure*, which changes Claudio to Claudia.[16] As this book went to press the Obie award-winning playwright Paula Vogel's *Desdemona: A Play about a Handkerchief* had its debut in New York.

The women who talk back to Shakespeare in the following chapters are not always consciously advancing a feminist agenda, but their insistence on talking back is characteristic of feminism's resistance to the representation of women from a male perspective. The male perspective and the Christian perspective together become targets for the many re-visions of *The Merchant of Venice* that I discuss in Chapter 2. These writers take an oppositional stance analogous to the stance of some women writers, as they rewrite Shylock from within a Jewish cultural and ethical context, view the play's Christian males from an unsympathetic remove, and appropriate Portia to advance their own arguments.

Studies of re-visions and appropriations, of the cultural history of Shakespeare and his characters, of the highly commercialized Shakespeare "phenomenon" (Terence Hawkes calls it "Bardbiz"),[17] of dissemination or "reproduction" in editions and classrooms and textbooks, all overlap and reinforce one another. The way British and American cultures have read their own values into the plays and fostered institutions and cultural practices to propagate those values is the subject of two wide-ranging social histories: Gary Taylor's *Reinventing Shakespeare: A Cultural History, From the Restoration to the Present* and Michael Bristol's *Shakespeare's America, America's Shakespeare*.[18] These works share the broadly historical perspective of Lawrence

Levine's influential 1984 essay, "William Shakespeare and the American People," originally published in *The American Historical Review* and recently reprinted in a collection entitled *Rethinking Popular Culture: Contemporary Perspectives in Cultural Studies.*[19] Levine argues that Shakespeare was not associated with high culture in America until the end of the nineteenth century; up to that point, the plays, or parts of them, were assimilated into minstrel and music hall shows, and inhabited the same milieu as magicians, dancers, acrobats, and comics. The "divorce" between Shakespeare and the "broader world of every-day culture," says Levine, lasted until the 1960s, when "young producers and directors like Joseph Papp began the process of liberat[ing] Shakespeare from the genteel prison in which he had been confined."[20] A recent collection, *The Appropriation of Shakespeare*, edited by Jean Marsden, contains essays that look at the way the mythologized "bard of Stratford" serves as a political figurehead and cultural emblem, at the assimiliation of Shakespeare references, allusions, and motifs into poems and novels, and at such acts of self-legitimation as Sir Walter Scott's characterization of himself as "the Shakespeare of novelists."

These cultural/historical studies share some of the pragmatic assumptions of reception theory. As Dympna Callahan, quoting Toril Moi, notes in one of the essays in *The Appropriation of Shakespeare*, appropriations are important not because of the origins of an idea but because of the "uses to which it is put and the effects it can produce."[21] The effects produced by some of the most contemporary transformations are at least as sensational and outrageous as they are ideological; they play on the disjunction between Shakespeare's "high-culture" associations and the "low-culture" uses to which his plots and characters can be put. I ran across a pornographic *Hamlet* published in 1987, in which Fortinbras, "with Horatio as his unwitting mouthpiece," emerges as the mastermind behind the murder of Old Hamlet and has duped, bought off, or seduced nearly everyone else in the cast.[22] In the same year, Erica Jong's bestselling *Serenissima* appeared; this is the ultimate woman's fantasy in answer to the question: "Was Will Shakespeare good in bed?" The heroine of Jong's *Merchant of Venice* offshoot is a twentieth-century actress who finds herself transformed into Jessica and living in sixteenth-century Venice, where she meets the young Shakespeare, who is yet to write his plays.[23] Lee Blessing also makes Fortinbras the central character in a cynical postmodern *Hamlet* sequel that had its first performance in 1991 at the La Jolla Playhouse in southern California. *Fortinbras* begins with the final tableau from *Hamlet*, starting with Hamlet's line "Oh God, Horatio, what a wounded name. . . ." Fortinbras enters, and the language shifts to colloquial American English as he refuses to accept Horatio's "story" and sets out to "make up the truth"—a story "that'll show people that everything that's happened up till now had to happen so that I could become king."[24] Appropriately, the Signature Theatre Company's October 1992 New York production of *Fortinbras* ran during the three weeks before election day, and its comic portrayal of a politician who invents a truth "that'll do something for us" talked back to the American political process at least a much as it talked back to Shakespeare.

In another recent play, *Goodnight Desdemona (Good Morning Juliet)*, Ann-Marie MacDonald shares some of Blessing's impatience with Shakespeare's characters but channels her impulse to talk back into a fantasy that sets out to transform the lives of her title characters. As she rewrites *Othello* and *Romeo and Juliet*, MacDonald interrogates the self-destructive behavior of tragic characters through farce. Even at its most whimsical, such talking back makes a serious statement about Shakespeare and the uses we make of him; irreverent appropriation in the service of cultural critique draws strength from Shakespeare's authority as a cultural icon even as it undermines that authority by mocking it. In a different medium, Jane Smiley's 1991 Pulitzer Prize-winning realistic novel *A Thousand Acres* talks back to the King Lear story with riveting seriousness about the dignity and complexity of women characters, the offstage and past events that get glossed over in the play, and the underlying sexual politics that shape it.

By the time this book appears in bookstores and libraries I will have discovered other transformations I would have liked to include. Why are so many playwrights and novelists attracted to Shakespeare? Literary history, said the aphoristic Jan Kott, "is, in a very literal sense, the eating and digesting of the classical texts."[25] As we feed off Shakespeare we participate in a process that has created an extraordinarily rich idiom of exchange, a common parlance of phrases, images, characters, and plots that cross boundaries of time and space, linking writers and audiences around the world. In our increasingly multicultural and anticanonical literary culture, Shakespeare remains the writer everyone has heard of, including, and especially, the students whose first readings are important barometers of the way Shakespeare changes as we do. Where once he was "that demi-god," "the god of our idolatry," in David Garrick's words,[26] he has gradually become a disembodied collection of names and associations and images that are accessible, replicable, versatile, seemingly timeless, and yet always timely.

1
Students Talking Back

Given the opportunity, many of my students talk back to Shakespeare, and I have learned to listen carefully to what they say. Their complaints, advice, questions, and firmly rendered judgments testify to a real engagement with the plays, however naive these might seem to a seasoned Shakespearean. I have noticed that an undirected first reading of a text, a reading that precedes the instructor's "official" pronouncements, is most likely to elicit this kind of talking back. When students confront a play on their own terms, making their own bridges to the values and conventions of a remote time and place, they frequently find themselves challenging the choices the characters make, guided by their own notions of appropriate behavior. Like other kinds of criticism, student writers' responses to Shakespeare are social and cultural statements of a particular kind. Every generation must formulate its own relationship with Shakespeare, Harry Levin has observed in an essay entitled "The Crisis of Interpretation." Wryly, he quotes from the first paragraph of T. S. Eliot's "Shakespeare and the Stoicism of Seneca": "About anyone so great as Shakespeare, it is probable that we can never be right, and if we can never be right, it is better that we should from time to time change our way of being wrong." For Eliot in 1927, the issue was the way critics construct a "Shakespeare" whose works can be explained in terms of the "influence" of Machiavelli, or Montaigne, or Seneca; for Levin in 1988, it was the current predominance of "trendy shibboleths" in literary theory which "glide past the methodological impedimenta of biographies, periods, and genres."[1] For this generation of university students,[2] the issues frequently have relatively little to do with literary influences, conventions, or interpretive strategies, and a great deal to do with the practical morality of social relationships.

Here is an example from an upper-level undergraduate Shakespeare course. Asked to write about the ending of *1 Henry IV*, several students said they felt uncomfortable with Hal's farewell to the seemingly dead Falstaff in act 5, scene 4. They described Hal as "cold" and chided him for not even checking to make sure that his friend had actually been killed. "I was angry at the Prince," one said, "because he seemed to feel no sorrow for Falstaff's death, only the need to move on in his own life." Many of these students heard Hal's words from Falstaff's point of view. "Falstaff realized that their relationship had ended," a young woman remarked, and another argued that we share his sense of being confused and hurt. This reader went so far as to propose a rejected but still loyal Falstaff who "kills Hotspur again for Hal," to make certain he is safely dead. The comments seem to reveal that students place a high value on friendship and that their commitment to this value can have the effect of eclipsing other ways of reading the scene. Out of about twenty responses, a very few saw regret and respect in Hal's parting words, and only two commented on Falstaff's lie, characterizing it as morally reprehensible. One of these was a student who had studied the play with me in another class the year before, which suggests that a second reading permits a more detached response to Falstaff and/or that it will be influenced by the student's recollection of the teacher's remarks. For the most part, the students were responding very directly to the characters and their perceived relationships with one another. Their readings had yet to be filtered through the protocols of academic reading that take into account historical or generic antecedents, literary conventions, thematic patterns, or the historical/ideological moment of the text's composition—all elements of a broadly formalist approach to literary study that continues to figure large in classroom and textbook approaches to Shakespeare. For them, "meaning" emerged from their own sympathetic identification with Falstaff at a particular moment in the experience of the play. Admittedly, judgments and allegiances like these take shape in process, before the readers know how the play (or, in the case of *1 Henry IV*, the tetralogy) ends; for this reason alone, these readings will be different from those of second or third readers, or of teachers who bring to the classroom an agenda shaped in part by a retrospective reading that moves backward from the ending.

Much reader-response theory and pedagogy builds on the work of I. A. Richards, who recognized fifty years ago in *Practical Criticism* that "the personal situation of the reader inevitably (and within limits rightly) affects his reading . . . the dangers are that such recollected feelings may overwhelm and distort the poem." He adds, however, that the readers' personal experiences "are not to be hastily excluded as mere personal intrusions, but that "they must be genuine and relevant, and must respect the liberty and autonomy of the poem." The question contemporary response theorists might ask of Richards is this: Who decides what is genuine and relevant? Richards goes on to discuss "stock responses," arguing that in life, as in literature, "an extensive repertory of stock responses is a necessity. . . . Clearly there is an enormous field of conventional activity over which acquired, stereotyped, habitual responses properly rule." Having said this, he notes that stock responses lead readers to object to a poem "for not being quite a different poem, without regard paid to what it is as itself."[3] This, I suspect, is what happens with many first readings of Shakespeare's plays. Faced with the combination of difficult language and seemingly familiar characters and situations, the students resort to stock responses as a way of "obliterating the difference or otherness of literature, domesticating or coercing into 'naturalness' the strangeness which defies and resists understanding."[4] This strangeness, for students in American schools, is especially evident in Shakespeare's plays, which may well be the only pre–nineteenth-century literary works they've encountered in high school English classes. For them, reading Shakespeare entails a particular kind of "indeterminacy," to use Wolfgang Iser's term; as they engage in the "transformation of signals sent out by the text," they reduce it to the level of their own experiences in order to "counterbalance" its indeterminacy, or lack of reference to "the objects of the external world or . . . the experiences of the reader."[5] Iser has subsequently characterized texts as "plays" to be "acted out by each reader, who by playing it in his or her own way, produces an individual 'supplement' considered to be the meaning of the text."[6]

To produce these "supplements," student readers apply interpretive conventions that frequently put a good deal of emphasis on characters as responsible members of society, accountable for the consequences of their behavior. These readers have somehow come to assume that reading is a reactive, judgment-making process, one in which the psychology and morality of social relationships tend to crowd out other aspects of the texts. Contemporary pedagogical practice has no doubt encouraged this approach to some extent. Alan Sinfield has noted with concern that when historical and theatrical contexts are disregarded in the teaching and testing of Shakespeare, "Individuals [become] the unproblematic source of action and meaning" and the plays are approached either in terms of the universal (e.g., "the problem of evil") or the individual, with "a yawning gulf between the two."[7] When students write about individual characters, they understandably try to imagine them as "real" people. It is difficult to imagine a college teacher today saying to students, as Maurice Charney did two decades ago in *How to Read Shakespeare*, that "Moral conventions in the presentation of character allow Shakespeare to ignore psychological realities." The handbook advises students that "We are willing to accept gaps in the presentation of Shakespeare's characters, quick changes in their development, and other moral conventions, because we are not committed to seeing them as real people."[8] Who, one might ask, are the "we" in this sentence? It may well be that student first readers do—and should—differ from their teachers as "interpretive communities" and that those differences can become a positive element in the teaching-learning process, not merely obstacles to be overcome.

By looking at student first readings as a legitimate form of interpretation from which we, as scholars, can learn, I am advocating a pragmatic approach that considers student first readers as a special class of readers with certain group characteristics that reflect the influence of our social and educational culture. I am not thinking of Norman Holland's "identity themes," an approach that focuses on each reader as a separate personality,[9] but rather of something like the "positions" identified by William Perry in *Forms of Intellectual and Ethical Development in the College Years*. Perry discovered that the early stages or positions of student development were characterized by "an urge to make order out of incongruities, dissonances, and anomalies of experience." Students confronted with the "dissolution of established beliefs" felt a desire to "retain hometown values" and resorted to a "dualistic absolutism," which eventually, as they matured, yielded to a more generalized relativism.[10] Although Perry's scheme may not apply precisely to students reading Shakespeare at the present time, more recent research on the reading process suggests a similar desire for this kind of "order." Inexperienced readers tend to "compose" a text "according to the code of [a] conventional narrative"; that is, they view the text as "proof" of the validity of a preexisting story, or formula, derived in part from "classroom structures of reading, but sometimes structures derived from the church or home or from any of the cultures outside our classrooms."[11] First readers try to make the text "mean" something, using what they know best, which frequently consists of received truths and rather prescriptive formulas about human behavior.

One such prescriptive formula emerged from an assignment that asked students to discuss the role of Fortinbras in *Hamlet*. The ten papers I received were remarkably unanimous in their admiration for the prince who receives Hamlet's "dying voice" and the throne of Denmark in the play's final scene. Fortinbras, my students said, was rational where Hamlet was given over to passion; he was determined, decisive, confident, proud, brave, prompt, and very much in control of the circumstances in which he found himself. Thwarted in his effort to invade Denmark, he listened to reason and redirected his energies against Poland, receiving, one student observed, a large sum of money from his uncle, the king of Norway, in the process. Indeed, he was "bought off," she remarked, unlike Hamlet, who "would not let Claudius buy him off with promises of gaining control of the crown." Although this contrast might seem to favor Hamlet, the student then went on to say, with unconscious irony, that Fortinbras is a "true soldier," who thinks in a "concrete, practical manner," as opposed to the "abstract" Hamlet; in sum, Fortinbras is the "business major" and Hamlet, the "English major." She concluded by saying that Fortinbras "manages to keep a handle on things with his strong, undefeated attitude . . . we are left with hope for Denmark [which] will be highly protected by this valiant soldier."

Although students have frequently been impatient with the way Hamlet seems to "delay," they have not until recently, in my experience, found a way out of their dilemma by attaching themselves, emotionally and ideologically, to Fortinbras. When I first studied *Hamlet*, in the 1960s, Fortinbras was an imperialist warmonger, risking the lives of "twenty thousand men [who] . . . go to their graves like beds, fight for a plot . . . which is not tomb enough and continent / To hide the slain" (4.4.60 – 65).[12] He was everything we despised in the Vietnam era, and our reading of act 5 viewed his triumphant entry and readiness to take charge as part of the melancholy and bitter tragedy of Denmark. Now, more than twenty years later, some of my students see Fortinbras as the brisk pragmatist who succeeds, and rightly so. They believe that Shakespeare intended him to serve as an unambiguously positive example for Hamlet, inspiring him, as one student put it, to "set a goal and proceed immediately" toward it. The word "goal" (another student spoke of Fortinbras's "single-minded pursuit of his goal") apparently applies equally to Fortinbras's fourth-act offstage invasion of Poland and Hamlet's contemplated revenge—many of the students did not seem to make any effort to distinguish between the two. *Hamlet*, viewed thus, begins to resemble a casebook study: two young men, out to avenge their fathers' deaths, define their goals. One succeeds in attaining his and becomes king, the other does everything wrong, and dies. Only one student of the ten started from the position that Fortinbras Senior might have been unwise to stake his possessions on the outcome of the battle and that his son was foolishly "jealous" and imprudent in his effort to retrieve them. Even though she remarked that Fortinbras accepts a "worthless piece of Poland" as a substitute for "the rich Danish crown," she concluded that

> Fortinbras ultimately shows courage and honor, where Hamlet shows procrastination and indecisiveness. Fortinbras acts like a man, while Hamlet acts like a madman. Hamlet hides behind curtains, talks to ghosts, deceives his friends and lover, while Fortinbras shows the nobility of an heir to the throne.

My first response to this group of essays was a wry and sardonic observation about student values. I wrote that

> The message seems to be that questionable motives and a willingness to be deflected from one's original goal are not grounds for failure in 1987. Fortinbras the business major succeeds in getting the crown, by projecting a strong self-image and never pausing to ask where he is and why.

I am now less sure that these words are fair to first readers who are dealing with a work that is unfamiliar and intimidating in at least three ways: it is at once a highly complex piece of poetry, an unannotated play-text with very little description of accompanying action or narrative "guide" and a social document belonging to an historically remote culture. Furthermore, a play such as *Hamlet* is encrusted with the sanctity of canonization, and so, as an unimpeachable "classic," it invites a mixture of awe, rebellion, and perhaps a perceived need to say something new and conclusive. Hence I now feel that a better conclusion to draw from these readings is that these students, like the students in Perry's study, felt uncomfortable with Hamlet's tolerance for ambiguity because it seemed to threaten their own need for certainty and order. They thus preferred Fortinbras's apparent decisiveness, though, on closer inspection, it is a decisiveness inferred rather than displayed, since Fortinbras himself is not given the opportunity to appear on-stage and announce his intentions.

First readers are reading quickly, "to see what happens next," as one of my students put it, and are unlikely to pause over the nuances of Hamlet's characterization of Fortinbras as one who "expose[s] what is mortal and unsure / to all that fortune, death and danger dare, / Even for an eggshell" (4.4.53–54). Where a sophisticated reader familiar with Elizabethan rhetoric might recognize the mock-heroic posturing of "all that fortune, death and danger dare," ironically undermined by the anticlimactic "even for an eggshell," a first reader may well be wondering what Fortinbras's presence has to do with the main action, and eagerly anticipating the outcome of Claudius's plot to use England to accomplish "the present death of Hamlet" (4.3.65).

Since the way we teach affects the way students read, I considered the possibility that my approach to *Hamlet* had led to this group of responses, so I asked a colleague to assign a paper on Hamlet and Fortinbras to an introductory Shakespeare class. Although not every paper celebrated Fortinbras at Hamlet's expense, the majority of responses were strikingly similar to the ones from my class. "Fortinbras remained dutiful to his country and national matters at hand while Hamlet was into his own pathetic suffering and outrage," said one student. Another described Fortinbras as a "clever, calculating character willing to wait for the opportune moment . . . while Hamlet . . . seeks immediate gratification of his vengeance." This reading offers an unexpected alternative to the age-old critical formula that views the events of *Hamlet* as a series of delays by the protagonist. The writer concluded that the play's ending shows "that perseverance and tactical reason lead to success." A third took the opposite tack, arguing that "the young Norwegian is quick to act [rather than "willing to wait"] in seeking revenge and when this is shown to be pointless he is able to rechannel his aggression against another enemy, Poland. Hamlet, however, is unable to control his emotions and as a result ends up destroying himself." She explains the play's ending like this, in language reminiscent of Lee Blessing's in *Fortinbras*: "Hamlet had to die to create a space for Fortinbras." Still others from this class talked back more explicitly to Hamlet, reproaching him for not having "made any concrete plans," and for "wallowing in misery," whereas they praised Fortinbras for self-control, taking action, and being "a doer rather than a thinker." The language of these judgments strongly reflects frequently used verbal formulas in the readers' subculture, and, I suspect, their experiences as well; one hears behind their assessments of Hamlet and Fortinbras the voices of parents, teachers, and peers, exhorting the reluctant adolescent in just such phrases. None of these students felt that Hamlet's reluctance to kill Claudius was uncharacteristic of him, an idea Blessing playfully proposes. When, at the end of *Fortinbras*, Horatio is still trying to tell his story, no one believes him:

> *Horatio.* I'm sick of the truth!! You know how many people I've tried to tell that story? You know how far I get?! Right up to the part where Hamlet walked directly past Claudius at prayer and didn't kill him!

But no one believes him: " 'Would've killed him,' they say! 'The Hamlet we knew would've killed Claudius then and there!' Any man would!!' "[13]

Even though Hamlet has certainly attracted his share of adverse criticism throughout the past two centuries, I imagine that most teachers would be tempted to declare these characterizations of Hamlet and Fortinbras to be misreadings, and make some effort to qualify or challenge them. Peter Rabinowitz has discussed the phenomenon of persistent or recurring misreadings in *Before Reading*, concluding that "we can therefore often uncover forces at work in a society by reading its misreadings, by studying the ways that readers have misappropriated the texts they live with." Curious about the "rules" readers apply when they attempt to discover the author's intended meaning (as my students

were doing), he advises that "we can illuminate the categories inform-
ing their thought, and consequently the ideological pressures working
on them."[14] The forces at work in American society that resulted in
these readings of *Hamlet* might not be much different from the ones that
produced Blessing's *Fortinbras*, with its similar, although much more
cynical, contrast between the pragmatic and opportunistic Fortinbras
and the passive and helpless Hamlet, an angry, brooding eye on the television screen whom an impatient and assertive Ophelia can "silence"
by turning off the sound.

The "ideological pressures" of the 1980s were undoubtedly responsible, in some way or other, for the *Hamlet* papers I received in 1987.
They reveal the students' intense preoccupation with worldly success,
as well as a systematic inclination to formulate dichotomous images of
the successful versus the unsuccessful man. Their approval of Fortinbras suggests a desire to emulate him—to be the decisive, self-con-
trolled man or woman of action whose story ends with the acquisition
of the modern equivalent of a throne.[15] In their instinct to apply what
Rabinowitz calls "rules of coherence" as part of the reading process,
they employ the strategy of "scapegoating," identifying Hamlet as the
wrongdoer who is punished as part of the closure or resolution with
which the play—and their relationship with it—concludes.[16]

The inclination to resort to scapegoating was equally evident, interestingly enough, in student responses to a play that contains one of
Shakespeare's most famous scapegoats. When I taught *Twelfth Night*
to a small, writing-intensive class of first readers in 1984, I was astonished by the vehemence with which students defended Malvolio and
lashed out at Sir Toby. The strongest instance of talking back to Shakespeare came from an older student who had worked for several years
before coming back to college. Sir Toby, he said, is

> not, on close examination, a harmless drunk. In fact he is far more offensive
> an individual than Malvolio. He is a malicious, self-serving parasite who
> exploits fellow human beings to his own ends. Indeed, his truly stinking
> nature may be seen near the end . . . [here he describes Toby's unexpected cru-
> elty to Sir Andrew in the final scene]. If Malvolio was deserving of his pun-
> ishment for his shortcomings, then Sir Toby, blight on society that he is,
> deserves ten-fold the punishment.

Others agreed that Sir Toby had played a "vicious prank" on Sir Andrew,
one which turns "harmless foolery into real injustice." As one student
observed, with evident frustration, "I wanted to see Sir Toby punished
because of what he did to Malvolio; he didn't deserve to live happily
ever after with Maria, but since he was a knight, no one could touch

him." Four years later, I taught the writing-intensive course again, and
again, a number of students felt that the joke on Malvolio was cruel;
indeed, two remarked that they hoped he would get revenge after the
play ended. These two students felt the innate need for closure described
by Rabinowitz, and they voiced their uneasiness about its absence in
Twelfth Night, wondering, for example, whether Olivia was going to
punish the tricksters after the play's last scene. I suspect that the comic
disorder of *Twelfth Night* disrupted both their sense of fair play and their
recently acquired notions of responsible, adult behavior. Reading it
was clearly an unsettling experience, but also one in which they found
themselves articulating and affirming their own values concerning
love, friendship and honesty.

Curious about how much first readings would change within a thir-
teen-week semester, I had my class read each play twice when I taught
the writing-intensive course for the second time. I assigned the plays
in this order: *Twelfth Night, Measure for Measure, Hamlet, Othello*, and
A Winter's Tale, and everyone in the class was required to keep reading
and rereading journals to record their responses, an assignment that
produced some remarkably good writing, as students talked back to
themselves, assessing, refuting, and expanding their own first readings. Eight weeks into the semester, one freshman who had initially
described Sir Toby as "a horrible person, a user, a money-hungry selfish man who was only out for himself" wrote in her rereading journal:
"Now, I see that Iago is by far the evil one . . . and can accept Sir Toby's
trick on Malvolio as part of the happy festive setting [of the play]." Yet
she could also talk about the "dark underside" of the play: the shipwreck, Antonio's arrest, Malvolio's imprisonment. In other words, she
had discovered that the play could not be reduced to a single, formulaic "interpretation." Her second reading echoed an illuminating discussion I had had two years earlier with a small group of students that
included the older, indignant student who had so resented Sir Toby
when he encountered him for the first time. This student had gone on
to become an English major and was among the best students in the
senior class. After observing that "you can't separate the reader from
what he is doing at the moment," he recalled that at the time he "was
involved with people who were experiencing madness" and so felt
affronted by what seemed to him to be a frivolous treatment of a serious subject. Moreover, "the outrage of an uninformed student" confronted for the first time with Shakespeare's language "is directed
against the fact that it is so hard for him to understand." He explained
that he was now able to see *Twelfth Night* as a lighthearted comedy that
deliberately violates our notions of logic in order to make a statement
about the irrationality of lovers. "The wit, the staging, the interaction

of characters are much funnier . . . then, I didn't know about comic conventions; I now read in a different way."

In an eloquent book published in 1970 that in certain ways anticipated later developments in literary theory, Walter J. Slatoff observed, "We usually fail . . . to consider the changes over time in the effects of particular qualities of a work." He goes on to hypothesize a reader of *The Sound and the Fury*, for whom the first reading might be "disturbed" and "groping" while the second reading

> is a quite different experience . . . as one brings to bear on earlier sections information and awareness gleaned from later ones. And with each successive reading, of course, this process continues. . . . This is . . . an extreme illustration of something which occurs with the rereading of any work as the effects of sequence and novelty wear off and one gains more and more sense of the work as a spatial entity . . . one might say that the work itself undergoes a transformation as one rereads it.[17]

Slatoff later draws attention to the reader's "discomfort" with *The Merchant of Venice*, because of the mixed signals we receive when we are asked to "delight in [Shylock's] torment" in act 4, after having earlier been encouraged to share his point of view. This leads to the speculation that the same kind of discomfort could occur with Malvolio: "Might there be those who resist sharing in the fun as he is mocked and tormented?"[18] There are indeed such readers, and they may well be seeing in Malvolio's role a mirror image of a humiliating experience they themselves have endured. This identification results in a particular kind of reading of the Malvolio scenes, one that isolates them from what Slatoff calls the "spatial entity," a space occupied, for instance, by the pattern of resemblances and echoes whereby Malvolio's self-absorption and posturing serve as an exaggerated reflection of Orsino's and Olivia's. In this era of deconstructed and destabilizing readings, dominated by dissonances and absences and subversiveness, Slatoff's conception of the work as a spatial entity is probably open to question; postmodern critics might argue, with good reason, that words like "disturbed" and "groping" and "discomfort" describe reactions that do not—and should not—"wear off."

First readings that demonstrate an unusual degree of sympathy for Malvolio could be partly the consequence of what Sinfield has characterized as an incomplete grounding in the literature, literary conventions, and the "historical field" of Shakespeare's age.[19] In other words, just as teachers and examination questions frequently isolate Shakespeare's plays from their cultural surroundings, student first readers take the process one step farther, and isolate characters like

Malvolio and Falstaff from their comic context in the play, transforming them into objects of pity and reflections of the reader's own real
or imagined experiences of persecution and helplessness. Students
bring a particular kind of intertextuality to bear upon the text; this
intertextuality is described by Jonathan Culler as "less a name for a
work's relation to particular prior texts than a designation of its par-
ticipation in the discursive space of a culture: the relationship between
a text and the various languages or signifying practices of a culture
and its relation to those texts which articulate for it the possibilities of
that culture."[20]

Presented with the opportunity to revise and expand upon their original responses to *Hamlet* or *Twelfth Night*, many readers engage in a
kind of "filling in," to use Slatoff's words, which contributes to the
changes their experience of the text undergo and which includes, among
other things, a "rounding out" of the characters.[21] Some of my students
used the rereading journal to give closer attention to characters they
had quickly dismissed, scenes they had rushed through, or issues they
hadn't noticed in the first reading. One young woman who had initially
described Gertrude as "shallow" and focused her attention on Hamlet
and Ophelia, devoted much of her rereading journal to Gertrude: "In
Hamlet's mind," she observed, "Hecuba's woes seem synonymous with
what Gertrude should have felt when Hamlet senior was killed." Her
discussion of act 4, scene 5 begins, "The Queen seems to be realizing
that her world is about to fall apart. Instead of playing an active role
she shuts herself away from the problems—e.g. she doesn't want to see
Ophelia." After examining Gertrude's "There is a willow . . ." speech
describing Ophelia's death, the journal entry concluded that Gertrude
was "a truly sensitive person" with "a touching perception of the world
. . . [and] the plight of Ophelia."

Seeing a stage or filmed version of the play almost always gets students to revise their first readings. Students who had been resistant to
comic conventions in *Twelfth Night* changed their minds after seeing a
university production of the play. One student observed that he had
despised Sir Toby and Feste for their cruelty before seeing the production; but in the course of the evening at the theatre, he "grew to love"
them, because of their sharp wit, hilarious practical jokes, and wonderful songs. Perhaps the best expression of this discovery came from
the student who remarked

> While reading *Twelfth Night* I didn't care for Malvolio; he seemed overbear-
> ing, pompous, and arrogant. After seeing the play I felt that he was still over-
> bearing, pompous, and arrogant, not to mention obnoxious, but now I see him
> in a comic sense. He isn't to be taken seriously.

A young woman who "found it difficult to understand how anyone could fall in love with another so quickly" and urged that "time is a necessity in the development of a true love relationship" discovered that she liked Olivia much better after seeing the play. "She displayed a great sense of assertiveness and charm which I hardly even noticed before," the student remarked. Again and again the students expressed their admiration for and identification with Viola in ways that revealed their own values: she was clever, determined, loyal, sincere and cared deeply for others. As one young woman said, "Most people have dealt with unrequited love but she does this gracefully . . . I deeply admire her courage and her willpower, [for] I know the feelings that this young girl is experiencing." Another said "the conflicts she faced in restraining her natural, feminine instincts while posing as Cesario must have been confusing . . . ; [after seeing the play] my respect for her doubled." Clearly these students were taking Viola seriously, yet without resisting the play's comic assumptions. Seeing a fellow student bring her to life on the stage undoubtedly helped. And although none of the students' papers specifically mentioned it, the director's decision to have Viola narrowly escape being assaulted by an Illyrian soldier when she makes her first entrance may also have contributed to their recognition that this was a young person not unlike themselves, forced to survive by wit and subterfuge in an unpredictable and possibly dangerous world.

Whether or not something is meant to be "taken seriously" constituted an ongoing issue for the students who talked back to *Twelfth Night*. When I spoke with a senior English major two years after she had taken my first writing-intensive course, the class that included the students so resistant to comic conventions, she commented that "I was seriously involved in a love relationship and was thinking a lot about my own sense of commitment at the time. I couldn't understand how Orsino could be so inconstant because I didn't want to think I could be." Two years later, she too can see that the play "isn't meant to be taken so seriously," although she still finds Orsino's change of allegiance inexplicable compared, for example, with Romeo's. "I can accept fantasy," she concluded, "but I can't throw out everything I believe in. Orsino still represents a challenge to my own beliefs."

This inclination to judge a character, either with approval or disapproval, illustrates one important characteristic of reader-response criticism—"a redefinition of the dynamics of didacticism from the point of view of the reader rather than the writer."[22] The assertiveness of such reader-generated didacticism testifies to the engagement student readers bring to the study of Shakespeare, an engagement that professional Shakespeareans may understandably view as marked by insufficient distinctions between highly complex literary constructs and the behavior one encounters in "real life." Student readers, in my experience, are remarkably unlike the readers posited by a well-known Shakespeare scholar in a remark about first readings:

> When we confront a play (or any other literary work) for the first time, we usually begin with the assumption . . . that its author is not fallible, that he has composed a flawless play whose various parts, if properly interpreted, will all be seen to cohere perfectly in a unified artistic whole.[23]

Just as common, among my students, at least, is the response that the play could be improved: "I still think a better ending would have been to have Iago killed," affirmed one reader's conclusion to a rereading journal that consisted of a series of questions about *Othello*. Students who felt uncomfortable with the portrayal of human relationships in *Hamlet* and *Othello* talked back quite unself-consciously to the characters and the playwright and offered alternatives in an effort to forestall the tragic outcome. This was especially evident in the response of women students to women characters; these students had become what Judith Fetterley calls "resisting readers," who, when "asked" by the text to identify with the male characters, respond by questioning its inherent values and assumptions.[24] "She shouldn't have listened to her father and brother," one young woman said about Ophelia, and added that the character indirectly brought Hamlet's bitterness upon herself. Another remarked indignantly, "I really think Ophelia should have told [Hamlet] off for the terrible things he said to her." The young women in the class were even more impatient with Desdemona. "Why doesn't Desdemona do anything?" asked one in her rereading-journal notes on act 4, scene 3. Earlier, speaking of Cassio and Roderigo, she said, "It doesn't seem as though the characters with problems are willing to solve them themselves." Here, clearly, is an important value that is being defined and asserted as part of the critical process. Another student began, "Maybe if Desdemona had confronted him and been a little more pushy instead of . . . just pretending nothing was wrong."[25] For her, the play is a tragedy because of "all the things that could have been solved" if Othello had acted differently. As she describes herself feeling "very aggravated" and "mad" at the outcome of events, she is, without realizing it, articulating an aspect of the tragic response which *Othello* inspires in its audience.

Othello almost always provokes strong responses from students inclined to talk back. As I read a set of papers from a large introductory Shakespeare course for freshmen and non-English majors a few years ago, I was struck by a recurring "pragmatic" approach, one which resorted insistently to familiar, and by now formulaic principles of social survival concerning such matters as sexual and professional jealousy, misplaced trust, communication breakdowns, and manipulative relationships. The students adopted the posture of advice-givers, proffering bits of received wisdom and personal opinions in a remarkably prescriptive tone of voice; hence they took Othello to task for "acting hastily, without first consulting several people," for not "communicating better with his wife," and for "being so foolish as to let jealousy get the better of him." They frequently assumed the authoritative voice of an advice columnist: "Communication is a vital part of sustaining a relationship," one young woman declared, after asserting that "in Othello's position I can safely say I would have consulted others, but not without consulting Desdemona." Another woman, speaking of "lack of communication" among all the characters, added "misunderstanding between couples is typical." And a young man, who concluded that the whole situation could have been avoided if Othello had listened to Cassio, pronounced the play to be "an example of what can result from lack of communication."[26]

Reading James Calderwood's essay on "Speech and Self in *Othello*" while thinking about these papers, I became interested in the similar conclusions yet complete differences in language and approach. Calderwood observes that Othello's style is "constitutionally opposed to dialogue," and that "monologue makes its own meaning"; moreover, that Othello is "logocentric" and "lodges all meaning in words."[27] Although my students were unable, or unwilling, to develop their interpretations out of close analysis of language patterns and specific scenes, many of them were, like Calderwood, finding pervasive patterns in the play. Their approaches to the writing process, though, were quite different: many, if not most, felt the necessity to see the play as an instructive statement for the audience's benefit, and to imitate or reinforce what they saw as the author's stance by drawing their own moral conclusions. Calderwood, by contrast, never makes a judgmental pronouncement; his role as critic, clearly, is to describe. The closest he comes to the type of reading I have been discussing is his remark that it is "perfectly natural" for Othello, as a stranger among the Venetians, "to situate as much meaning as possible in words, and especially in his own words."[28] In other words, as my students might say, he was not listening to others.

The "pragmatic" responses represent one aspect of the students' readings of *Othello*. But the papers also revealed another, quite different stance. Many of the first-time readers described strong feelings of anger, helplessness, indignation, and disgust, as they entered into an emotional relationship with the play.[29] Responding to it became a way of articulating their own anxieties about relationships, their sense that people like Iago do exist and pose a serious threat to social stability, and their frustration at being in a position of knowledge yet unable to intervene. Students found themselves wanting quite literally to talk back to the characters: "I felt like screaming to Othello not to listen to Iago"; "I knew exactly what Iago was going to do, but I couldn't yell out and warn anyone. To put it simply, Iago made me feel quite helpless"; "I would have loved to have been there with them in Cyprus, to . . . tell Cassio he was being set up . . . Shakespeare keeps our attention by frustrating us"; "I really had an urge to enter the play and tell Othello and Cassio of Iago's knavery"; "I wanted to shake [Desdemona] and say: 'Look at your husband and do something to help yourself instead of trying to help Cassio.'" Whether they realized it or not, these five students seemed to be dealing with their reaction to Iago as a "frightening" or "disturbing" character by wanting to oppose him directly. If this response has a certain "naive" quality, suggesting an insufficient distinction between art and life, it also testifies to a strong need to believe in one's own ability to take charge and restore order.[30] Further, it reveals an uneasy relationship with the play's prevailing irony, and a feeling, as one student put it, of being manipulated. *Othello* employs dramatic irony to an unusual degree, and first-time readers sometimes have to go back and look at exits and entrances to remind themselves of how much more they know than the various characters do. Such knowledge can confer a sense of moral superiority or authority on students who are accustomed to feeling humbled by the linguistic difficulties of first readings. But knowing more than the characters can also become an emotional burden, one which could, if pushed too far, trigger frustration, impatience, and even contempt. Writing about the play intensifies this effect, for writing, particularly when it takes the form of talking back, can be a form of exerting authority and control over the text, particularly if one can define (or, we might say, redefine) the play's central issues in a familiar vocabulary.

First-time readers are less likely to use quotes from the text to make their points than more experienced readers, resorting instead to a significantly small group of loaded words and phrases. Foremost among these recurring words and phrases were references to order and self-control. One student stated that "Shakespeare is telling us that to avoid tragedies within our own lives we must keep in touch with the events and actions that make up our life." Another, who initially viewed Othello as a clearheaded, even-tempered father figure, said that he felt like a child who discovers that his father is "a bum." "He threw it all away— beliefs, ideas, loyalty, trust, faith, and let himself be manipulated like a piece of clay." He found a similar message in Othello's tragedy: "We must take a step back and reevaluate our conclusions and see how foolish they are." "Even-tempered levelheadedness," he felt, "should be our goal." In sum, as one student concluded, "the play expresses a basic fear of loss of control." At the end of the term, when the students looked back at *Othello* after reading *Hamlet* and *The Tempest*, this emphasis on order and control was, if anything, even greater. Several of the students praised Prospero for his "restraint of emotions" and "evenheadedness" and for his ability to "reason correctly" and arrive at "a rational solution through language rather than violence." Unlike Othello and Hamlet, Prospero, in the words of one student, can evaluate before acting. "Many aspects must be considered and evaluated," the student approvingly generalized, "before extreme steps are taken." (The passives lend a tone of bureaucratic prudence to this utterance.) Another student noted that Prospero and Iago shared "an almost perfect control" of their respective plays, while Othello "did not control his situation." Or, as another put it, Othello "was quick to act before he had all the facts." ("Hamlet," she said, "was too slow in acting.")

For many of the readers, order and control occur when people talk things out and trust one another. Viewed thus, *Othello* becomes a statement about trust in marriage. One impassioned young man spoke of having "always been taught that when you say 'I do' that means forever. Now if you are going to spend your life with someone you are going to have to trust that person with all your heart and soul. Even if there were a chance of that belief backfiring, I would have to believe my wife over anyone." This trust, he seems to feel, is the only absolute in a perilous world. Even a long, intelligent paper on the way symbolism and imagery shape our responses to Othello as an "outsider" who elicits our sympathy concludes that "Othello brought his downfall upon himself." In the accents of a marriage counselor the writer observes that "Any marriage will not survive without trust and honesty on the part of both husband and wife. . . . Everyone who reads *Othello* should examine his mistakes and try to avoid them in his own relationships."

The students in this class tended to ignore historical or cultural differences and regarded the characters as if they were our contemporaries. I was surprised to find an almost complete absence of references to racism or racial identity in the papers, especially since we had had a rather lively discussion of Shylock's Jewishness only a week or so earlier. At a time when "cultural diversity" is a catch phrase on college campuses, one possible pragmatic response to Othello might attribute his behavior to his African origins and view the "failure of communication" from a cultural perspective. With only two or three exceptions the students who were so quick to scold Othello for listening to Iago said nothing about his position as a Moor, unfamiliar with the ways of European culture. Nor did anyone mention racism on Brabantio's part, or attribute Iago's behavior to xenophobic or racist motives. One student who did see "a racial issue" in the play wrote that Othello reverts to a "lower, bestial self," but she, too, resorts to the familiar 1980s psychospeak: Othello's love for Desdemona wasn't "strong enough," because his "sense of confidence and self-worth were weak," while Desdemona's love was "obsessive and based on novelty." These first readings suggest that the students were not paying much attention to the black/white imagery in the play's opening scene and that the words "Moor" and "Venetian" did not signify much to readers for whom both cultures are equally foreign and without any very clear associations. In other words, these responses are quite different from those of a Jacobean audience, which would presumably come to the play with some acquired notions and prejudices about Venetians and Moors. Similarly, the students seemed to approach *Othello* assuming that troubled marriage relationships were the "fault" of the participants but that these relationships could be "fixed." As in the readings of *Hamlet*, the students felt that the principal characters have more control over their lives than they care to exercise.

When each reader "plays" the text in his or her own way, to return to Iser's description of the reading process, a text can veer off in unexpected directions. One young man said that the only person he sympathized with was Brabantio: "I tried to put myself in his place; how would I feel if my daughter, who I loved and thought was so honest and trustworthy, just packed up and left one day?" But he added that Brabantio had put his daughter in a difficult position: "She is so high on a pedestal that the slightest thing she does wrong will cause her father's heart to break." It is difficult to know how to respond to a reading like this one without seeming to dismiss a serious and heartfelt response to a character who may appear less to blame for his suffering and loss than Othello and Desdemona. This is an instance in which the student reader resists the "implied reader's" role, by distancing himself from the major characters and focusing rather narrowly on a relatively minor character whose role is confined to the play's first act.[31] This first reader had read *A Midsummer Night's Dream* and *Romeo and Juliet* and heard me discuss the conventional comic, irate father as a character type who opposes the heroine's desire for autonomy and true love; yet he did not read *Othello* from that perspective. Rather, his reading placed Brabantio in a contemporary "realistic" framework and took him seriously as a developed, sympathetic character—and in doing so rejected the possibility that Desdemona and Othello could have similar, though perhaps irreconcilable, claims on his sympathies. If I were able to talk to this student further, I would try to discover what combination of reading strategies and individual inclinations led him to focus so exclusively on Brabantio.

Many of the students, especially the women, talked back to Emilia in *Othello*. One expressed her annoyance that Emilia "just gave Desdemona's handkerchief to Iago. I would have been more loyal to Desdemona, because she treated Emilia better than Iago did." And another spoke of feeling "the pain and guilt Emilia must have felt because she did contribute to Iago's schemes unknowingly." A strong-minded young woman who felt disappointed by Desdemona ("I wish she had been more aggressive, more demanding; everyone lacked bravery and accepted too much") found it easiest to imagine herself in Emilia's role. "I would have questioned Iago and not given him the handkerchief until he gave me a good reason." But she adds, "But I'm not sure I would know whether he was lying to me." Interestingly, one male student spoke passionately of how Emilia risked her life to clear Desdemona and of how it felt "to watch her in agony over the death of her friend, and then discover that her husband is the cause . . . I didn't expect Othello to murder his wife, but I was really troubled when Iago kills Emilia. This caused me to stop admiring his skill and start hating him."

The words "stop" and "start" in this sentence are revealing; rather than describing mixed or contradictory responses to a character, as a more experienced reader attuned to the complex texture of the play might do, this student records his responses serially, employing black-and-white terms like "admire" and "hate" to do so.[32] It occurred to me, reading the first-time reader responses, that the students and I were operating at cross-purposes. The students wanted to demystify the text, to cut a path through the difficult language and unfamiliar speech patterns to arrive at a clear sense of meaning, whereas I, as teacher, wanted to explore its multiplicities and contradictions. If I saw *Othello* as a floating mass of possibilities, they wanted it to be a solid object against which they, as young adults, could test the moral and social assumptions they were in the process of formulating. The ambivalence and contradictions professors of English are so receptive to in literary texts seem unsettling to many first readers. For them, submitting to the clear control of a morally unambiguous text was an experience they were more likely to expect when reading "great books" than entering into a labyrinth of incongruities, discordances, and unanswerable questions.

The moral and social assumptions my students read into *Othello* were frequently articulated aphoristically, in easily invoked phrases. When I asked a colleague to elicit some first readings of *Othello* from her class to see how they compared with my students', the pattern of responses was revealing. A recurring phrase used by five of the twenty-three students to express the play's theme or message stood out. The phrase, "don't jump to conclusions," encapsulates or "packages" a stock response in a form easily understood by speakers of English who recognize the extensive conventional wisdom that lies behind the cliché. In its epigrammatic brevity, "don't jump to conclusions" employs a formula familiar to us at least since the Ten Commandments: by admonishing us *not* to do something, it alludes indirectly to a pattern of behavior that will make us morally and socially successful human beings. The five students who used this phrase, and several others, spoke urgently of the importance of checking the facts, rejecting rumors or hearsay, and being careful about whom you trust. As in the student responses I had looked at earlier, the tone was frequently prescriptive and sounded rather like an official document; for example, "Do not always take what 'seems' to be true for being so and do not react without thoroughly contemplating end results," said a student who viewed the play as a statement about trust, both in others and in one's own judgment. Another remarked that "this play reaffirmed my belief that you should never listen to rumors and always get the story from the source." She added, "we should not let the passion of jealousy and revenge take us over"—like so many of her generation of first readers, she seems to believe that we can control our emotions. Several students defined tragedy as a situation that could have been avoided. In *Othello*, as one young woman put it, people died "who didn't really need to"; there could have been a way of "working out the misunderstandings." Another proclaimed that "Jealousy is inherent in human nature, so all must learn to control it." These readers shared my earlier class's concern with order and control, though as a group, they put less emphasis on the issue of communication and trust in marriage and more on Othello's susceptibility to Iago's machinations. One of my questions invited them to explore the relevance of *Othello*'s themes to their own lives and some responded in very moving ways. "Be wary of who you call your friend," one young man urged, adding that "there are manipulative people today who will do anything to get ahead." This statement allies Iago with people who are determined to "get ahead," a stock response which would, one hopes, later be probed and revised in class discussion.

The student who sees Iago as someone who will do anything to get ahead is bringing the preoccupations of his own culture to bear upon his reading of the play. Eleanor Rowe's fascinating study of the reception of *Hamlet* in Russia reveals that Shakespeare's plays have long had this effect on readers and audiences, especially when they come to the plays with very little of the historical preparation Sinfield spoke of. Rowe ends *Hamlet: A Window on Russia* with the following observation: "Perhaps partially because of the trauma of her history and the collective and individual pain of her people, Russia has tended to react to *Hamlet* by reaching for immediate applicability, by assigning to the play and its hero an immediate moral and social value."[33] As each new generation of Russians reinvented its own *Hamlet*, so each generation of student readers will read Shakespeare's plays somewhat differently. Only a few of these students will proceed from first to second and third and fourth readings. When they do, they may discover, as one of my most thoughtful students did, that "I now realize that I could never act as rationally as I had originally wanted Othello to act. I am now much less critical of his character . . . and have a better feeling for the entire play . . . each time I read the play I reevaluate my feelings and that's what keeps me going back."

2

Shakespeare Transformed:
The Merchant of Venice

The prefix *re* has assumed a prominent place in contemporary Shakespeare criticism. The plays are represented, reproduced, and reinvented by legions of readers, actors, directors, writers and academics, who regularly find new ways of rethinking the body of work we continue to refer to as "Shakespeare." This process is hardly new. F. E. Halliday's chapter headings in his 1957 book *The Cult of Shakespeare* provides a witty rundown on the fortunes of Shakespeare from the 1630s onward. "Shakespeare Eclipsed" gave way to "Shakespeare Reformed," and thence to "Shakespeare Refined," "Shakespeare Restored," "Shakespeare Celebrated," "Shakespeare Fabricated," "Shakespeare Eviscerated," "Shakespeare Incorporated," "Shakespeare Commemorated," "Shakespeare Disintegrated," and onward into the early twentieth century, culminating with "Shakespeare Reintegrated."[1] Since the 1950s Shakespeare Reintegrated has become Shakespeare interrogated, psychoanalyzed, and politicized. The new revisionists, as Grace Ioppolo describes herself and other textual scholars investigating authorial reworking and revision, have produced "a new conception of the author as a creator and re-creator, viewer and re-viewer, writer and re-writer of his dramatic world."[2] And then, of course, there is Shakespeare in performance and Shakespeare on television and film. All of these revisions, representations, reproductions, and reinventions are ways of talking back to—and through—Shakespeare; taken together, if such a project were possible, they would constitute a particular kind of social history of our times.

The critical practices associated with the prefix *re* have a corollary in the writerly practices associated with the prefix *trans*. How could Halliday have omitted "Shakespeare Translated"—translated into more languages, very likely, than any other literary text? Since Charles and Mary Lamb, the plays have been repeatedly translated and transformed for children, or for anyone who wants to read them in prose narrative, nondramatic form. The plays have also been transformed—some would say debased—through parodies, travesties, and burlesques, enough to fill hundreds of volumes, but many of them ephemeral and unpublished. The transformations that are of most interest to contemporary readers, however, are those that, in Alan Sinfield's words, "approriate and confront the Shakespeare myth" in one way or another.[3] Charles Marowitz's "Shakespeare Recycled," a 1987 retrospective essay on his Shakespeare variations and their reception (recently reprinted as the title piece in a collection of his essays), defends the collages as part of an ongoing process by which "Shakespeare has been renewed, rekindled, and rejuvenated" by revisionists who recognize that "no play possesses exclusivity of meaning, and the greater the play, the more meanings it is able to engender." To account for "extrapolations" and "variations" and other kinds of "departures" made possible by the "malleable material of William Shakespeare," he proposes a couple of medical metaphors:

> What happens to a work-of-art is that, with the passage of time, it becomes steadily infected by the germs that multiply from one generation to another. The work-of-art that weathers those infections emerges a much healthier specimen; and there is no question that over the centuries, the works of Shakespeare have withstood some pretty devastating plagues and national epidemics.

Shakespeare's greatness, he triumphantly concludes, "is nothing more than the sperm-bank from which we must spawn our own offspring."[4]

A writer like Marowitz is bound to appeal to students—or at least wake them up. Not unexpectedly, the Marowitz of 1968 was considerably more rhetorically audacious than the Marowitz of 1987. One late Friday afternoon I took *The Marowitz Hamlet* to my writing-intensive Shakespeare class and proceeded to read aloud from the part of the introduction entitled "Open Letter to Horatio." The letter begins:

> Dear Horatio,
> I know the world esteems you a "good friend", but in my opinion you are a rotter. A good friend doesn't let his good friend continually delude himself. A good friend says: you've got everything on your side, and if you kill the King and wrest control everyone will support you, but if you continue to indulge in amateur theatricals and walk around with your head up your arse you will lose what small dignity you still possess.
> You are the most obnoxious Yes-man in the Shakespearian canon. . . . I

loathe your muttering obsequiousness, your "Aye, my lord" and "No, my lord" and "Is't possible, my lord?"

It is no wonder Hamlet thinks so highly of you. You possess the very same fault that cripples him: the inability to permit conviction to give birth to action. You lack the moral gumption that makes a man forsake fruitless intellectual roundabouting for the sharp, straight path of direct action. To say that your "blood and judgement" are so well commingled "that they are not a pipe for Fortune's finger / To sound what stop she please" is only another way of saying there is no impulse so naturally overwhelming that you would not be able to rationalize its reversal or abandonment.

My reading ended, two paragraphs later, with Marowitz's final sentence, banishing Horatio from his version of the play: "I hope you will not take this too personally; but the fact is that until further notice your services will no longer be required."[5]

Inadvertently, I had just created my first "talking back" assignment. With no prompting from me, a freshman's subsequent journal contained a very thoughtful and eloquent letter to Escalus in *Measure for Measure*, in which she chided the character for allowing himself to be drawn into the corruption that surrounded him: "You allowed yourself to be bested by even a common bawd . . . you stood by in silence [while] the greatly wronged Isabella and Mariana petitioned the Duke for yet another life." She ended her letter with a splendid rhetorical flourish that reveals the cumulative effect of a semester of reading Shakespeare's language: "There is remedy for injustice, but there is none for honor tarnished through negligence."

I went on to devise other alternatives to the conventional critical essay, among them an invitation to transform a Shakespeare play; students were asked to submit a synopsis, an annotated cast list, a sample scene, and a commentary. This assignment works well with upper-level students, who are more comfortable with Shakespeare's works and more confident of their own abilities as writers than most of the students quoted in Chapter 1. Some of the transformations have been little more than translations, not unlike the set and costume designs in Shakespeare festivals around the country—for example, setting *The Taming of the Shrew* in the Wild West, as The Public Theatre did in New York's Central Park in 1990. But most of the students who choose this assignment attempt to say something, using Shakespeare as the medium, and some do so in inspired and original ways. One young man located his *Richard II* in the Vatican, with Richard as a newly anointed twentieth-century pope presiding over a church whose influence is declining. Cardinal Bullingbrook seeks to stop the decline in church membership by reaching out to the third world, whereas Cardinal Mowbray and his faction resist change. The author was intrigued by

Shakespeare's treatment of the king's two bodies and attempted to explore this idea by having his Richard undergo the transition from an ordinary man to a leader "who truly believes that he rules under divine right and guidance." The author's commentary began with the observation that many people in our class had dismissed as "silly" the belief that the king ruled by divine right. He explained that "By drawing a direct parallel [to the Papacy] . . . I attempt to show in my play that the idea is very much alive today . . . [so that] people will be better able to identify emotionally with the idea of 'divine right.'" Like many of the student transformations, the synopsis also attempts to make sense of events Shakespeare passes over with what seems like insufficient explanation. For instance, the Gloucester in this transformation is a cardinal from San Salvador, one of six cardinals whom Richard, working through Mowbray, arranges to dispose of in such a way as to make it seem that left-wing rebels were responsible. The scheme is intended to embarrass Bullingbrook, who knows what happened but cannot prove it. The transformation follows Shakespeare's first act fairly closely; Mowbray and Bullingbrook are both banished, Mowbray to a hospital in Africa, and Bullingbrook to a small communist country. On his deathbed Gaunt warns Richard that he must change the church or it will lose whatever power and stature it has left. Bullingbrook uses his new position to speak out on behalf of the working classes, and his message is taken up by intellectuals and church officials throughout the world. Eventually Richard is forced to invite Bullingbrook back into the Vatican and adopt his policies. The play ends when Richard dies mysteriously of a heart attack, and Bullingbrook becomes pope.

Some of my resisting readers' transformations have come to the defense of Shakespeare's women characters as a way of talking back to the patriarchal assumptions under which the plays were originally written and performed. A carefully adapted and reconstructed *Antony and Cleopatra*, written by a senior English major, was designed to "make a statement about women in power." In act 1 Antony responds to the news of Fulvia's military activities by angrily asking Enobarbus, "What right has a woman to do battle in her husband's place?" The scene with the soothsayer has Iras and Charmian react indignantly to the suggestion that they might want to know about their husbands and children; these women are only interested in Cleopatra's political fortunes. In an added scene between Octavia and Caesar, she proposes the marriage to Antony, for her own political as well as personal gain. Caesar dismisses the idea scornfully, then publicly presents it as his own. The other scenes in which Octavia appears are altered so that she appears "more assertive"; in act 3, scene 4, when she leaves for Rome, she is "a woman who knows what she wants and won't put up with Antony's behavior." Enobarbus's famous description of Cleopatra on her barge has been changed only slightly, to emphasize her "intellect," through "an anecdote describing a strategic maneuver she once used." She is distraught but not childish in the scenes with the messenger, and gives good reasons for her flight from the sea battle in act 3, scene 11. When Enobarbus decides to leave Antony, it is because he is frustrated that his master "doesn't see when she is right"; this blindness, Enobarbus realizes, will bring about his downfall. In act 4, Charmian "will really have to push" Cleopatra to send Antony the news of her death, and in their final scene together at the monument he acknowledges his stubbornness as the cause of the tragedy. Caesar treats Cleopatra contemptuously, "as a prize and a toy," but she dies "with dignity and grace." The author explained that she didn't want her Antony to come across as a "male chauvinist pig."

> I want him to know what is right. I want the audience to see him strive for that, but he is human and falls short. In this day and age, I don't think there are too many "pigs" out there. I feel most men are like Antony, they are struggling with what they know is right. However, they are fighting against their upbringing.

Enobarbus and Dollabella, she adds, are the kind of men who "can look at Cleopatra as their peer without feeling insecure around a powerful woman." This young woman is using her transformation to steer a middle course through the intensely debated sexual politics of her generation. She deliberately avoids a reductive portrayal of men as "the enemy" and dwells instead on the strong women in her play. Octavia is important to her transformation, she remarks, because unlike Fulvia and Cleopatra, she does not die: "I didn't want to leave the impression that death was the successful woman's fate." The commentary ends with a justification for adding a new character, Caesarion.

> There is a myth that the "working" woman cannot be a good mother. I wanted to contradict that. I looked at a biography of Cleopatra, which said she was indeed a good mother. She loved Caesarion very much and she tried to secure his rightful place as Caesar's heir.

A very different transformation of *Antony and Cleopatra* was submitted by an imaginative, enthusiastic student who had difficulty with conventional exams and assignments. She envisioned the play as a science fiction film set in the year 2026. Mark Antony lives on the planet Caesar, ruled by Caesar, and in the course of the play becomes obsessed with the planet Cleopatra, "known for its serenity and utter bliss." While visiting that planet, Antony becomes "interested in philosophy, perhaps the philosophy of war" and begins to question the importance of conquering new lands. This upsets Caesar and eventually leads the two men to battle. The author mentions none of Shakespeare's characters except Enobarbus, who leaves Antony, is rejected by Caesar, and "drifts off into deep space alone." The play remains a love story, the commentary emphasizes: Antony blows up the planet he loves so much because he cannot bear the thought of losing "her." The author suggests that this is a form of madness and that Antony sees a female ghost, or illusion, who speaks to him only when he is on his planet. The influence of *Hamlet* is evident here, but the transformation is revealing in other respects. Like the other *Antony and Cleopatra*, this work resists Shakespeare's depiction of women but finds a way out of the dilemma by resorting to science fiction fantasy. Shakespeare's gloriously contentious, willful, self-dramatizing queen has become a desirable but essentially silent abstraction without visible form, dwarfing the embattled men of the play. The writer has consciously or unconsciously pursued Shakespeare's "world" imagery; Cleopatra, so often synonymous with Egypt, has literally become a world in this version of the story, but in doing so, she loses her human quality.

The last transformation I will mention here is in some ways the most radical one I received. It was submitted by an English honors student who said in her final exam that she had become interested in the multiple roles characters assume (Hamlet, for example) and in the way those characters are endowed with the ability to reinvent themselves. Her transformation was entitled

THE REAWAKENING OF JULIET
1989
HEY! ROMEO IS A JERK

The first scene takes place in a college classroom where about twenty students are reading aloud in unison from their Riverside Shakespeares. "Suddenly in one of the back desks appears a ghost-like apparition in the form of Shakespeare's Juliet." As the students read Romeo's lines about Rosaline in act 1, scene 1, she "jumps out of the play and into the front of the classroom," demanding to know "who this other woman is." The astonished students and professor attempt "to shut her up," so that they can proceed in an orderly way to prepare for the final exam. Juliet will not be silenced, however, and continues to comment acidly on Paris's intentions ("all he thinks about is mothering") and Romeo's pathetically self-indulgent behavior. Finally she announces that "I'm not doing the tomb scene today. It is just too much to handle after all of this misery and faithlessness." Once the students stop worrying about what they need to learn for the exam and support her position, she returns to the play and the reading continues. When Paris appears at the tomb in act 5, scene 3, there is Juliet, alive and waiting for everyone to arrive so that she can deliver the final speech. The author's commentary explains that "I intend to hand the authority of her fate and Romeo's over to Juliet." She is "awakened to Romeo's childish characteristics and saves both of them from impending doom," in an "updated comedy that retains the tragic framework of the original." In her final speech, Juliet announces that "I am going to eat, drink, and be merry because the next time that a student picks up this play I will let myself die. It is much easier that way and whenever I feel the need I will change the play again because now that I have the knowledge, the authority is mine." What makes this transformation especially interesting is the way it formulates the idea that a text does not need to be the "same" each time it is read or performed and that its variants can reflect the participant's need—projected onto the character—to assert herself in the face of authorial authority. The writer also explores the implications of the character's limited knowledge of the events in the play, as well as the past and present lives of other characters, drawing attention to the function of dramatic irony in the process.

*   *   *

After using this assignment for a few semesters, I decided to break with the traditional format of the undergraduate Shakespeare course and ask my students to read a contemporary transformation in place of one of the plays I would normally assign. I devised an assignment for an upper-level Shakespeare course that entailed the following month-long sequence: Students read *The Merchant of Venice* and wrote a response journal which they submitted for comments; we then discussed the play for a week or so, and they read Arnold Wesker's *The Merchant* on their own and wrote another journal. Finally, they reread *The Merchant of Venice* and wrote a paper about how their reading of the play had changed over the past month. As they were doing this, I embarked on a more extensive exploration of *Merchant of Venice* transformations and variations. There are few plays in the Shakespeare canon that have inspired as much highly charged talking back. *The Merchant of Venice* is particularly susceptible to sequels, for this is a story that invites speculation about all three of its plotlines. Bassanio and Portia's courtship differs from the extended courtships in the other middle romantic comedies, so much so that the ring business of act 5 can easily be seen as the beginning of the process of accommodation and adjustment that leads to a stable union rather than as an ending. Readers and audiences also want to know what will become of Lorenzo and

Jessica's intermarriage, and of course they—we—are curious about Shylock.

To extend another author's play into the future is a way of talking back to his or her decisions about closure. St. John Ervine used this strategy in his 1924 play, *The Lady of Belmont*, which returns to Belmont ten years after the conclusion of *The Merchant of Venice*. Ervine's play is an attempt to answer some questions a skeptical reader might pose about the aftermath of Shakespeare's fourth- and fifth-act resolutions. The three couples, Bassanio and Portia, Gratiano and Nerissa, and Lorenzo and Jessica, now inhabit a country-house-weekend-inspired Belmont, where the quickly contracted marriages of *The Merchant of Venice* have succumbed to sophisticated matter-of-fact twentieth-century bickering, indifference, and infidelities. When Shylock unexpectedly faints at Portia's gate on the day a festive dinner is being prepared in honor of her cousin Bellario's visit, the characters are forced to remember and relive the events of ten years earlier. Antonio has become the pathetic and garrulous unwanted houseguest, obsessed with recounting his brush with death. Bassanio is virulently anti-Semitic and an irresponsible womanizer: he tells Jessica, with whom he is having a rather weary affair, that "I'll love you as long as I can. No one can promise more. An active gentleman that has his health and strength, when there are no wars, must have variety of love."[6] Shylock has been transformed by the outcome of the trial into a highly respected and prosperous Venetian Senator, outwardly Christian but, like so many European Jews in Shakespeare's time, secretly faithful to his religion. He has come to Belmont to get a glimpse of the grandsons he has never met and will, at the play's end, succeed in taking them and their parents back to Venice. After a night of deception, detection, and revelations, Portia says to Shylock, "You see us all here as we are: Nerissa with her drunken, faithless husband, Lorenzo deceived by Jessica, and I married to a husband I despise! . . . Oh, sir, you've won your pound of flesh! We must seem very despicable in your eyes" (93). But for Shylock the pound of flesh and the revenge it embodies are no longer important. He rejects the "bitter-minded man" he once was, while acknowledging that "sometimes, still, I am full of anger when I hear my race derided. . . . We are a proud and narrow race, and our pride and narrow minds have ruined us. I have the power to govern men. . . . But I'm condemned, because I am a Jew, to be a usurer and spend my mind on little furtive schemes for making money" (94). And yet he tells Portia that "I must forgive," and on that note the play ends, inconclusively in respect to the three couples but with an affirmation of hope for Christian-Jewish relations symbolized by the friendship and mutual respect Shylock and Portia share.

Ervine attempted to solve the ethical problems *The Merchant of Venice* poses for modern audiences by positing a world of mostly contemptible Christians and an admirable Jew, a solution other writers and directors have opted for as well.[7] Portia is the only Christian who earns our respect, but her strengths have little scope; other than her fierce insistence on preserving Shylock's dignity, her role is confined to that of the aggrieved wife. Jessica, as in so many interpretations of *The Merchant of Venice*, is sharply contrasted with her father: Ervine, in a stage direction, describes her as "*still the mean little sweep she was when she ran away with LORENZO. Her beauty is slightly marred by lines of discontent about her eyes and mouth, and she is more obviously sensual than she was ten years ago*" (42). Shylock tells Portia in their final scene together that he has "few illusions left" about his daughter but affirms "I am a Jew, and every Jew has a passion for posterity." The closure Ervine offers here is the prospect of a better life for the three grandsons who will inherit Shylock's property. "When I lose hope in one place, madam," he tells Portia, "I try to find it in another" (93). Ervine, as we shall see, was not the only writer to endow his transformed Shylock with grandsons, an investment in the future that has the power to alleviate the painfulness of the present.

The insistent polarities *The Merchant of Venice* seems to invite (good Christians, bad Jew; good Jew, bad Christians) were confronted head-on by Arnold Wesker in 1976. *The Merchant* radically realigns the plot's central axis by presenting Antonio and Shylock as the closest and most mutually generous of friends. Wesker also tries to make sense of the Shylock-Jessica relationship and the reservations modern readers might have about the casket plot and Bassanio's and Portia's roles therein. Curiously enough, Marowitz makes no mention of *The Merchant* in either the *Shakespeare Survey* or the *Shakespeare Quarterly* articles when he urges the modern theatre to embark on "a whole slew of new experiences and new artifacts which can be spawned from the original sources, in exactly the same way that Shakespeare spawned his works from Holinshed, Boccaccio, Kyd, and Belleforest."[8] And yet Wesker, perhaps more than other transformers of Shakespeare's plays, has reconstituted Shakespeare's fables and the fables that preceded them by reaching back to *The Merchant of Venice*'s antecedents in folklore and history for the materials from which to create his version of the ancient Flesh Bond tale. He also involved students in the process. In an interview, Wesker describes the experience of watching Jonathan Miller's 1973 production of *The Merchant of Venice*, "which I didn't like, and I certainly detested Olivier's 'oi, oi, oi' sort of Jew. When Portia suddenly gets to the bit about having a pound of flesh but no blood, it flashed on me that the kind of Jew I know would stand up and say,

'Thank god!'"[9] So he decided to write a new play, the point of which would be "to explain how he [Shylock] became involved in such a bond in the first place.[10] A teaching engagement in Boulder, Colorado intervened, and as he taught "The History of Contemporary British Drama" Wesker began to feel

> very fraudulent, because I didn't really want to talk about my contemporaries. I just wanted to talk about this new play I was going to write, and perhaps that might tell them more about the new British drama than anything I might say about other writers. So I involved them all in the background research that I would otherwise be doing, and some of the students wrote papers. And one student in particular wrote a very long and, I thought, brilliant paper, in which she gave me one of the pillars on which my case rested, about how you couldn't have dealings with a Jew except through a contract.[11]

The Merchant was subsequently dedicated to the student, Lois Bueler. A certain amount of talking back seems to have been part of the research process. In the playbill for the American production, Wesker spoke of how the drama students "wrote papers, prodded, questioned, and finally found they could support my approach."[12] Having convinced his students, and armed with the Arden edition of *The Merchant of Venice* and the works of Cecil Roth, whose *Jews in the Renaissance, Essays and Portraits in Anglo-Jewish History* and other books he used extensively, Wesker retired to the Welsh mountains to read and write.

Wesker's unpublished diary indicates that he became familiar with the sources John Russell Brown included in the Arden edition.[13] The imprint of Shakespeare's principal source, *Il Pecarone*, is evident in his version of Bassanio, who is Antonio's godson, unknown to him until a letter arrives from his old friend in Milan. Unlike Ser Giovanni's Ansaldo, who greets Giannetto with "Welcome my dear godson, whom I have longed for so much," Wesker's Antonio frets to Shylock that "he's probably a swaggering young braggart" (6).[14] When Bassanio arrives at Shylock's house, where Antonio has spent the night, he does indeed justify Antonio's uneasiness. He has never met a Jew before, and is visibly uncomfortable about the prospect of borrowing the three thousand ducats from Shylock, whom he persists in referring to as "the Jew" (21). Wesker's irrepressibly generous and hospitable Shylock shrugs off this behavior: with a burst of laughter, he observes that "there are a hundred million people in China who've not met a Jew before" (22). He is delighted with the prospect of being able to do a favor for the beloved friend who shares his pleasure in books and has been helping him catalogue precious volumes that have been hidden for ten years. Shylock refuses to draw up a contract for the loan of the three thousand ducats, even though, as Antonio tells him, "the law demands it." "That law was made for enemies, not friends," Shylock rejoins. When Antonio quotes the law, Shylock quotes the Deuteronomic code back to him: "Thou shalt not lend upon usury to thy brother." Finally Shylock proposes "A lovely, loving nonsense bond. To mock the law"— a "barbaric" bond to mock barbaric laws. The scene ends with the two friends laughing like children, tickling and goosing one another's pounds of flesh (23–26). Later, in the courtroom scene, the Doge is prepared to release both men from the bond, but Shylock and Antonio refuse. Neither wants to "bend the law" and set a precedent; in their private scene together before the trial Antonio had said to Shylock "Your yellow hat belongs to both of us" (63). The undisguised Portia finally interrupts the trial, explaining that "the contract is not binding because—impossible." Wesker's reworking of *The Merchant of Venice* has brought him to the point he had envisioned before his research began: Shylock cries "Thank God!" and embraces Antonio, then extravagantly praises Portia, who sadly anticipates what will follow. As in the original courtroom scene, the Doge cites the law that condemns to death any alien who plots against a Venetian citizen, and then offers to confiscate Shylock's goods and let him live. The "goods" are the scholar's beloved books, and without them, he is empty, "a bitter man," consumed by the passionate contempt for men he had spoken of earlier to Antonio: "Seeing what men have done, I know with great weariness the pattern of what they will do, and I have such contempt, such contempt it bewilders me. . . . My contempt, sometimes, knows no bounds. And it has destroyed me" (63–64).

For his portrait of Shylock, Wesker drew heavily on his research, rejecting what might be viewed as the "old historicist" rationalizations that absolve Shakespeare of anti-Semitism by regarding his portrayal of Shylock as "only" a reflection of his culture's ignorance about Jews and prejudices against moneylenders. Rather like the Shakespeare of the cultural materialists, who, as Jonathan Dollimore describes them, attempt to "subvert, interrogate, and undermine the ruling ideologies,"[15] Wesker armed himself with the tools of the historian and set out to interrogate our culture's cumulative image of Shylock the Jew. As Efraim Sicher observes, he "does not so much rewrite or reinterpret Shakespeare as answer him"; his Shylock affirms his "Jewish destiny" by choosing loyalty to his community over his friend.[16] From Roth, Wesker learned of scholarly loan-bankers for whom money-lending was a part-time occupation that left time for studying and of Christians like Pico della Mirandola who sought out Jewish scholars and entered into close friendships with them.[17] In contrast to Shakespeare's solitary Shylock, whose "sober house" must be protected from festive music, Wesker's Shylock throws open his doors to a large collection of visitors in the opening scenes. With his older sister Rivka, he welcomes the Portuguese Marranos, or Anusim, Solomon Usque and Rebecca da Mendes, the latter inspired by the distinguished Portuguese Jew Gracia Mendes.[18] The family circle also includes Roderigues da Cunha, a young architect who is drawing up plans for a new synagogue Shylock is helping to build, Shylock's partner Tubal, and Jessica, a willful young woman who dismisses her highly respected father as an "intellectual snob" and feels oppressed by his passions, ideals, and dogmas and the "tight restricting little codes" with which he imposes them on her (8, 9, 24). Wesker enables the reader to feel sympathy for both father and daughter as he dramatizes the intergenerational conflict between two strong-minded antagonists. Through Jessica, Wesker poses a familiar question to readers of Shakespeare: "At what point is the child's right of movement and taste taken into consideration? Does she only become whole when taken from the possession of her father to the possession of her husband?" (36).[19] Usque, observing this debate, which ends with Jessica storming out, warns Shylock that he will drive her into a hasty marriage. But Shylock is not listening; the stage direction indicates that his ever-active scholar's mind "is thinking of other things" (37).

Jessica rebels by running off to Belmont with Lorenzo but soon begins to regret her choice. When Lorenzo says "I will make you a wife, a woman and a Christian" she responds *with controlled fury.* "Sometimes I think the sadness in my eyes comes from the knowledge that we draw from men their desperate hates. . . . That is my doom! to know that secret: that at any time, for any reason, men are capable of such demented acts" (67). She finds a kindred spirit in Portia, who had told Nerissa in their first appearance

I feel I-am-the-new-woman-and-they-know-me-not! For centuries the Church has kept me comfortably comforting and cooking and pleasing and patient. And now—Portia is no longer patient. Yes, she can spin, weave, sew . . . . But Portia reads! Plato and Aristotle, Ovid and Catullus, all in the original! Latin, Greek, Hebrew—(48)

Determined to work hard at farming to restore the family's decayed estates, and driven by the energy she inherited from her peasant mother, Portia suspects that her eccentric but dearly beloved father's "caskets will bring me down as his other madnesses brought down my mother" (47). And yet she abides by his wishes. After Bassanio chooses the lead casket, she briefly embraces him, then sends him away and confides in Nerissa, wondering if she will tire of him, fully aware of his faults. Rather like Jessica, she resists the arrogance and presumption which make men, in Nerissa's words, "such clumsy things." "What feeble and pathetic arts they have," Portia adds. "And we must pretend!" (52). In the final scene at Belmont, Portia tells Antonio "I'll look after Jessica. My marriage is a parent's will, not hers, though. Mine can't be held back, hers, I will see, never takes place" (83). The last words of the play belong to Nerissa, a confident intellectual like her mistress, who, in a witty variation of the "Tell me where is fancy bred" song, was reading aloud from Seneca's letters while Bassanio contemplated the caskets. "And heroes you are, sirs," she says mockingly to Bassanio, Graziano and Lorenzo as she brings them drinks in the Belmont garden. "True, true heroes, indeed. True. True, true, true. Heroes!" (85).

It should be evident by this point that Wesker problematizes the *Merchant of Venice* marriages just as pointedly as he does the Flesh Bond story. Like Ervine's Portia, this Portia is left at the end to face an unromantic future with a man she does not respect. There is more hope for the Portia of the 1970s than there was for her less interesting 1920s counterpart, however. To her newfound friend Antonio she confides

> I'll fill my house with poets and philosophers, and politicians who are poets and philosophers. Bassanio will come to know his place, accept it, or leave it. I am to be reckoned with, you know, not merely dutiful. Although, something in me has died struggling to grow up. (84)

Something has died in Shylock as well, Wesker implies; his parting words at the end of the courtroom scene could almost have been spoken by Portia, Jessica, or Nerissa: "I am so tired of men" (82). He will embark on a pilgrimage to Jerusalem, where Antonio hopes to "visit him once, perhaps, before I die" (83). The language of weariness and death, mingled as it is with the *"inane conversation"* of the three young men and the *"distant sad singing"* of a woman singing a Sephardic song, brings the play to a melancholy conclusion, although the three women's self-preserving energy qualifies that melancholy somewhat. Writing in the mid–1970s, just as feminist readings of Shakespeare were beginning to challenge many widely held interpretations of the plays, Wesker seems to be suggesting that women as a community may succeed where Jews have not in resisting the impositions of ruling ideologies.

The Merchant had a successful premiere in Stockholm in 1976, followed by a short run on Broadway in 1977. This ill-starred enterprise was doomed by the sudden death of its leading actor, Zero Mostel, after the first preview night in Philadelphia. A British production was mounted by the Birmingham Repertory Theatre in 1978, but the play has never been given the attention it deserves.[20] Jeanne Addison Roberts saw the American production at the Kennedy Center in Wash-

ington; her brief review in *Shakespeare Quarterly* describes it as an
"ambitious effort" with "occasional brilliance" but one that "finally
foundered on the absurdity of the trial itself. If the bond was a joke,
why could it not be dismissed?" She ends by speculating that "there
is little reason to suppose that Shakespeare would have rejected the
darker version," a roundabout endorsement, on the Bard's behalf, of
Wesker's "vision," if not of his plotting.[21] A decade later, the climate
in Shakespeare studies had changed. Alan Sinfield, an important presence among British cultural materialists, took a different view of
Wesker's experiment. He begins his essay on "appropriation and confrontation in recent British plays" by discussing the "cultural space"
any writing needs and the way a dramatist's "bid for cultural space"
constitutes "an attempt to take part in the making of culture." (Culture, for Sinfield, following Raymond Williams, is "an amalgam of the
current stories of who we are . . . and especially, about the power relations between us.") Like Marowitz, Sinfield reminds us that "Shakespeare altered, often hugely, all the stories he dealt with"; by doing
so, he "was working politically, making his culture. And our subsequent work with the idea of Shakespeare and with Shakespearean texts
is the same kind of activity."[22]

Wesker, then, is making culture, and his bid for cultural space on
behalf of Jews grows out of his own experience as a Jew who became
"unforgiving of [Shakespeare's] play's contribution to the world's
astigmatic and murderous hatred of the Jew."[23] No matter that Shakespeare's portrayal of Shylock may have been "a product of its time" that
"verges on the sympathetic," as *The Jewish Chronicle* reported in 1981.
Wesker responded to this by saying in an article that first appeared in
The Guardian in 1981 and serves as the preface to the Methuen student
edition:

> I don't understand the logic of that argument. If we are presenting the play in
> "our times" what is the relevance of pointing out it was a sympathetic vision
> in past times? We're not living in those times. (Li)

And so, as Sinfield remarks, after a brief discussion of *The Merchant*,

> People sometimes say: "But why tinker with Shakespeare? Why not write a
> totally new play?" I think *The Merchant of Venice* is sufficiently interesting,
> and its topic sufficiently important, to indicate the answer. The racism of *The
> Merchant of Venice*—for all that criticism can unearth qualifications, hesita-
> tions and complexities—must not be ignored. While we have a competitive
> economic and political system rooted in differentials of class, gender, sexual
> orientation and race, this will manifest itself at the level of culture. Subordi-
> nate and dissident groups make their culture in the space left by the hegemonic

culture—there is nowhere else. Shakespeare is a powerful cultural token, and hence a place where meaning is established and where it must be contested.[24]

Classrooms are also places where meanings are established and contested. The unwritten history of *The Merchant of Venice* in British and American school curricula is alluded to in passing in the opening sentence of Wesker's *Guardian* piece. "Once again *The Merchant of Venice* is on school syllabuses." A few Jews have in the past and will no doubt again demand that the play be withdrawn from school syllabuses, he continues, although the majority, "if they know what's good for them, will keep quiet."[25] Wesker's play, in this context, is a deliberate effort to get them to talk back.

A large number of my students are from the metropolitan New York area, the world's largest Jewish community. Some have encountered *The Merchant of Venice* in high school, although they are more likely to have read *The Taming of the Shrew* or *Twelfth Night* or *A Midsummer Night's Dream*.[26] Like every teacher of the play, I have had to steer carefully among their initial responses to what some of them, with Wesker, would no doubt regard as "the play's irredeemable anti-semitism." As one might expect, the *Merchant of Venice*-Wesker assignment generated a good deal of talking back to Shakespeare, some of it preceding and some of it inspired by the experience of reading *The Merchant*.

There were a few instances of the kind of advice-giving talking back I discussed in Chapter 1, though fewer than I generally encounter in introductory Shakespeare classes. One young woman, for example, said of Shylock that "He should learn to channel [his anger] in more useful ways, but he has been severely humiliated." This student had been "bored" by the first reading ("I kept waiting for something to happen") and disturbed by the anti-Semitism. A serious feminist, she also disliked Shakespeare's "sexism," though she would "tolerate his portrayal of women only because I know that he was only depicting the way it really was." She was "captivated" and "delighted" by Wesker's play and quickly identified with the characters. Speaking of Antonio's admiring envy of Shylock in the opening scene, she remarked, "If you have ever had a friend as active and vibrant as Shylock, you've felt this way." Not unexpectedly, her "favorite parts" of *The Merchant* were the scenes in which Portia appears. The rereading journal begins by commenting on what a "different experience" rereading the play had been and later returns to the "strangeness" of "coming off *The Merchant* and reading *The Merchant of Venice*." She ends with "I'm no longer bored—I think Shakespeare had a lot to say."

This student's sympathy for Wesker's Shylock—qualified somewhat by her recognition that "being Shylock's daughter would be tiresome

and irritating"—is what enables her to return to Shakespeare's Shylock
and understand the humiliation that drove him to revenge. She now
feels that "he's justified in his anger." Another student expressed similar feelings. "At first I saw Shylock as an evil, bitter man. In my second reading, however, I found him to be a much more pitiful character.
He is a Jew living in an anti-Semitic society and had to adapt in order
to survive." *The Merchant*, she continued, "forces its audience to question the motives of the people who are hostile to Shylock." She brought
that questioning attitude back to *The Merchant of Venice* and "wondered
if the hostility is due to his religion." Many of the students were
shocked by what they learned from Wesker about life in the sixteenth-
century Venetian ghetto. Reading *The Merchant* made them confront
the historical realities behind what they had originally seen as Shakespeare's stark antithesis between Christians and Jews. An Italian-
American student said "I was really amazed that Wesker's Shylock had
to hide his books for the past ten years. It was also appalling to discover that the Jews had to reside in the overcrowded Ghetto Nuovo . . .
Wesker really made me see the inhumanity done to Jews." A Jewish
student with many years of religious education behind her said that
she'd never known about the yellow hats. Another non-Jewish student
said that "*The Merchant* really made me think about society's attitude
towards Jews and what it must be like to be Jewish." And a young man
who originally dismissed Shylock as a "Scrooge-type character" used
his rereading journal to express his indignation at the way the Christians expect and "demand" mercy from a man they have treated so poor-
ly. He made a serious effort to account for Shylock's obsession with
wealth: "he has taken money so intimately into himself that it has
become part of his value system." Shakespeare, he says, faults Shylock for his values, not his religion.

   This last student, who had undoubtedly been taught in high school to
revere the Bard, was troubled by Wesker's characterization of Shakespeare as an anti-Semite. For him, as for many of the other students,
the assignment was a disruptive experience but disruptive in productive ways. As one student put it:

> What shocks me most concerning my rereading of the play is how much bit-
> terness and cruelty I missed the first time through. Perhaps it was the pres-
> sure of expectations subconsciously associated with comedy (good will tri-
> umph over evil, happy resolution, etc.), but after a second reading the only
> comic resolution I see is forced.

   This student had originally viewed Antonio as "the hero" and Shylock as "the villain." He now sees that these terms are inadequate and

is reading Antonio's behavior far more critically. "By unwisely making promises," he moralizes, "Shylock and Antonio both put themselves into situations that nearly destroy them." He condemns the "candied cruelty" disguised as mercy the Duke and Antonio show to Shylock during the trial, and remarks that "Shakespeare portrays a world where the lines between good and evil are sharply drawn, and no treatment is too cruel for the enemy." This drama, he concludes, is "a dialogue in which the values and judgments of a whole society are called into question."

One of the most interesting papers focused on Wesker's handling of "the seemingly impossible question" of the relative claims of "the life of the innocent man on one side of the scales (moral principles) versus the integrity of the law (the traditional rule of trading families) on the other." The writer wonders what would have happened "if Portia had not attended court with her loophole." The conflict between what is morally right and what is legally right is a crucial contemporary question, he notes, adding, "I must say that the more I think about this, as the question has been debated in my head since the finishing of *The Merchant*, the more this question intrigues, fascinates, frustrates, and frightens me." The paper concludes with Bassanio's line "to do a great right do a little wrong" as part of a meditation on the way "the decision makers" make "value judgments." There is no inherent "rightness" in one interpretation or another, he decides, which is why "Wesker's Shylock was right. The nature of power *is* knowledge."

For most of the students, moral issues turned on human relationships, and interestingly, Shylock's and Jessica's parent-child relationship received more attention than any other. The 1989–90 Peter Hall production of *The Merchant of Venice* was playing in New York while the course was in progress, and I had told the class how Dustin Hoffman and Francesca Buller played act 1, scene 5, the scene in which Shylock instructs Jessica to "Lock up my doors" as he takes his reluctant leave of her. Hoffman's Shylock was the devoted, affectionate, and apprehensive father in this scene, while Buller's Jessica was seemingly responsive to his warm embraces. The audience became increasingly aware of her duplicity as she remained silent while he talked on, and then sprang to life and delivered her unpleasantly dismissive couplet after his departure ("Farewell, and if my fortune be not cross'd, / I have a father, you a daughter, lost" [56–57]). The effect of the scene was to make the audience feel sympathy for Shylock and a corresponding wariness about Jessica, a wariness intensified by Hall's direction of her scene with Lorenzo in act 3, scene 5. Jessica seems uneasy about her elopement; Lorenzo's line, "How cheer'st thou, Jessica?" takes note of her unhappy mien after Launcelot's anti-Semitic jesting about the price of pork. When Jessica elaborately praises Portia, concluding "for the poor rude world / Hath not her fellow," Lorenzo's rejoinder "even such a husband / Hast thou of me as she is for [a] wife" strikes a discordant note, and the two go off to dinner in a state of suspended hostility (82–84). They are still at odds in act 5, scene 1 in the opening exchange which invokes unfaithful and unhappy lovers: Troilus and Cressida, Thisbe, Dido, Medea and Jason. Jessica is clearly brooding on her betrayal of her father when she says "In such a night / Did Jessica steal from the wealthy Jew, / And with an unthrift love did run from Venice . . ." (14–16). They become reconciled by the time Portia arrives, although we are never entirely sure that Jessica is comfortable with her situation as a Jew among Christians.

Hall's production could be characterized as an interpretation that talks back to *The Merchant of Venice* and its critical history without actually changing a word. In this respect it differs from ideologically inspired transformations or translations, while sharing with them the impulse to work against the grain of conventional staging and characterization. Hall's staging of these three scenes hints at a complexity in Jessica that Wesker had developed much further. My students were quite affected by Wesker's handling of this aspect of the play, and returned to *The Merchant of Venice* with questions and challenges for Shakespeare. A very eloquent first reading, which couldn't "decide if the play is anti-Semitic or is using anti-Semitism as parody as a way of denouncing it," expressed a desire for a more complete comic closure. "I would have liked to see Shylock reunited with his daughter or forgiven by the others for a real happy ending. I liked the play but it disturbed me, especially the end." In her rereading journal the student remarked that she preferred Wesker's treatment of Jessica. "It always seemed a little wrong that she just up and abandons her entire life, family and religion. . . . Like any young girl who has run away from home, she is having second thoughts; she is sad, lonely, and confused. This does not come across well in Shakespeare." Although she is reassured about the prospect of Jessica being "reunited with her family" rather than marrying Lorenzo at the end of *The Merchant*, she concludes that in other respects "this ending is all wrong. Lorenzo, Bassanio and Graziano should be the unhappy ones . . . [and] Antonio and Portia should get married. Stranger things have happened." This curious mix of resisting Shakespeare's comic closures and yet wanting to impose a comic closure of their own occurred in other papers. The feminist student "loves it" when Wesker's Jessica ignores Lorenzo in the final scene but is disappointed that Shylock and his defenders "give up too easily." Another student remarked that she was "happy" when Wesker's Jessica gets angry at Lorenzo for suggesting that she convert and adds that "Her insistence on converting in *The Merchant of Venice* bothered me more than Lorenzo's asking her to convert in *The Merchant*."

Many of my students found Wesker's portrayal of five strong women

characters and the solidarity, the sense of a mutually supporting community among them, to be a welcome relief from the male Shakespearean worlds in which women are on the periphery except when they
resort to disguise and subterfuge in their roles as love objects. While
they admired Wesker's Portia for her strength, independence, shrewd-
ness, and sense of humor, they kept returning to Jessica, in whom they
could see familiar character traits. Two young women scolded Jessica
for being a "spoiled brat" who did not respect her father; by contrast,
a rather sophisticated senior English major who started off wondering
if Jessica was "jealous" because she did not get much attention from
Shylock later felt that

> she had a right to feel as she did . . . I was proud of her for leaving, and was
> very pleased that she did not end up with Lorenzo. I saw her as a somewhat
> strong character, especially when she did not give in to Lorenzo's request that
> she convert. She took a risk in leaving her father, yet it was a carefully
> thought-out risk. . . .

Later in her paper she remarked parenthetically, "Shakespeare's Jessica and Portia were much weaker." Another young woman poses some
questions about Shakespeare's Jessica in her first reading journal:

> In act 2, scene 3, I tried to establish if Jessica was ashamed to be Shylock's
> daughter because he was a Jew or because of the way in which he conducted
> business. If she was ashamed of the way he treated business associates, why
> would she give up her heritage so easily?

She was "annoyed" at first, then "sorry for" Wesker's Jessica, who does
not give her father the "respect" he deserves and, like the students in
Chapter 1, worries about "her tendency to make rash decisions out of
passion rather than out of wise thinking." She "should have thought
more about a decision as great as leaving her family." Still another student, who devoted much more attention to Jessica than to Shylock in
her journals, was clearly put off by Jessica's cynicism about the value
of the books and her "lack of manners" when she is late for a portrait
sitting in *The Merchant*. She characterized this Jessica as "a typical
1960s rebelling teenager." But Shylock, she realized, offers his daughter "no freedom . . . he is trying to raise the perfect daughter and Jessica resents it." After a brief digression expressing admiration for Portia, who is independent and "accustomed to hard work," she resumed
her analysis of Jessica: "She seems like a bitter girl, or maybe she is
desperate to find a solution to her problems, and frustrated with her
father's persistent lightheartedness." She "pities" Jessica at the end,
and hopes that she will reconcile with Shylock. Father and daughter

are alike, she observes, in that "they both run away from their problems." Reading Wesker made her unable to see Shakespeare's Lorenzo and Jessica as "moonstruck lovers" just as she now doubts the sincerity of the love between Portia and Bassanio.

The Merchant, this student concluded, is a "dark play," and some of its darkness seems to have carried over to her rereading of *The Merchant of Venice*. The student who was initially annoyed by Jessica had a similar response. When she reread *The Merchant of Venice*, she was struck by the lack of remorse in that Jessica; Wesker's Jessica "seems much wiser and more compassionate by comparison." Portia and Antonio are also "wiser for the experience" at the end of *The Merchant*, she notes approvingly, whereas in *The Merchant of Venice* "no one seems affected by the tragedy which has occurred."

The notion that *The Merchant of Venice* is a tragedy—Shylock's tragedy—has been an important shaping force in the play's production history, one that calls into question the conventional distinctions among genres that have until recently shaped much teaching of and writing about Shakespeare. Reading *The Merchant* caused some of my students to question their previously held assumptions about tragedy and comedy and to view both Shylock and the other characters as tragic figures of a modern kind, not noble princes or leaders who fall from positions of power, but ordinary people caught in the webs of troubling relationships. A *Merchant of Venice* transformation of 1987, the York Theatre Company's musical *Shylock*, attempted to present the play in this light. Described by its author/composer (and leading actor) Ed Dixon as an attempt to explain Shylock's motivation sympathetically, *Shylock* ends with a scene between Shylock and Jessica. Shylock is leaving his house with his few remaining belongings and encounters Jessica, alone. "No news of you, and you know not what's spent in the search," he tells her, and then, a few lines later, "No sighs but o' my breathing, no tears but o' my shedding." Their duet ends with her line "Fare thee well, wish me well," and then she exits, as he begins "walking in place as all sense of time and location fades away, leaving him wandering through eternity." Like Wesker, Dixon has emphasized the pain both Shylock and Jessica felt as a consequence of her elopement; earlier, when Shylock recognizes her voice in the courtroom scene (she is dressed as a man and accompanies Portia and Nerissa), he delivers a moving rendition of the "Hath not a Jew eyes" speech, at the end of which she runs from the court.[27]

The sympathetic and tragic Shylock of stage history is at least as old as Edmund Kean's interpretation, first performed in 1814, which presented a suffering, extraordinarily human Shylock who "left the courtroom with the audience on his side." By 1900, M. M. Mahood notes, "a kind of synthetic *The Merchant of Venice* had replaced Shakespeare's in playgoers' minds. It was above all a character study of Shylock, who emerged from its events as a tragic hero, even 'a heroic saint'" (Ellen Terry's words). Throughout the period, the play frequently ended with Shylock's departure at the end of act 4, and was referred to as "Shakespeare's Tragedy of *The Merchant of Venice*."[28] Henry Irving's Shylock, first performed in 1879, departed from the stage "a retreating, broken old man" in early performances, although later, Irving's portrayal reportedly became less sympathetic, and act 5 was reinstated.[29] More recently, an account of two Israeli productions describes Aharon Meskin's post–World War II Shylock, whose heroic revenge was shown to be justified, and who was "left miserable and penniless on the stage while his victors celebrated unjustifiably," and a daring 1970 production in which Shylock was "a poor little anti-hero," "a little Jewish sinner" who was also "partially in the right." Of this latter production, Gershon Shaked observes

> That the Jewish protagonist erred or sinned or was cruel does not give his enemies the right to persecute him. That was more of less the purport of Yezraeli's reinterpretation: it was a translation of Shakespeare's world, with its prejudices and conventional meanings (along with the interpretative tradition imposed on the play in particular after World War II) to the conditions and needs of the independent Jewish state, which was capable of saying to itself that Jews need not be perfect in order not to be persecuted.[30]

According to Toby Lelyveld, *The Merchant of Venice* is the most often performed of Shakespeare's plays, after *Hamlet*, in English-speaking countries.[31] The production history of the play elsewhere is equally revealing; for instance, fifty or more productions recorded in Germany between 1933 and 1944 enlisted Shakespeare's authority in defense of anti-Semitism.[32] This kind of appropriation, while it may not change the language of the play much, constitutes a particular form of talking back, one motivated by a single-minded ideological agenda. Needless to say, it prompted pro-Jewish reappropriations in various forms, notably some very politicized critical studies of the play.

Hermann Sinsheimer's *Shylock: The History of a Character* was written in Hitler's Germany in 1936–37 and eventually published in London in 1947. Sinsheimer's historical approach to his subject places Shylock in the context of medieval and sixteenth-century Jewry, with sections on Gerontus, the Jew in William Wilson's 1584 morality play *The Three Ladies of London*, Marlowe's Barabas, Joseph of Naxos, Queen Elizabeth's physician Roderigo Lopez, and Thomas Nashe's Zachary and Zadoch in *The Unfortunate Traveler* (1594). In 1962 another historical study of *The Merchant of Venice*, by the popular teacher and poet Bernard Grebanier, looked at contemporary portrayals of Jews in Elizabethan literature in order to prove that Shakespeare "stood like an Everest above his contemporaries by dint of his unequalled humanity, and that he therefore was capable of any number of sympathies centuries in advance of them. But . . . his contemporaries by no means all shared the cramped bigotry of the medieval mind."[33] Sinsheimer, like Grebanier, defends Shakespeare's "superb craftsmanship," which puts into the mouth of a medieval figure the "pronouncements and arguments of a future and more progressive time and spirit." His Shylock is a "tragic hero" whose "Hath not a Jew eyes" speech "proclaims something like the equality and the equal rights of man"; he is "the usurer turn[ed] teacher and preacher understood by the people."[34]

Several years earlier, Jacob Lopes Cardozo had taken an historical approach in his *The Contemporary Jew in the Elizabethan Drama*, arriving at *The Merchant of Venice* by way of a detailed study of other stage Jews and the many versions of the Flesh Bond folktale. Cardozo's book was written in Dutch and originally published in Paris in 1925. Interestingly, Cardozo was more negative than either Sinsheimer or Grebanier about Shakespeare's ability to mingle medieval and modern ideas. After discussing the genealogy of the Flesh Bond story, which appeared in over twenty editions of the popular medieval collection, the *Gesta Romanorum*, he gloomily announced that "the more highly organized an art-creation grows, the more destructive to its inner truth become the vestiges of a primitive legend of which it purports to be a modernization." His conclusion follows: "It is impossible to modernize a legend." When Shylock's ancestor, the medieval Mercator, or merchant, was simply called Dyabolus, he was "nearest to reality."[35] It was not until much later that the creditor became a Jew; ironically, if Shakespeare had used the English *Gesta*, from which he borrowed the story of the three caskets, instead of *Il Pecarone* for the Flesh Bond tale, the merchant would not have been Jewish.[36] A more recent historicist approach to *The Merchant of Venice*, Walter Cohen's "*The Merchant of Venice* and the possibilities of historical criticism," takes a position similar to Cardozo's. Shylock, Cohen says, is "a figure from the past, marginal, diabolical, irrational, archaic, medieval"; in refusing to take interest he acts like a figure from folklore rather than a typical usurer.[37] Even the "typical usurer," whether Jewish or Christian, may no longer have been a "morally relevant figure" at the time when *The Merchant of Venice* was written. Laura Stevenson's study of the popular literature that praised merchants, industrialists, and craftsmen argues that "the greedy, heartless usurer was a stock figure left over from an earlier age."[38]

How different, one wonders, would the history of *The Merchant of Venice* have been if the protagonist had been simply a diabolical merchant, or even a usurer who was not explicitly identified as a Jew? Still another kind of transformation, motivated less by ideological convictions than by a desire to make Shakespeare "presentable" for children, deals with Shylock's Jewishness by omitting it from the story. Edith Nesbit's tale of "The Merchant of Venice" appears in *Twenty Beautiful Stories from Shakespeare* ("The Official Text for Members of the National Junior Shakespeare Club"). Nesbit was a celebrated author of children's books, and her prose adaptations of Shakespeare's plays, first published in 1897 in both England and America, were reissued both individually and as collections many times by several publishers up until 1926. With their Raphael Tuck illustrations that make all the characters look like children, these transformations are clearly intended for the very young.[39] Nesbit describes Shylock as "a rich money-lender," who submitted to the "harshness and scorn" of Antonio "with a patient shrug," hiding his hatred for the man who "both hurt his pride and injured his business." The word Jew is never mentioned in Nesbit's story; in the trial scene, when he is condemned for seeking to take the life of a Venetian, he is referred to only as a foreigner, with no further explanation. Jessica's elopement is handled in a sentence or two, concluding with "Shylock's grief and anger were terrible to see."[40] Nesbit's transformation is clearly addressed to a society anxious to avoid anti-Semitism, or the appearance thereof, especially in literature for children. Whereas adults, under the tutelage of Cardozo or Sinsheimer or Grebanier, could view Shylock in the context of the Flesh Bond folktale or the Lopez incident, children would presumably respond to the play in terms of contemporary culture and its prejudices. A study of the many adaptations of Shakespeare for children would no doubt uncover many similar re-visions of elements that might inspire disturbing instances of talking back by young readers inclined to ask embarrassing questions about the characters and situations they encounter in books.

*   *   *

The best-known *Merchant of Venice* transformation, *The Last Days of Shylock*, was a Book of the Month Club selection when it first appeared in 1931.[41] Its author, Ludwig Lewisohn, was then a popular writer of fifteen works of fiction and criticism, including a powerful autobiographical novel written in Paris that shared with *Ulysses* the distinction of being banned for obscenity by the U.S. Postal Service. Lewisohn's corpus eventually included three autobiographies, several books of literary criticism, essays on Israel and Judaism, several more novels, and a number of anthologies and translations from German. Lewisohn's approach to *The Merchant of Venice* was strongly affected by the auto-biographical imperative, a feature it shares with the two *Hamlet* trans-formations to be discussed in Chapter 3. *Up Stream*, the first and best of his autobiographies, describes his upper middle-class childhood in the Berlin of the 1880s, followed by his family's emigration to Ameri-ca when he was seven. Lewisohn and his parents settled in South Car-olina, where they led a lonely existence. Young Ludwig enrolled in a Baptist school (there was no public school in the town they lived in before they moved to Charleston) and later, under the influence of a neighbor, attended Baptist Sunday school, withdrawing instinctively, he remarks, from his less genteel cousins and the other Jewish children in the village. In Charleston, he briefly became infatuated with Catholi-cism, again, through the influence of neighbors; and in high school, he joined the Methodist Church. By then, he says, "my Americanization was complete." Not until he experienced the effects of anti-Semitism as a graduate student at Columbia University in 1904 –5 did he begin to rediscover his Jewish heritage. Rejected for teaching positions in English literature because he was Jewish, he eventually taught Ger-man, first at the University of Wisconsin, and then for six years at Ohio State University. He was forced to resign, however, after being attacked as pro-German and a pacifist during World War I. Embittered by a "Christian-capitalist civilization" condemned to decay because "at its core festers a cancerous lie," he rejected the "rigid and unnatural lives" and "sapless pleasures" of the American middle class and eventually went to live in Paris, where he continued to write books that were pub-lished and widely read in America.[42] From the publication of *Israel* in 1925 onward, Lewisohn was an outspoken Zionist, an advocate of a multilingual, culturally diverse Jewish state in Palestine. During his later years as a columnist, editor, and teacher at Brandeis, he was iden-tified as a "Jewish writer"; *The Island Within* (1928), frequently regard-ed as his best novel, ran through thirty printings and has been widely praised as an example of the Jewish-American novel.[43]

The Last Days of Shylock appeared as Lewisohn's popularity was beginning to wane. All of his earlier fiction had dealt with the con-temporary scene, so this was a first experiment in writing historical fic-tion. Grebanier, in his final chapter on "Other Men's Shylocks," refers to it as having been "much spoken of for a while."[44] Oddly, his summa-ry of the novel skips over the historical events Lewisohn wove into the life he invented for Shylock after the trial and his departure from Venice. Lewisohn did the same kind of historical research Wesker was doing forty years later; indeed, it is altogether possible that he read Cecil Roth's *History of the Jews in Venice*, which had been published in

1930 and which describes incidents Lewisohn included, such as the pretended messiah David Reubeni's arrival in Venice in 1524.[45]

Lewisohn begins his novel where *The Merchant of Venice* ends, with Shylock's return to the Ghetto after the trial. As his friends Tubal and Chus await his return, they provide the reader with clues to his character. Tubal says

> "The loss of the child has robbed him of reason and prudence: it will go ill with him."
>
> Chus had thrown up his hands in despair. "He always tortured his soul beyond reason; he could never reconcile himself to injustice; he dreams of a Messiah to right our wrongs." (2)

The resettlement of the Venetian Jews in the Ghetto Nuovo in 1516 had taken place when Shylock was a child, the only son of a prosperous physician. Lewisohn describes the painful moving day, with drunken Christian carters maliciously tossing about the sacred objects, and the process of building a synagogue and houses of study among the rickety houses of the Ghetto (17–19). As a young man, now fatherless, Shylock became rich in his dealings with the prodigals on the Rialto, guided by Tubal, who provided him with introductions to banking houses in Antwerp, Frankfort and Muscovy.

> He grew in power as well as in hate. For always there were pious fools who cursed him for the taking of interest and always he had to witness the jeers, the blows, the shames with which his brethren of the poorer sort were daily stained and wounded. Often while he was on the way to a notary with a Christian civil enough to him, the man would stop to throw a stone at some cringing Hebrew by the wayside. (25)

These local injustices paled beside the

> expulsions and woes of all Israel and chiefly of the horrors endured through the long years by those Marranos or secret Jews whom the cruel King and Queen of Spain had driven forth from their dominions. Hundreds, nay, thousands of these had been sold into slavery by the masters of the ships on which they fled and still, in those younger years of Shylock, moneys would be sent through him to ransom from Venice, the gate to all the East, an aged parent or once tender child who had languished long under the whip of some Berber chieftain or some pasha of Egypt. . . . (26)

This Shylock is the Jew Lewisohn was becoming: outspoken on behalf of world Jewry, he uses his influence to help his people, in concert with other prosperous Venetian Jews. Shakespeare's brooding and isolated Shylock, Wesker and Lewisohn realized, was the invention of a culture that lacked a Jewish community with the coherence and vitality of the sixteenth-century Venice that emerges from the pages of Roth's history. Lewisohn places his Shylock at the center of the international network of influential Jews that brought the powerful Mendes family from Lyons to Venice in 1535 and makes him the trusted agent of Gracia Mendes, sending and receiving funds and jewels, and buying the Venetian palace she lived in briefly, before being arrested on charges of "Judaizing." When the Mendes family moved to Turkey, under the protection of the Sultan Sulaiman the Magnificent, Joaº Miguez, Grazia's nephew and son-in-law, became Joseph of Naxos, whose "amazing career," says Roth, "embodies the quintessence of sixteenth-century romance." By 1566, he was the sultan's prime favorite, more powerful than the grand vizier and a diplomat "almost on terms of equality with the kings and princes of Europe." As duke of Naxos and prince of the Cyclades, his most memorable achievement "was the obtaining of a grant of the city of Tiberias in Palestine, where he endeavored to build up a Jewish settlement, being thus a forerunner of Zionism."[46] The story of Joseph of Naxos nicely dovetailed with Lewisohn's own commitment to Zionism, and hence it is not surprising that his Shylock follows the Mendes family to Constantinople and becomes Joseph's fiscal agent on the Palestinian expedition, an episode which constitutes nearly one-fifth of the novel.

Shylock's departure from Venice occurs midway through the novel at the end of a searing chapter depicting his forced baptism in the Church of San Marco, accompanied by the cruel and scornful Gratiano, the "plump" Bassanio, "debonair and gay" Salanio and Salarino [sic], and the conciliatory Antonio (97). These characters are lightly sketched, however; the narration focuses on Shylock's torment as he goes through the motions of the conversion ritual, with a halberdier at his side to ensure his compliance. Afterward, he returns to the synagogue to "let his sore heart take refuge with its God," only to find that the Rabbi and the synagogal court have grave doubts about

whether a public recantation in face of the congregation and public acts of penitence for his baptism could be spared him. But if he performed these he was guilty of relapse from Christianity and but food for the fires of the Inquisition; if he performed them not, he would be an outcast from his own people. . . . There was no tarrying for him in Venice. (107)

Thus begins his new life in a new country, a life in which he no longer feels distrusted and humiliated by the dominant culture. When the Palestinian settlement ends in failure, subverted by treacherous Arabs and overrun by Bedouins, Shylock returns to Constantinople.

In the final episode of the novel, he embarks for Cyprus, at Joseph's request, as the almoner of a naval campaign to wrest the island from the Venetians. Cyprus, Joseph hoped, would become a haven for fugitive Turkish Jews and the Jews flocking to Turkey from elsewhere in Europe.[47] After several months in Cyprus, Shylock is ready to depart when a ship of Jewish fugitives arrives from Venice, bearing Jessica and her three sons. Silently, he gives her his blessing and takes her home with him to have his grandsons circumcised. The story of her unhappy life with Lorenzo is briefly recounted. In the final chapter Shylock and his family are back in Constantinople, dwelling peacefully "for sundry years" in a house "at the foot of his master's garden" (221, 214), where the boys attend a Hebrew school founded by Gracia Mendes. Distancing his protagonist from "the tumult and the cruelty of the years of the reign of Murad," during which Joseph died and nearly all the fortunes of the Nassi were confiscated, Lewisohn closes his novel with the aged Shylock's gentle yielding to "an eternal sleep" in the arms of his daughter (222).

It would be easy to dismiss *The Last Days of Shylock* as a historical novel about sixteenth-century Venice and Constantinople which simply appropriates the name "Shylock" without in any way coming to terms with the people, plots, and ideas in Shakespeare's play. In a sense, this is so; Lewisohn shows no interest in any of Shakespeare's characters, except Shylock, and his novel is a conventionally structured account of the early life and later adventures of its protagonist. The novel sets out to "supplement" Shakespeare's play, inasmuch as the main event, the ill-considered flesh bond and its consequences, occurs offstage. Lewisohn provides ample historical justification for the hatred a Venetian Jew might feel for a Christian merchant, but he does not account for the poor judgment that made him vulnerable to Christian laws after a lifetime of success in the Venetian mercantile community.

The Last Days of Shylock does not entirely "work" either as a novel or as a transformation, because everything about it is so clearly determined by its polemical purpose: to reclaim the name "Shylock" from the associations that have gathered about it for the past three centuries. More than any other Shakespearean name except for Pandar or Caliban, "Shylock" has passed into the English language as a term with a life of its own: "Shylock" is a widely used byword for the grasping, usurious Jew. Consider, for instance, the opening sentence of a recent scholarly study entitled *Shylock Reconsidered: Jews, Moneylending and Medieval Society*, by Joseph Shatzmiller: "With the stage performance of *The Merchant of Venice* in 1605, Shakespeare established for centuries to come the image of the Jewish moneylender as an execrable, pitiless usurer."[48] Everything about this sentence reveals how little

Shatzmiller knows about *The Merchant of Venice*; even the briefest introduction to a student edition would have told him that the play was written and performed in the 1590s and that from the early nineteenth century onward Shylocks on stage have been far more sympathetic and complex than the words "execrable" and "pitiless" imply (although the performances in the legitimate theatre may have made a less lasting impression on European and American culture than the countless parodies and travesties on the popular stage). Yet Shatzmiller's statement is telling, for it reflects popular assumptions about the set of associations denoted by the word "Shylock" that exist independently of any firsthand acquaintance with the play, much less its sources and predecessors. In its own way, Shatzmiller's project is analogous to Lewisohn's and Wesker's; his twenty-five years of historical research serve to illustrate "the other face of medieval society: sympathy for and appreciation of Jewish moneylenders," specifically in France from the thirteenth to the fifteenth centuries, but elsewhere in Europe as well. The Jewish moneylender, he asserts, was frequently perceived as "a benign and even benevolent" professional in "a society in which virtually everyone was permanently in debt." He reminds his readers that after the expulsion of the Jews from England in 1290 moneylending went on without them; documentary evidence shows that the Bishop of Coventry and the Archbishop of York lent money on hundreds of occasions to people from all ranks of society.[49]

All of the writers discussed in this chapter have been talking back in one way or another, although much of their talking back has been directed at the way Western culture has read Shakespeare, rather than at Shakespeare's intentions.[50] For some of them, writing about or rewriting Shakespeare's *The Merchant of Venice* is a way of talking back to a world in which what it means to be Jewish is quite different from anything Shakespeare could have imagined. A few months after the Stockholm premiere of *The Merchant*, in May 1977, London's Open Space Theatre presented Charles Marowitz's *Variations on The Merchant of Venice*, the last of five adaptations and collages written and produced by Marowitz since the 1960s. In his introduction, Marowitz notes that

> It is difficult, almost impossible, to come to a play like *The Merchant of Venice*, whose central character is an orthodox Jew, without bringing to the experience all one has learned and read about the Jews in the past 2000 years; difficult to obliterate from the mind the last seventy-five years of Jewish history which includes European pogroms, the Hitler "death camps", the rise of

Jewish Nationalism and the Arab-Israeli conflicts. Of course, Shakespeare had no knowledge of any of these things and it is undeniable that none of these factors enter into *The Merchant of Venice*—and yet, can they be excluded from the consciousness of the spectator who attends the play?[51]

Marowitz chose to set his *Merchant of Venice* in Palestine in 1946; the opening scene consists of a voice-over accompanying slides of the bombing of the British Military Headquarters at the King David Hotel by a group of Zionist terrorists. Antonio becomes the "ready-made villain," identified with Ernest Bevin, the British Foreign Secretary, and Shylock becomes a "cold, Talmudic stoic" who plays the caricature Jew in the presence of the Jew-baiting Christians in order to work most effectively for the Zionist cause. The introduction continues: "As a result of this reorganization of character, and sections lifted from Christopher Marlowe's *Jew of Malta*, it becomes possible to arrive at that detestable trial scene and make it turn out differently" (23). In a response to the critics who were negative about his play, Marowitz said that he was trying to "make sense" of the bond, in a way analogous to my students' talking back. To a critic who dismisses the *Variations* as a "frivolous" and "literary" "exercise" that resituates an "unpleasant play," Marowitz answers that "every classic is automatically translated into another time and ambiance simply because it is *playing* in another time and ambiance."[52]

Unlike Ervine, Wesker, and Lewisohn, Marowitz constructs his transformation from speeches and scenes taken directly from Shakespeare's play. His collage technique relies heavily on stage directions that radically recontextualize the original language; in Marowitz's version of act 3, scene 1, for instance, Shylock *"feigns weeping"* as he bewails the loss of his daughter and ducats. Solanio and Salerio thus become dupes in a scene dominated by Shylock and his fellow nationalists Tubal and Chus. The speeches are rearranged so that the scene ends with Shylock's menacing words "To bait fish withal / If it will feed nothing else, it will feed my revenge" (3.1.47–48). Marowitz adds "I will have the heart of him if he forfeit," but reserves the "Hath not a Jew eyes?" speech for later (254).

Marowitz's appropriations from *The Jew of Malta* entail, among other things, conflating Jessica with Marlowe's Abigail. This enables Marowitz to make sense of Jessica's romance with the Christian Lorenzo. A committed Zionist like her father, Jessica follows Shylock's instructions to "Use him as if he were a Philistine. / Dissemble, swear, protest, vow to love him" (229).[53] Unlike Abigail and Shakespeare's Jessica, Marowitz's Jessica is in league with her father to the end of the play, where, according to the stage direction, she silently "*leaves Lorenzo's side and takes up a defensive position with Shylock*" in the trial scene.

Marowitz's trial scene employs more interpolations from *The Jew of Malta* in order to disrupt the rhythm of the play in its original form. After the Duke upholds Antonio's request that Shylock become a Christian and record a gift of all his wealth to Lorenzo and Jessica, Marowitz cynically undermines the Christians' pardon by shifting to act 1, scene 2 of *The Jew of Malta*. Marlowe's hypocritical Christian Governor of Malta has summoned Barabas and the other Jews to demand increased taxes in order to raise funds to pay his tribute to the Turks. Marowitz's Duke assumes the Governor's role, moralizing about how the scorn heaped upon Jews "is not our fault, but thy inherent sin" (280; cf. *The Jew of Malta* 1.2.112). Indignantly, Shylock delivers Barabas's powerful rebuttal, which begins: "What? Bring you scripture to confirm your wrongs? / Preach me not out of my possessions . . ." When the Duke-Governor proclaims piously, "Excessive wealth is cause of covetousness, / And covetousness, O 'tis a monstrous sin," Shylock-Barabas quickly responds "Ay, but theft is worse" (281) [cf. *The Jew of Malta* 1.2.126–28]. It becomes clear that *The Merchant of Venice* has veered off in a new direction, foreclosing any possibility of a return to Shakespeare's comic closure. The dialogue is broken off when "*an explosion is heard outside. It shatters the courtroom and causes the Union Jack to fall. Chus, Tubal and Others suddenly reveal weapons.*" Chus steps forward and delivers an adaptation of Barabas's speech from the final scene of *The Jew of Malta*, in which he triumphantly reveals his "policy" to the Governor:

> First know, there is an army sent before
> Enter'd the garrison and underneath
> In several places are field-pieces pitch'd
> Bombards, whole barrels full of gunpowder,
> That on the sudden shall dessever it,
> And batter all the stones about your ears
> Whence none can possibly escape alive. (282)
> [cf. *The Jew of Malta* 5.5.26ff]

Shylock closes the scene with the "Hath not a Jew eyes" speech, after which shots are fired, the stage goes dark, and the voice-over describes, in the manner of a news report, the bombing of the King David Hotel with which the play had begun.

Marowitz, like Ervine, cannot resist modernizing the casket plot as well. Ervine's transformation took its cue from *Il Pecarone*. After twice losing his ships and cargo, according to the terms of the love test,

Giannetto borrows a third time from Ansaldo and returns to Belmont. One of the lady's maids takes pity on him and in a whisper tells him not to drink the drugged wine before going to bed. He is thus able to remain awake so as to "give the satisfaction of wedlock," the requirement for winning the lady's hand. Ervine's Nerissa likewise helps the handsome suitor, who lacks the wit to help himself, to please her mistress and win Gratiano for herself. During the evening's festivities at Belmont, while Gratiano is dancing with a young and pretty girl, the jealous and resentful Nerissa tells Antonio "I told Bassanio which casket he must choose, and thus he won Portia." Antonio responds, "And so her father's will was defeated. You young always circumvent us, scheme how we may" (51–52). Marowitz's *Variations* entails an analogous act of circumvention, but now the trickster is Bassanio himself. He arrives disguised first as the Prince of Morocco, then as Arragon. It is not clear whether the audience is meant to recognize the disguises at the beginning of the Morocco scene, but presumably they would at the end. The stage direction calls for some slapstick *"salaams"* between Bassanio and Gratiano, concluding with a kick in the backside (248). Later stage directions indicate that Portia may suspect the disguises; when she greets her second suitor, she *"raises her glasses to examine Arragon who is, of course, Bassanio—shakes her head and then proceeds"* (257). The romantic third casket scene is undermined by Portia's and Bassanio's irritated and incredulous reactions to Gratiano's and Nerissa's betrothal. This Portia is a spectator in the trial scene, her lines spoken by Balthazar, who is silently introduced in an earlier scene donning his Barrister's garb. As he dresses he listens to what *"sounds like a Sunday sermon"* on the wireless, the speech about how "The world is still deceiv'd with ornament" that Shakespeare's Bassanio delivers as he contemplates the caskets (261).

Marowitz's *Variations* on *The Merchant of Venice* grafts a Marlovian irony onto Shakespeare's play, distancing the audience equally from the calculating, subversive Jewish community and the hypocritical and coercive Christian one. The play expects us to bring our knowledge of post-1946 events to the experience of the play: the British Christians eventually left Palestine to the Jews, whose independent state of Israel bears a small but significant resemblance to the fortress-like Venetian ghetto as Lewisohn depicts it. When the *Variations* were first performed in 1977, the precarious balance of power in the Middle East was as potentially explosive as it is today, with no possibility of comic closure in sight. Substitute Palestinian terrorists for Zionists, and the Israeli government for the British military force, and the political dynamics might look uncomfortably similar from a disinterested vantage point. Because Marowitz's appropriation of *The Merchant of*

Venice lacks the obvious pro-Jewish stance of Wesker's and Lewisohn's transformations, it is undoubtedly more disturbing and controversial, but also, perhaps, a better reflection of contemporary political culture.

I will conclude this chapter with a telling instance of the way Shakespeare appropriations, allusions, and the performance history of the plays are breaking down the barriers between academic and nonacademic approaches to Shakespeare. *Shylock: A Legend and Its Legacy*, by the theatre critic and former editor of *The Times Literary Supplement* John Gross, came out in the spring of 1993, just as I was sending this book off to press; the appearance of the American edition coincided with the fiftieth anniversary of the destruction of the Warsaw ghetto and the opening of the Holocaust Museum in Washington D.C. Written for a broader audience than the readers of academic studies, and published by a commercial press, *Shylock* immediately became available in public libraries and bookstores. Gross's book begins with a compendium of disparate information: he provides, for instance, a handy overview of the history of Jewish moneylending, a synopsis of Marlowe's *The Jew of Malta*, and a page or two on the origins of the Venetian ghetto, interspersed with reference to and quotes from the play. Much of the subsequent two sections consists of an international performance history of the play, but unlike standard performance histories, this one expands outward to include allusions and appropriations in its depiction of Shylock's afterlife. These range from Maria Edgeworth's *Harrington* (1817), a novel with an anti-Semitic protagonist who falls in love with a Jewish woman while attending a performance of *The Merchant of Venice*, to brief references to Jewish characters whose indebtedness to Shylock is shadowy at best—Meyer Wolfsheim in *The Great Gatsby*, for example.

Gross includes a paragraph or two on the transformations discussed here, though he reserves his longest discussion for Erica Jong's *Serenissima*. Gross also introduces his readers to the standard twentieth-century critics, from A. C. Bradley and Arthur Quiller-Couch and Sidney Lee to Mark Van Doren, who described Shylock's voice as ugly, "nothing but a snarl, an animal cry" in 1939 ("to write in such a way at such a time was chilling," Gross observes), to Frank Kermode and M. C. Bradbrook and Terry Eagleton, who imagines an innovative director's "re-vision" in which Shylock "never really expected to win in the first place" and "throws the audience a knowing wink when Portia produces her knockdown argument."[54] Gross concluded with a long look backward at the cultural history of his subject, reemphasizing the indissoluble link between that history and the history of anti-Semitism:

Invested with Shakespearean power and, in time, with Shakespearean prestige, Shylock the Jewish villain became part of world mythology. He may not have added anything to existing stereotypes, but as the most famous Jewish character in literature he helped to spread them and to keep them vigorously alive. He belongs, inescapably, to the history of anti-Semitism.[7]

We cannot, in other words, separate Shylock from the uses people throughout time have made of him. And as the history of anti-Semitism continues to be rewritten and added to, so will the transformations of its most important lightning rod.

3
American Hamletology: Two Texts

Hamlet, as everyone knows, is a transformation of an indeterminate number of prior texts. *The Historiae Danicae* of Saxo Grammaticus commissioned by the Archbishop Absalom of Lund at the end of the twelfth century contains the earliest inscribed version of the Amleth saga, although the tale itself and its analogues may have undergone many transformations by the time Saxo heard it.[1] François de Belleforest used Saxo in preparing his *Histoires Tragiques*; the fifth volume of this collection, containing an expanded and moralized version of the Amleth saga, appeared in at least ten editions from 1570 onward.[2] This text, in turn, was presumably the source of the lost "Ur-Hamlet" of the late 1580s, frequently attributed to Thomas Kyd. Looking back at Saxo's Amleth from a perspective framed (to extend Eleanor Rowe's window conceit) by nearly four centuries of Hamletology, one's attention is irresistibly drawn to the long, triumphant victory speech in Saxo's saga for which there is no counterpart in Shakespeare. Saxo's Amleth has plotted and schemed and dissembled for over a year, eluding traps and tricks through his cunning, wisdom, and perseverance, when he finally achieves his revenge by means of an elaborate trap that involves the sharpened sticks he had begun whittling shortly after his father's death. The speech, which constitutes more than 10 percent of the entire saga and nearly 20 percent of the part that deals with the events culminating in Feng's (Claudius's) death, is a masterpiece of heroic self-vindication and celebration. He asks his audience to "pity" his "stricken" mother, "this weak woman," and proclaims that

> It is I who have wiped off my country's shame; I who have quenched my mother's dishonour; I who have beaten back oppression; I who have put to death the murderer; I who have baffled the artful hand of my uncle. . . . . Acknowledge my service, honor my wit, give me the throne if I have earned it; for you have in me one who has done you a mighty service, and who is no

degenerate heir to his father's power; no fratricide, but the lawful successor
to the throne; and a dutiful avenger of the crime of murder.[3]

The people are moved to compassion and tears, and promptly proclaim
him king. He subsequently has a shield made for himself depicting all
of his epic exploits in exquisite detail (the description of the shield is
nearly half as long as the speech). If the Amleth saga were to end here,
it would be a tale of unambiguous triumph for its heroic protagonist,
with no trace of what we think of as tragedy. But like *Beowulf*, the epic
continues with another round of conflicts, ending with the death of
Amleth in battle. His wife Hermutrude immediately "yielded herself
up unasked to be the conqueror's spoil and bride," prompting the narrator to comment that

> Thus all vows of women are loosed by change of fortune and melted by the
> shifting of time; the faith of their soul rests on a slippery foothold, and is
> weakened by casual chances; glib in promises, and as sluggish in perfor-
> mance, all manner of lustful promptings enslave it, and it bounds away with
> panting and precipitate desire, forgetful of old things, in the ever-hot pursuit
> after something fresh.

"So ended Amleth," the narrator concludes. "Had fortune been as
kind to him as nature, he would have equalled the gods in glory, and
surpassed the labors of Hercules by his deeds of prowess."[4] Nowhere
does Saxo hint at any character flaws or tragic errors in his depiction
of Amleth. However, the misogyny that would continue to attach to the
character of Gertrude is clearly evident in the narrator's digressive
remarks about women in the final paragraph of the saga. If there is
anything tragic in the ending, it stems from the wife's infidelity to the
memory of the dead hero.

When Belleforest expanded the closet scene between Amleth/Hamlet
and his mother he added a new element: Geruth attempts to explain to
her son why she remarried.[5] After a long speech of reproach and accusation by Hamlet, she responds in a spirit less of reproof than of "joy . . .
to behold the gallant spirit of her son," admitting to the "great wrong"
of marrying Fengon but explaining that she had no alternative, due to
the "treason of the palace" filled with "courtiers all wrought to his will."
She promises to help him and looks forward to rejoicing in his vengeance.[6]
No further mention is made of her from that point onward. The serial
construction of the saga limits Geruth, like most of the other characters,
to a single brief appearance. It was left to the playwrights—the author
of the "Ur-Hamlet" and Shakespeare—to construct a plot in which characters repeatedly interact with one another throughout the drama.

In the annals of Hamletology Gertrude's reasons for marrying Claudius have at times become a major crux that drives the interpretation of the play. Indeed, when *Hamlet* moves from one culture to another fascinating things happen; for example, a 1953 BBC radio broadcast described the reception of *Hamlet* in the West African bush in a way that "reinvents" the story. The anthropologist Laura Bohannan describes her attempt to tell the story of Hamlet to a circle of seasoned storytellers who repeatedly resist and contest her account, engaging in a kind of talking back that threatened to subvert the storytelling process altogether: " 'In our country,' " she explains,

> "the son is next to the father." I rushed on. "The dead chief's younger brother had become the great chief. He had also married his elder brother's widow only about a month after the funeral."
>
> "He did well," the old man beamed and announced to the others, "I told you that if we knew more about Europeans, we would find they really were very like us. In our country also," he added to me, "the younger brother marries the elder brother's widow and becomes the father of his children. Now if your uncle, who marries your widowed mother, is your father's full brother, then he will be a real father to you. Did Hamlet's father and his uncle have the same mother?"

Bohannan confides that she was "upset and thrown . . . off balance by having one of the most important elements of *Hamlet* knocked straight out of the picture." Her rather naive belief (paralleling the old man's) that "human nature is pretty much the same the whole world over" has evidently been severely undermined.[7] An essay entitled "Hamlet in Tamil" in the *Hamlet* volume of *Shakespeare Worldwide: Translation and Adaptation*, observes that the Indian theatre has "an inborn resistance to tragedy" because Tamil culture believes that "the world makes sense" and "harmony finally prevails." The Tamil tradition "could never consider *Hamlet* as part of their heritage . . . no Tamil would accept the remarriage of Gertrude to Claudius."[8]

Between these diametrically opposed and culturally determined responses to Gertrude's remarriage lies the "western" realm of tragic choice—choice that is psychologically believable but morally questionable, choice that rebounds on the agent and the community to which she belongs. The two relatively unknown twentieth-century American *Hamlet* offshoots I have chosen to examine in this chapter are less interested in Hamlet's character and dilemma than they are in the complex motivation and sequence of events behind Gertrude's marriage to Claudius. *Hamlet* is a long play, but these texts are longer, and their greater scope permits an extensive imaginative reconstruction of the characters and the nature of their relationships. Lillie Wyman's

Gertrude of Denmark: An Interpretive Romance is a synchronous transformation that describes Gertrude's early years and marriage to King
Hamlet, then follows the events that occur or are referred to in the play
and ends with Gertrude's death. Percy MacKaye's *The Mystery of Hamlet, King of Denmark* is a diachronous offshoot covering a period that
begins shortly before Hamlet's birth and ends where the first act of
Hamlet begins. I have coupled these two texts because they illustrate
a particular aspect of talking back that can be traced to the primacy of
the novel and biography in nineteenth- and early twentieth-century
America. These two genres reflect the pervasive influence of Darwin
and Freud: both tend to emphasize origins, making some effort, at
least, to begin at the beginning of a character's life, rather than *in
medias res*, and both put great stock in a character's actions, often
accounted for in terms that emphasize heredity and psychological motivation. Parentage, childhood experiences, inherited personality traits—
all these become crucial elements in the makeup of a character. Wyman
and MacKaye talk back to Shakespeare out of a felt need to give his
characters fuller lives than they appear to have. As writers they attempt
to fill in the gaps, to provide a more naturalistic sense of character, in
ways that parallel the concerns of Bradley and other early twentieth-
century critics. And they do so with much of the same respect and rev-
erence for the work and its authors as that which motivates those critics. This, then, is a different kind of talking back from the irreverent
and ideologically-inspired back talk of many of the contemporary playwrights discussed elsewhere in this book. This is a talking back that is
cooperative in spirit, seeking to augment the canonical text rather than
challenge its claim to canonicity.

My decision to pair *Gertrude of Denmark* with *The Mystery of Hamlet* also stems from a curious kinship between their authors, both of
whom, I suspect, found in *Hamlet* a creative outlet for their own complicated feelings about their respective prominent and charismatic parents. Just as Wesker's identity as a Jew led him to rewrite *The Merchant
of Venice*, so Wyman's relationship with her mother and her son and
MacKaye's with his father helped draw them into this most famous and
puzzling of plays about a heroic father and his duty-bound child.
Wyman and MacKaye wrote their *Hamlet*s late in their lives, after they
themselves had married and become parents, and so it is as wife and
husband, child and parent, poet and observer of the human drama, that
each entered into a dialogue with nineteenth- and early twentieth-century Hamletology.

"Was it in a dream or reverie," asks the narrator of *Gertrude of Denmark*, "that Gertrude of Denmark came and begged me to tell her story

to the world?" Prince Hamlet, the Gertrude-ghost remarks, had Horatio "to report him and his 'cause aright.' I had no chance, before I died,
to ask anybody to protect me from the writers, the critics,—and the
actresses."[9] Thus begins Lillie Buffum Chace Wyman's "interpretive
romance," a *Hamlet* transformation that appeared in 1924 when its
author was seventy-seven years old. As Wyman rewrites the Hamlet
story, she explores and interrogates the nineteenth-century cult of the
devoted, self-sacrificing mother, a cult that, as Ann Douglas has
remarked, enabled American women "to exonerate almost any action
performed in the sacred name of motherhood."[10] Gertrude is defined
by her role as a mother:

> She was not quite sixteen when Hamlet was born. She became a Madonna at
> once. There were two or three children afterwards, but not one of them lived
> many hours. She had not quite come out of her gulf of maternal pain, before
> each of those children had turned itself into the memory of a thwarted hope. It
> was Hamlet therefore always with her—Hamlet first and last and all the time.

One afternoon, Wyman continues, the two brothers see Gertrude sitting on a high-backed chair holding her child on her knee.

> "She looks like the Holy Mother," said the King. "I think that I will give her
> to the church here to take the place of their wooden image of the Mother."
> "She is the most sacred creature on earth," answered Claudius, as he
> whirled on his heels and walked away. The King came nearer, yet not very
> near, to Gertrude, sat down, told her of the little colloquy and then declared
> that he was jealous of her love for "that baby."
> She gazed at him wonderingly, went across the room, kissed him, returned,
> took up the child and bent low over it so as to hide her face. After a while,
> the King laughed, and departed for the hunt.

The two men view Gertrude as the quintessential idealized mother,
here represented by the conventional icon of the self-effacing madonna
with the child at her breast. *Uncle Tom's Cabin*, a book Lillie Wyman
allegedly read at age six (though she doubts the truth of this family legend), told the story of salvation through motherly love to a culture that
sanctified motherhood and the family and celebrated the redemptive
power of "motherly loving kindness."[11] Lillie's childhood reading
included the works of Louisa May Alcott and could conceivably have
also included the books on the mothers of famous men—George Washington's mother Mary, for instance—which became immensely popular
in mid–nineteenth-century America.[12] Jane Tompkins has suggested
that *Uncle Tom's Cabin*, while seemingly a conservative novel harking
back to "an older way of life," is actually radical in its "removal of the

male from the center to the periphery of the human sphere."[13] Wyman's *Gertrude of Denmark* and the biographies of famous men's mothers do likewise; they replace the male hero with the mother at the center of the text, thus effectively rewriting an old myth from a new perspective.

As Wyman depicts her, Gertrude is devoted fiercely to her only son but extends her mother's arms to Ophelia, Laertes, and even Osric as the story unfolds. For Gertrude, motherhood is a supremely reward-ing—and sensuous—state of being; in her imagination, Hamlet will always remain the little boy on her lap. As he announced his intent to return to Wittenberg, "she remembered just how soft his little body had felt, and how he had been wont to gaze at her and then lay his head on her shoulder" (15). Her refusal to relinquish the past suggests the emptiness of the stereotypical mother's life once her child no longer needs her. The narrator tells us, with characteristic understatement, that "When her husband died, Gertrude had been a queen for thirty years. She did not know how to be anything but a queen with a prince for a son—both of them upheld in their station by a king" (14).

This re-vision of *Hamlet* constitutes a critique, not so much of Shake-speare's "text," but of the play's performance history and the lore sur-rounding it, a Hamlet-centered tradition that Lillie Wyman observed from her own distinctively feminine (if not entirely feminist) perspec-tive. Wyman was able to create a fictional work of criticism in a way that links her to the nineteenth rather than the twentieth century, a time when criticism was not yet the purview of a class of academic special-ists and was instead written for the "cultivated public and disseminat-ed in editions of the works, public lectures, books, and—above all—in magazines and newspapers." So observes Hugh Grady, who adds that the plays "were assumed to be the intellectual property of men (and increasingly of women) of any cultural pretensions."[14] Wyman's text not only implies the incompleteness of Shakespeare's, it resists every reading of *Hamlet* that dismisses Gertrude as a relatively unimportant character while Hamlet occupies center stage and an undisputed claim on the reader's or spectator's sympathies.

But Wyman's re-vision, while drawing on the cult of motherhood, also interrogates its inherent assumptions. Just as a certain ambiguity attaches to the role and obligations of the hero-revenger as the *Hamlet* story changes through time, so Gertrude's role as the self-sacrificing mother is treated with a certain ambivalence. For a woman to define herself wholly as a mother, Wyman seems to imply, is to risk losing her sense of self when the child, now an adult, no longer needs and depends upon her. Building upon the sixty-eight times Gertrude speaks in Shakespeare's play, Wyman probes the inner life of Hamlet's mother in the form of a romance, a text women readers experience privately in their homes rather than publicly in the theatres. And in doing so, she speaks to women readers, not only about the way a male-dominated theatrical establishment has long represented this particular mother and wife but also about their own experiences as mothers and wives.

Every literary transformation creates its own sets of rules and works within them to lodge a challenge to the original author and to the cumulative community of readers that have conferred meaning on his or her work. Wyman has written a particular kind of transformation, bound by rules that are clearly stated in an Appendix:

> I felt constrained to take the material furnished by the tragedy of "Hamlet" exactly as it is in the version which has been accepted as standard. I have treated this version as though it were an absolutely true historical narrative, but one with which I had not the historical novelist's privilege to tamper.

Although she has "taken no liberties with the text itself," she "felt entitled to give what seemed to me reasonable interpretations of the actions and speeches provided by the drama." Wyman goes on to say that she has added a few imaginary scenes, which are consistent "with my own conception of the personages in the tragedy" (232–33). She has not rewritten the "plot," or recast the characters (as Arnold Wesker does in *The Merchant*), nor has she dismantled and rearranged the play, as Charles Marowitz does in his collages. She begins with the characters and events of the play, assuming the reader's acquaintance with Shakespeare's text, but fleshes them out according to the conventions of the nineteenth-century novelist. She adds a few scenes, but only when Gertrude is involved; most of the additions take the form of the narrator's commentary. Just as Tom Stoppard places Rosencrantz and Guildenstern in the foreground of *Rosencrantz and Guildenstern Are Dead*, expands the roles of the players, and relegates the major characters, including Hamlet, to minor roles, so Wyman enlarges the roles of Gertrude, Claudius and Ophelia, and removes Hamlet to the periphery of the novel. Wyman occasionally records Claudius' and Ophelia's unspoken thoughts and feelings but almost never includes Hamlet's. As in Stoppard's play, the redistribution of attention constitutes a statement about the relative "importance" of men and women, princes and attendants, "heroes" and minor characters.

Gertrude of Denmark is clearly intended to be read as an interpretation of *Hamlet*, one that challenges the received opinions of a male critical establishment. Wyman's analysis of Hamlet's character explicitly seeks to refute the views of readers "enamoured of Hamlet" (241). The brief and maddeningly undocumented statement of method in the Appendix alludes to critics Wyman read (for the most part after completing the manuscript, she confesses) and gives some insight into her approach to "the critic's business" of discovering what Shakespeare "meant" or "intended" (233–34). For example, she challenges critics to apply to the characters in *Hamlet* the same standards they would adopt in "real life." Surely, she argues, "a man, and especially a prince, who becomes insane or who willfully puts on 'an antic disposition,' should be the subject of careful observation both by his responsible kindred and by the servants and rulers of the State" (241). Hence it is a mistake to accept Hamlet's characterization of Rosencrantz and Guildenstern and Polonius as "sponges" or "spies"; Wyman would firmly disagree, for example, with C. L. Barber and Richard Wheeler, who maintain that *Hamlet* "calls for an identification with the hero's alienation that excludes critical perspective," so that we can see Hamlet only from his own vantage point.[15] What about Gertrude's and Ophelia's alienation, Wyman seems to be asking—the alienation experienced by misrepresented and largely ignored women in a world both dominated and imaginatively recreated by men? The Hamlet legend, from Saxo Grammaticus onward, has been told and retold from the male perspective of the hero, and it is how Gertrude's remarriage is perceived, not why and under what circumstances it occurred, that mainly interests both authors and readers. Working in a tradition of women novelists writing for women readers, Wyman recognizes that some members of *Hamlet*'s audience may well find themselves identifying with the mother whose son is enmeshed in tragedy, and want to know more about her. Why and how did she come to remarry? How does she regard both her first and second husbands and her son? What lies behind her public words? What is she doing and thinking when she is silent or offstage?

Lillie Buffum Chace Wyman was born in 1847, the eighth of ten children in a family of New England Quakers. Her mother, Elizabeth Buffum Chace, was a well-known activist in the abolitionist and women's rights movements, an indefatigable woman who lived to the age of ninety-three. In 1914, Lillie and her son Arthur Crawford Wyman published a two-volume biography entitled *Elizabeth Buffum Chace: Her Life and Its Environment*. This was not Lillie's first literary endeavor; she had published collections of short stories and poetry (*Poverty Grass*, 1886, and *Interludes*, 1913) and a collection of essays entitled *American Chivalry* (1913), memoirlike portraits of her mother, her husband John Crawford Wyman, her mother's sister Rebecca Buffum Spring, and her mother's friends Wendell Phillips and Sojourner Truth. Phillips and Truth were among an extraordinary collection of nineteenth-century notables Lillie met in her parents' home: the biography refers to, and contains letters from, Elizabeth Cady Stanton (whose friend, Paulina Wright, got Elizabeth Chace involved in the new Women's Rights movement in the 1840s), William Lloyd Garrison, Stephen Foster, John Brown, and Frederic Douglass. Lillie says remarkably little about herself in *Elizabeth Buffum Chace* and *American Chivalry*; the impression one gets is of a self-effacing daughter overshadowed by her powerful mother, a daughter who had chosen the private occupation of writing rather than public service as her life's work.

Although the biography focuses on Elizabeth Chace's public life, Wyman's study of her mother as a *mother* is especially revealing. Mrs. Chace (as the Wymans refer to her in their narrative) was born in 1806, married Samuel Chace in 1828, and had five sons in the early years of her marriage, all of whom died in the late 1830s. After an interim of several years, during which time she was very active in the New England Anti-Slavery Society (founded by her father, Arnold Buffum, with William Lloyd Garrison and others in 1832), Mrs. Chace had five more children, from 1843 to 1852. Of her mother, Lillie says that

> she grew to be a dominant, though intensely feminine monarch . . . a brooding and solicitous rather than a caressing mother. Perhaps she was different as to that in her younger life, but I remember her as personally demonstrative only to her very youngest son, the ninth of her ten children; and yet I am certain that an older one was really her best beloved child while his brief, beautiful life lasted.[16]

Lillie recalls having had whooping cough when her brother Edward was born; because he was a sickly baby, her mother "never left him" for six months, thus effectively abandoning her fifteen-month-old daughter (1:115). Lillie's son Arthur was born in 1879 or 1880, the only child of her marriage to John Crawford Wyman, a widower twenty-five years her senior. The biography offers glimpses of both Elizabeth and Lillie as devoted, self-sacrificing mothers of sons. Like Wyman's Gertrude, the Lillie that emerges revered her much older husband but was probably closer to her son, although, unlike her mother and the Gertrude of her interpretive romance, she does not seem to have lost any children to early death.

The biography contains an incident that Wyman later adapted in *Gertrude of Denmark*: in 1889–90, the Wymans spent the winter in Georgia, and the ten-year-old Arthur was "dangerously ill for many weeks." A letter from Lillie to her mother describes her in conversation with the sick child, who, "looking at me with big, misty eyes," said, "I can't bear to have my Mama get so tired" (1:238). In an invented recollection, Gertrude remembers

a morning hour, seven and twenty years before, when she came alone through
that door and found, lying there, the child Hamlet, a little figure that seemed
to be all curls and white garments around a small pale face.

He was feeling slightly sick . . . [and] she stayed beside him all that day,
singing, telling him stories, listening to his chatter, feeding him, soothing him,
kissing him awake, watching him sleep. . . . (144–45)

The door alluded to is the one through which the grown Hamlet has just
left, at the end of the powerful closet scene. Gertrude's memory is
prompted by Hamlet's "yearning, almost childlike" parting words,
"Good night, mother," at which her "heart melted. She started toward
him as towards her baby—then stopped motionless, as before a mystery" (144). The image of the mother comforting and being comfort-
ed by the angelic male child, softened and rendered helpless by illness,
had been part of Lillie Wyman's consciousness since her very earliest
memories of her mother in the infant Edward's sickroom.

We can speculate that Lillie Wyman was drawn to the Hamlet story
at least in part by her own complex identification with the characters:
she is at once the widowed Gertrude to Arthur's Hamlet and the motherless Ophelia to Elizabeth's Polonius. As much as she admired her
accomplished and charismatic mother, she never ceased to resent her
indifference to a daughter's childhood needs.[17] Speaking of the close
friendship between her mother and her husband, Lillie acknowledged
that her mother "was better fitted by nature to get on with men than
with women" (2:103). Such a mother was clearly, from Lillie's point of
view, something less that the idealized maternal presence of nineteenth-century popular fiction.

A chance remark about Lady Macbeth in *American Chivalry* hints at
Wyman's inclination to read Shakespeare against the grain. Wyman is
describing the actress Helena Modjeska, whose rendering of Lady Macbeth's line "But in them Nature's copy's not eterne" had a profound
effect on her. The words

sounded like a cry of despair; she spoke and acted as though a sudden realization had come to her, that Macbeth meant to murder Banquo and Fleance,
that they did not possess earthly immortality, and that she herself was power-
less to check her husband's murderous impulses which were now passing far
beyond her original intention, and exciting pain and horror in her mind.[18]

This is a highly unusual reading of a line generally regarded as Lady
Macbeth's toughminded effort to reassure her distraught husband.
Much as *Gertrude of Denmark* would later do, this reading opens up
possibilities implicit in the text; it follows from Lady Macbeth's previous line, "You must leave this," and prepares for her next one, "What's

to be done," to which Macbeth answers, "Be innocent of the knowledge, dearest chuck." Wyman's image of Lady Macbeth, inspired by Modjeska, is not unlike her Gertrude; both are women whose nurturing instincts resist the reckless destructiveness of their husbands, although Gertrude is "innocent of the knowledge" from the outset in a way that sets her apart from Lady Macbeth.

The autobiographical allusions in *Elizabeth Buffum Chace* and *American Chivalry* provide no further insights into Lillie Wyman's decisions to rewrite *Hamlet* as her final, and most original, literary effort. The romance has less in common with the many male-authored adaptations and transformations of Shakespeare that appeared from the seventeenth century onward than it does with three nineteenth-century works by women. Both Anna Jameson's *Characteristics of Women, Moral, Poetical and Historical* (1832) and Mary Cowden Clarke's *The Girlhood of Shakespeare's Heroines* (1850–52) attempt to explore and account for the personalities and motivation of the female characters in Shakespeare's plays, in ways that somewhat anticipate Wyman's.

Gertrude does not figure in either Jameson's twenty-three portraits or Cowden Clarke's fifteen novellalike tales, however; she is referred to only in passing by Jameson in her section on Ophelia. Wyman had read Jameson[19] and would certainly have taken issue with her characterization of Gertrude as a "wicked queen" who is nevertheless "not so wholly abandoned but that there remains within her some sense of the virtue she has forfeited." Jameson's Lady Macbeth is a more sympathetic figure, praised for her superior intellect, her eloquence, her "splendid imagination," and her "touch of womanhood; she is ambitious less for herself than for her husband." A maternal wife, she is tender: "she sustains him, calms him, soothes him," while at the same time the "towering bravery of her mind disdains the visionary terrors which haunt her weaker husband." Much of this language implies assumptions about female virtues and wifely devotion that Wyman shares. It is curious that Jameson made no corresponding effort to get beyond the standard male appraisals of Gertrude. Wyman's portrayal of Gertrude resembles Jameson's description of Constance in *King John*:

Whenever we think of Constance, it is in her maternal character . . . the maternal affections are a powerful instinct. . . . We think of her as a mother, because, as a mother distracted for the loss of her son, she is immediately presented before us, and calls forth our sympathy and our tears; but we infer the rest of her character from what we see, as certainly and completely as if we had known her whole course of life.

Constance, says Jameson, experienced "a mother's heart-rending, soul-absorbing grief" at the death of Arthur, a grief as "natural" as her ambitions for her son, proud as she was "of his high birth and royal rights, and violent in defending them."[20] This Constance's grief anticipates the self-sacrificing devotion Wyman's Gertrude would feel toward her son, a devotion felt inwardly rather than expressed passionately.

Feminist Shakespeare critics have rediscovered writers like Anna Jameson and Mary Cowden Clarke. In a recent essay on Jameson as a critic, Christy Desmet draws attention to the way she speaks of Constance's "power—power of imagination, of will, of passion, of affection, of pride."[21] It may be that Gertrude's powerlessness made her uninteresting to Jameson. Wyman, by contrast, makes no claims for her subject's heroism or moral power but finds her interesting precisely because she exemplifies the kind of woman who lacks the imagination and assertiveness Jameson finds in Constance and Lady Macbeth. Gertrude, Wyman's narrator remarks, was "not a profound thinker nor a very wise judge of the motives which actuated people around her. Yet not commonplace was the personality of this woman, whom a great king had loved and trusted all his life."(4)

It is difficult to believe that Lillie Wyman was unacquainted with Mary Cowden Clarke's reconstructions of the early lives of Shakespeare's "heroines," for the two works, although published at a remove of seventy years, approach literary characters from a common vantage point.[22] As Cowden Clarke states in her preface to *The Girlhood of Shakespeare's Heroines*, her intent is "to imagine the possible circumstances and influences of scene, event, and associate . . . which might have conduced to originate and foster those germs of character recognized in their maturity"(xi). Nina Auerbach's *The Woman and the Demon*, a study of Victorian women writers, observes that the *The Girlhood of Shakespeare's Heroines* allows its subjects to "move freely in the conditional tense"; Desdemona, for instance, is "freed from her author's single-minded cause."[23] Cowden Clarke

> frees the heroines from the boundaries of their plays, endowing them with rich lives of their own whose autonomy is impinged on by neither Shakespeare nor the man his play will make them love. . . . Until her history is ended and begun by Shakespeare's words, each heroine lives as herself alone, appropriating fleeting suggestions in Shakespeare's text to her own richly unfurling life.

Cowden Clarke's "overwhelming popularity," Auerbach continues, "reminds us of the widespread intensity with which the autonomous literary character was believed in."[24] Many of the other transformations discussed in this book testify to a perpetuation of this belief since Cowden Clarke's time, even in the face of a literary culture that stresses the fictionality and incompleteness, not only of invented characters, but of autobiographical or historical ones as well.

The mother-child bond is clearly as important to Cowden Clarke as it is to Wyman and Jameson; equally important is the conviction that childhood experiences are crucial in shaping the disposition of the adult. Cowden Clarke's story of Lady Macbeth, for example, depicts a motherless girl (like Wyman's Gertrude) whose childhood was spent longing to "pour some of her own spirit into that placid nature" (104) of her "unmanly" father. The tale begins with the birth of Gruoch's second child, a daughter, to her intense disappointment. We are later told that a son born a year after the marriage had died a few months later, and that "after the loss of her son, the habitual gloom that settled upon her brow" caused her to be known as "the dark lady of Moray" (85). Gruoch rejects her daughter, until one day she sees the infant, while grasping at sunbeams, catch and kill a moth. Roused momentarily from her malaise, she embraces and praises the child, and then dies instantly. Young Gruoch eventually grows up to be the proud and ambitious wife of the admired hero Macbeth, yet her marriage does not satisfy her aspirations: she always wishes she had been born a man. Like Elizabeth, Lillie, and Gertrude, Gruoch nurses a young son through an illness, but "fate decreed that he shall not live." She suffers "fierce pangs for the loss of her offspring," but bears it "with stern composure, that she may stimulate her more irrepressible husband" (147–48). The tale ends where Lady Macbeth's role begins in the play, with the letter announcing the witches' prophecy. Cowden Clarke's portrait of Lady Macbeth, like Jameson's, emphasizes her subject's passionate nature and desire for independence, qualities that Wyman's Gertrude does not possess.

Although Cowden Clarke's Lady Macbeth and Wyman's Gertrude are clearly very different characters, what the two women share are a series of influential events in their past lives as daughters, wives, and mothers, which make their behavior in the "present" of each play's main action seem both understandable and inevitable. It should be noted that Wyman employs this same approach to character as the consequence of formative past events in her handling of characters other than Gertrude. For example, as Hamlet looks upon the kneeling Claudius in the prayer scene, "odd memories" come back to him and he recalls that as a child "he had often heard his father mock at Claudius a little for his athletic failures . . . the boy Hamlet, with the uncomprehending, almost innocent cruelty of childhood, had delighted in his father's taunting raillery" (118).

The third woman-authored text that provides a context for *Gertrude of Denmark* is Helena Faucit's *On Some of Shakespeare's Female Characters*, published in 1885. Faucit was a British actress who had played many of Shakespeare's women during the nineteenth century, and her book of profiles of Ophelia, Portia, Desdemona, Juliet, Imogen, Rosalind, and Beatrice was reissued several times during the 1880s and 1890s. Faucit's approach to Hamlet is similar to Wyman's: She only "touch[es] upon his character so far as it bears upon Ophelia," and condemns his behavior toward Ophelia as a "wilfulness, even insolence," that "not even his affectation of madness can excuse." As Cowden Clarke does, she believes that "we must go back to [the] youth of Shakespeare's women in order to understand them," and so, for instance, she imagines an early life for Portia at Belmont, in which her father "train[ed] her to succeed him in his high position." She also imagines her characters' futures, for "I could never leave [them] when the curtain fell and the audience departed" (her Portia, interestingly, "goes alone to [Shylock's] wretched, lonely home," repeatedly, bringing food and wine and reminding him of his sympathetic, beautiful wife Leah).[25]

Faucit's treatment of Gertrude is in many respects more sentimental than Wyman's, but it shares with Jameson, Cowden Clarke, and Wyman the emphasis they place on the strong, nurturing wife/mother figure. Wyman will use this characteristic in filling out some of the gaps in *Hamlet*, those moments when the inner life and feelings of her subject go unnoticed. For example, she offers an elaborate gloss on a single line, Gertrude's "I will not speak with her," in act 4, scene 5. Gertrude dreads an encounter with Ophelia because

> to face another encounter with a lunatic was horrible to this woman who, except for that frightful hour with Hamlet, had throughout all her adult life been cloistered in splendor and sheathed in courtesy.

Uncertain of herself, she

> feared, as she had from the beginning, that, if she saw the daughter, she would in some way reveal the awful secret of that stab through the arras. This fear, and the knowledge from which it grew, wrought an uneasiness like that of guilt within her. (161)

Yet Gertrude's maternal instincts overcome her fear and guilt, and she steps forward, saying 'How now, Ophelia?' in a spirit of pity and love (162). This moment of moral courage anticipates an even more impressive one later in the scene. As before, Gertrude derives strength from

her maternal role at a crucial, and potentially dangerous moment.26
Laertes has just entered the room, hurling angry threats at Claudius:

> Gertrude let go of the King's hand, went close to the young man and took hold
> of his. She had often held him on her knee when he was a child. Custom par-
> alyzed him. He stood still.
>   "Calmly, good Laertes," she said with a smile, that was only a little more
> dauntless than it was gracious. (167)

In constructing a life for Gertrude before the events of the play *Hamlet*
begin, Lillie Wyman confronts head-on a crucial unanswered question:
How did Gertrude come to marry Claudius after her husband's death?
Wyman depicts Gertrude as a soft and sheltered woman "bruised" at
the thought of being "any kind of personage" other than a queen. When
Polonius hints that "the position of an abbess would be most seemly for
a widowed queen," and a court lady informs her "that speculation was
busy in the palace as to whom the new king would marry, for marry
now and speedily he must," Gertrude retreats to her closet for ten days
of intense and agonizing reflection (14 –15). "No son of Claudius shall
ever sit in my Hamlet's place," she resolves, then recoils in horror from
an image of herself "with fell intent stealthily approaching an unguard-
ed infant" (19). As "her brain was still whirling," a messenger comes
from the king to "beg" an interview. This fortuitous event presents her
with an opportunity she might not have sought on her own.

> They were entirely alone. "Gertrude," he said, "marry me! The people who
> loved my brother best will see, in such a marriage, a plain augury of my future
> policy. You and I will front the world, clothed in double dignity. The nobles
> elected me king. Through your clasp of my hand, my brother will bestow his
> blessing. . . . Your Hamlet will become my son; no other son will ever be born
> to me. His princely future lies in your hands, Gertrude. Together, we will
> persuade him not to go back to Wittenberg and lead a bookish life. At our
> side, he will become a seasoned prince, fit to share my power as I grow old,—
> certain to win the election after my death."

As Gertrude walks into his outstretched arms, the narrator observed
that "perhaps he was sincere for the moment, perhaps he had even for-
gotten his guilt for that instant. He had refrained from unholy expression of love for this woman so long." Gertrude sees nothing but ten-
derness and solace. "Mother of God, I thank thee . . ." she murmurs,
"Hamlet's father has sent you to save my boy and me" (20 –21).
    This Gertrude is not an idealized, heroic woman; rather, she is a
more familiar and human character, the suddenly widowed woman confronted with choices for the first time, with no one to turn to for help

and advice. That she agrees to marry a man she has known for her entire adult life, a man whose devotion she has probably recognized and taken for granted, is hardly surprising.[27] There is nothing in Shakespeare's text that absolutely discredits this reading, particularly if one accepts Wyman's skepticism about the character of King Hamlet, a skepticism skillfully woven into the romance at various points.

For her portrait of Gertrude to be convincing, Wyman must first of all clear her of the charges of adultery. Speaking of Hamlet's encounter with the Ghost in act 1, scene 5, the narrator firmly asserts that "there is no word in this scene or elsewhere, in the whole of Shakespeare's dramatic rendition of the story, which even intimates that the King, during his existence upon the earth, had ever doubted his wife's fidelity" (52). This interpretation lodges a direct challenge to the formidable Shakespeare scholar A. C. Bradley, whose *Shakespearean Tragedy* (1904) had become widely influential by the time Wyman published her romance. Bradley proclaims that it is "practically certain" that Gertrude was "false to her husband while he lived," though he adds that "she was not privy to the murder of her husband, either before the deed or after it."[28] To this Wyman's Gertrude would respond, as her ghost cries indignantly to the narrator, "Whatever Claudius may have done, there was one indecorous thing he never would have done. He would never have made his mistress the queen of Denmark" (53).

Wyman doesn't try to explain why Claudius killed his brother, perhaps because she knows that such an explanation is beyond her skill. She speaks briefly of his ambition, of the "kind of self-love which makes a man at once brave and cowardly," of the parts played by both hatred and love in "his onward progress toward criminality." Passing quickly over both "the deed which entailed upon him the 'primal eldest curse' and his election to the throne" (11–12), she dwells instead on his role in bringing about Gertrude's "fatal mistake." This "mistake" is made as convincing as possible. Gertrude's hesitantly whispered objections to the immediacy of the marriage are swept aside by Claudius's shrewd awareness that his advisers might try to pressure him to marry a woman of childbearing age. When Gertrude asks about "the notion that such a marriage was incestuous" Claudius assures her "that he has seen the priests, and everything has been made right as to that," an ambiguous response Gertrude accepts because "she held a solemn conviction that angels . . . had inspired Claudius to offer the ring which would insure her own and her son's future safety and dignity" (23).

This response is very characteristic of Wyman's Gertrude; like many self-deluding tragic characters, she believes that which most comfortably supports her own self-image and aspirations, and willingly accepts what she was told without further inquiry. Yet like other tragic characters, she remains plagued by doubts. When Hamlet violently accuses her in the closet scene, she experiences

> this feeling coming upon her and gripping her throat . . . had she, after all, been moved to that marriage by the slightest unworthy desire? Oh God, had she? Had she in the least, wanted throne and royalty, for herself, and not merely for Hamlet? This thought hissed its awful question in her ears.

The question is an "awful" one because it is very hard for Gertrude to accept the truth that "she wanted something for herself. She had preferred life to stagnation. . . ." Wyman is fully aware that other possibilities existed: "There were, indeed, women, even in her period, who, as spinsters or widows, could, and did carve out and carry on interesting careers for themselves in politics or other action." The "interesting career," a medieval version of Elizabeth Chace's career, perhaps, is utterly beyond Gertrude, as the narrator realizes. Gertrude was "not that kind, and nothing, in her experience as King Hamlet's wife, had fitted her to become such." Neither, perhaps, was Lillie. And so the narrator concludes, defending her heroine in an understated way: "She had made the normal choice" (135–36).

In her Appendix, Wyman observes that "the critics have generally denounced Gertrude's second marriage as sinful in its very nature. It is rather absurd to echo Hamlet so completely as to this. . . ." She goes on to remind the reader that the Catholic Church upheld the marriage of Catherine of Aragon to Henry VIII after the death of his brother Arthur and that Shakespeare "did not represent Katherine as a loathsome creature in his drama on that subject" (238). The novel presents Gertrude as a sheltered, rather childlike woman, trained to defer to male authority, with little knowledge of the world outside her palace garden. Gertrude is placed "amid tragical circumstances," as Wyman says in the final paragraph of the Appendix, not the least of which are the circumstances created by an uprearing from which she emerges as a passive, dependent woman, able to act assertively and confidently only when she assumed her maternal role on behalf of another. Equally tragic, perhaps, is the way her beloved son misunderstands and misrepresents her, abetted by a ghost who had "develop[ed] a posthumous but unfounded suspicion and jealousy" (250). This son is a "monstrous egotist, who could question all things in the Universe, himself included, but who could not see the answers to his questions, because his egoism imposed itself like a tangible substance between the eyes of his mind and everything in the Universe" (222). This sentence is in some ways the most startling instance of talking back in Wyman's transformation of *Hamlet*, not because it is so unusual for a reader to denounce

Hamlet as an egotist, but because one hears in Wyman's voice a passionate appeal to Gertrude and women like her. Women, Wyman seems
to be saying, must recognize and resist the egotism of their sons and
husbands, rather than nurture and encourage it.

In order to transform Gertrude's story in *Hamlet* into a character
study that adhered to the conventions of nineteenth-century narratives,
Wyman needed to invent a turning point for Gertrude, a moment of revelation that marked her growth as a character. The death of Ophelia
serves as the catalyst, since Ophelia has been an important character
in this Gertrude's life. Left motherless a year before the events of the
play began, the sixteen-year-old Ophelia realizes early on that "it had
been ignoble for [Hamlet] to make love to her without proffering the
wedding ring" (45). Gertrude and Ophelia are thus allies in the face of
Hamlet's egotistical selfishness, and Wyman invents a tender little
scene between them after act 2, scene 3. Gertrude "gathered the motherless girl like a trembling blossom to her bosom" and questioned her
laughingly about Hamlet. "I give you a mother's blessing," she says,
then "babbled of her boy," recalling his beauty as a baby. "We are going
to marry him—to you, little Ophelia,—to you" (78).

Wyman's elaboration on the relationship between Gertrude and Ophelia prepares the reader for Gertrude's intense grief when Ophelia dies.

> Suddenly, all the poetry in Gertrude's nature awoke, like a spirit, arising from
> the sunken depths of unconscious being. It was a strange psychical experi-
> ence,—but it came to her, this woman of primal instincts. She had lived
> among conventions, she had thought the thoughts which courtiers, princes and
> abbesses had taught her to think. She had not possessed the intellect, which
> would have enabled her to unthink them. Love and dignity had sufficed to
> quiet all impulse towards self-expression. But the stone, which had covered
> the sanctuary of her inner life, was now rolled away. Tragedy touched and
> transformed her into one who must sing aloud.

This paragraph prepares the reader for Gertrude's extraordinarily
poetic account of Ophelia's death, a speech unlike any other Shakespeare has given her (5.1.166–83).

We do not see Wyman's Gertrude again except at the public funeral
and subsequent duel. Her posture during the duel is that of a pleased
mother, enjoying the prospect of "her darling . . . restored to health,
lovely in his powerful manhood . . . her son . . . her perfect creation . . .
and he loved her . . . rapture of raptures, he loved her once more!" (217).
The narrator speaks of "a mystical kind of vision" that comes over her,
and it is in this mood of exultant self-affirmation that she drinks to
Hamlet, and then, a few lines later, realizes that she is poisoned. As
she lies dying, "Some sort of awareness came to her."

"No, no,"she groaned, "the drink, the drink—" She thought she felt her son's arms around her. The supreme passion of her life asserted itself. "O my dear Hamlet," she whispered.

"Then," says the narrator, "a mother died" (220).

Wyman's Gertrude lives and dies in a world where the only socially acceptable or legitimate reason for the marriage would be the selfless one—to protect Hamlet's claim to the throne. To expiate the sin of having possibly acted selfishly, Gertrude feels she must immerse herself in selfless, wifely ministrations to a king whose love, the narrator observes judgmentally, was "selfish, unmoral love . . . [an] overdevelopment of aestheticism, which rots downward into the heart of man, and turns the love of anything which is beautiful . . . into self-love and the desire for self-gratification" (177). Although she cannot achieve the perfect selflessness and womanly devotion to the interests of husband and child to which she feels she should aspire, the romance convinces us that her desire to remain in the court world where she has lived all her adult life is understandable and forgivable, particularly when her husband and son are so undeserving of her attentiveness and self-sacrifice. The sympathy for Gertrude that Wyman allows her narrator to voice might appear as a critique of a society that placed unfair expectations upon women. Wyman's upbringing among feminists and abolitionists could easily have prepared her for the role of social critic, but it would be a mistake to view *Gertrude of Denmark* as an overtly ideological work. The dominant tone of the romance is one of gentle, decorous sympathy and respect for a character left unfinished by her original creator.

Rather than a victim of society, Wyman's Gertrude can be seen as a casualty of the limitations of a play centered on its male protagonist. The romance interrogates the "maleness" of *Hamlet* as a sacrosanct canonical text far more than Jameson, for example, does: Jameson's portrait of Ophelia speaks of its subject's "relative beauty and delicacy when considered in relation to that of Hamlet, which is the delineation of a man of genius in contest with the powers of this world." Hamlet, Jameson continues, has "an immense intellectual power [which] renders him unspeakably interesting . . . undoubtedly Shakespeare loved him beyond all his other creations."[29]

In 1924, the year *Gertrude of Denmark* appeared (although we have no way of knowing when it was actually written), Agnes Mure MacKenzie published *The Women in Shakespeare's Plays: A Critical Study from the Dramatic and the Psychological Points of View*. There are certain similarities between her portrait of Gertrude and Wyman's:

the whole tragedy has its root in Gertrude's weakness—weakness, not wicked-
ness, for she is not at all an evil woman. She is passive and obtuse, and she
loves comfort—one always pictures her as being a little fat, with podgy white
fingers heavily beringed—but she is nothing worse, at bottom. Only that
"nothing worse" is the direct cause of nine violent deaths, besides a hell of
agony for her own son.

MacKenzie condescends to Gertrude, something Wyman never does:
"She has the qualities of a pleasant animal—docility, kindliness, affection for her offspring, a courage in the defense of her mate." The
urgency of Wyman's felt need to tell Gertrude's story may owe something to the unfairness of MacKenzie's view of her, particularly her
final, extraordinary paragraph. Gertrude, she concludes, "kills both
husbands, she kills Ophelia, she kills her son . . . [and] Rosencrantz and
Guildenstern . . . and Polonius. . . . And she has not a particle of ill-will
or ill-intentions in her. Simply she is stupid, coarse, and shallow."[30]
The review of *Gertrude of Denmark* in *Theatre Arts Monthly* (August
1924) lamented that Wyman's "frankly intuitional and sentimental"
presentation "weakens the value of what critically and historically handled might be an interesting contribution to the study of *Hamlet*." Other
reviewers were more positive: *Bookman* called it a "friendly, 'civi-
lized,' humorous, beautiful, and assertive entry into the lists of Shakespeariana," and *The Springfield Republican* observed that "whether we
are convinced or not, this romance of Hamlet and his mother . . . is likely to stay in our memory."[31] *Gertrude of Denmark* does not seem to have
had any influence on Shakespeare criticism, however. When Carolyn
Heilbrun published her defense of Gertrude in *Shakespeare Quarterly*
in 1957 (reissued in 1990 as the title essay in a volume called *Hamlet's
Mother and Other Women*), there was no mention either of Wyman's
book or the ideas contained within it. After surveying the critics'
assessments of Gertrude, Heilbrun concludes that without exception
they agree to define Gertrude by her "frailty." The best they can say of
her is that she is "well-meaning but shallow and feminine in the pejo-
rative sense of the word: incapable of any sustained rational process,
superficial and flighty." Heilbrun sets out to refute this view, by looking at everything Gertrude says and every scene in which she appears.
She asserts that Gertrude's speeches are "human," "direct," "courageous," and that except for her "single flaw," she is a "strong-minded,
intelligent, succinct . . . [and] sensible" woman. The flaw that stands
against and undermines all these fine qualities is "lust, the desire for
sexual relations," which causes Gertrude to cry "O Hamlet, speak no
more! / Thou turn'st my [eyes into my very] soul," when he accuses her
of shameless and "compulsive ardure." (3.4.86 –90). Heilbrun sees

this as a moment of recognition for Gertrude (she knows "that this is her sin") and as a key element in the plot ("Gertrude's flaw of lust made Claudius' ambition possible").[32] It would be interesting to know what the Heilbrun of the 1990s would say about Wyman's theory of the "normal choice," a natural preference for the married state that resists the imposed constraints of widowhood. Curiously, Heilbrun says nothing about Gertrude's maternal feelings; perhaps she was making a deliberate break with the ideology of the 1950s and anticipating the feminism of the next decade.

By 1980 it had become possible once again to depict Gertrude as a devoted mother. Rebecca Smith's essay on Gertrude in *The Woman's Part* emphasizes Gertrude's "persistent extreme love for her son," a love that conflicts with her love for Claudius (hence the "heart cleft in twain" of the essay's title). Gertrude is "merely a quiet, biddable, careful mother and wife," a "compliant, loving, unimaginative woman whose only concern is pleasing others," one "easily led and [who] makes no decisions for herself except, ironically, the one that precipitates her death." Smith ends by saying that if Gertrude "were presented on stage and film as only her own words create her, she might become another stereotypical character: the nurturing, loving, careful mother and wife—malleable, submissive, totally dependent, and solicitous of others at the expense of herself."[33]

For a reader familiar with Wyman's Gertrude, Smith's conclusion that Gertrude is a solicitous mother who experiences no inner conflicts is just as unsatisfying, in its own way, as Heilbrun's emphasis on Gertrude's recognition of her sinful lust in the closet scene. One wonders how either Heilbrun or Smith would have reacted to Wyman's description of Gertrude's thoughts as Hamlet delivers his long and excoriating speech. Gertrude's conviction that she had made the "normal choice" falters in the presence of Hamlet's fury, so that "it seemed that every motive which had influenced her must have been stained through by some terrible stream of selfishness." Gertrude returns to her earlier "moral question":

> Was the marriage really one that was forbidden by God's law? And, if it were, had she herself become an odious creature? Then it was that she sobbed,
>   "O Hamlet, speak no more. . . ."
> Out of her very innocence, as many another stormily distracted one has done, she confessed to a comparatively small fault, in language which sounded like the admission of a great sin. (136)

The "terrible stream of selfishness" that torments Gertrude is in many ways a more interesting "sin" than Heilbrun's lust, precisely because it is a more ambiguous one, originating as it does in a misguided effort to preserve her own identity as a queen and protect her son's future.

And yet Wyman does not attempt to present Gertrude as a tragic figure. *Gertrude of Denmark* sets out to dislodge Prince Hamlet as the hero of the play, but without offering his mother in his place. Gertrude never becomes a heroine who invites the reader's profound sympathy and admiration, partly because she remains constrained by Wyman's decision not to add extensively to or alter the words Shakespeare gave her. Wyman imposed a very restrictive set of rules upon her enterprise, for she viewed herself as an interpreter who "had no right to alter [the play] in order to harmonize it with my fancies" (233). Wyman's book is thus a curious hybrid, at once a critical challenge to the literary establishment's adulation of Hamlet, a romance exhibiting many of the traits of nineteenth-century novels written for and about women, an indirect analysis of the limitations inherent in Shakespeare's view of women, and a record of Wyman's own ambivalence about the problems women face when they define themselves as wives and mothers.

How would the students who reacted so strongly to Wesker's *The Merchant* respond to *Gertrude of Denmark*, one wonders? Since the romance is out of print and unavailable in most libraries I have been unable to assign it to classes, but several years ago one of my students did undertake the project of transforming parts of *Gertrude of Denmark* and Shakespeare's closet scene into a staged reading for three actors, a narrator, a Gertrude, and a Hamlet. When this piece was performed for an undergraduate Shakespeare class, they came away with a new perspective, not just toward *Hamlet* but toward other plays as well. One young man said that the staged reading made him rethink his reactions to some of Shakespeare's other women characters and speculate about the effects of gender reversal; for instance, "Lear's daughters' rejection of their parent could be seen as natural if they were three boys who were victims of their mother's madness." A young woman found herself wondering about Lady Macbeth: "The audience knew that Macbeth had second thoughts about killing Duncan, but not Lady Macbeth. Wyman helps the reader to wonder if Lady Macbeth was actually as strong as she seemed." Another was inspired by Wyman's invention of an earlier life for Gertrude to speculate about Isabella: "If we knew that Isabella had been sexually molested as a child, and was deathly afraid of any contact with men at all maybe we would understand her actions in *Measure for Measure* better." Several students discovered, through watching the staged reading, that the *Hamlet* they knew represented Gertrude almost entirely from Hamlet's point of view. One young woman commented that "*Gertrude of Denmark* is great because it doesn't make Gertrude the scapegoat," and another said she now realized that Hamlet's "constant slander of Gertrude definitely affects the way we see her character. She is viewed as an accomplice to murder and a woman committing incest." Still another wished there were similar adaptations of other Shakespeare plays from the woman's point of view, for *Gertrude of Denmark* made her realize what Shakespeare's plays tell us about how his culture viewed women.

The adapter/director of the staged reading (who also served as the narrator) and the actress who played Gertrude told me that the project made them much more aware of the discovery that occurs when Gertrude realizes that she is poisoned. They had become less interested in Hamlet's response—his realization that he can now kill Claudius with a clear conscience—and much more aware of Gertrude, who must speak her line about the poisoned drink in such a way as to convey a powerful and intensely tragic flash of recognition. This new, Wyman-inspired Gertrude registers in her face and voice a sudden realization that she has been duped all along by Claudius, and her consequent horror and disgust leave a profound impression on the audience. I pointed out to them that Wyman might not have agreed with their interpretation, since she seems to feel that Gertrude's loyalty to Claudius is never shaken. It is nevertheless the case that *Gertrude of Denmark* acted as a catalyst for new staging options for *Hamlet*, much as a particularly convincing critical interpretation might do.

I suspect that Percy MacKaye's *The Mystery of Hamlet, King of Denmark*, or *What We Will*, would have a similar effect; that is, it might make it difficult for students to return to their earlier readings of *Hamlet* without questioning their assumptions and responses. I have yet to find the opportunity to introduce students to this massive work, a tetralogy in prologue to Shakespeare's *Hamlet* that begins thirty years before act 1, scene 1 of Shakespeare's play and ends, 650 pages later, with Claudius's opening speech of act 1, scene 2. MacKaye spent most of the 1940s composing his final work for the theatre, which was staged only once, by the Pasadena Playhouse in 1949. The full text of the plays appeared in the following year, in a beautifully designed limited edition. The best way to describe the tetralogy is to invoke Northrop Frye's concept of encyclopedic form, a form characterized by expansiveness, mythmaking, cyclical movement, "a tendency to be exhaustive in technique and subject matter," and an inclusiveness that incorporates instances of various genres or modes into larger aggregates.[34]

The tetralogy is no more obviously a product of the late 1940s than Wyman's *Gertrude of Denmark* is of the 1920s; indeed, as Ruby Cohn has observed, MacKaye's plays "might have been written over a century earlier."[35] What Cohn dismisses as pretentious and "old-fashioned" Romantic mysticism does indeed take some getting used to, for MacKaye's work occupies a distinctly artificial realm filled with insistent symbolism and highly fraught emotions. The tetralogy is filled with song and accompanying musical notation; indeed, the work as a whole has a masquelike quality, not surprising since MacKaye's most important theatrical works had consisted of civic pageants, called masques by their author and clearly indebted to the Elizabethan and Jacobean masque in respect to their subject matter and theatrical strategies.

The only published article devoted to *The Mystery of Hamlet* appeared shortly after the Pasadena Playhouse production, in the Shakespeare Association Bulletin (now *Shakespeare Quarterly*). In his remarks on "this extremely unusual adventure in playwrighting, play producing and publication" Henry Wells observed that although the plays "bear some likeness to earlier Shakespeariana" they are "distinctly unlike what MacKaye himself or anyone else has thus far done." He speculated that the four plays "will also be unlike what will come after them; the mythology of Hamlet may be endless, but MacKaye has explored almost to the limit this particular province."[36]

Discovering MacKaye's tetralogy shortly after having read Wyman's *Gertrude of Denmark* was an uncanny experience for me, largely because of the fascinating parallels between these two authors' histories. Both Wyman and MacKaye came to the Hamlet story late in their lives, having both spent a large portion of their earlier years amassing exhaustive, two-volume biographies of a famous parent. If anything, MacKaye's life was even more powerfully dominated by his father's mythic status and accomplishments than Wyman's was by her mother, and his own career more clearly reflects his father's influence. Both of these parents, judging from the biographies, were extraordinarily charismatic, idealistic, and widely known public figures during the second half of the nineteenth century. For their respective children to be drawn to the tale of a mythic character forever identified as the son of a mysterious and heroic father whose name he shares seems somehow appropriate. In a very real sense, Percy MacKaye and Lillie Wyman led Hamletlike existences, for they were associated with their dominant parents in their own eyes and in those of others. Both devoted their literary energies to inscribing those parents' lives, transforming what remained of oral memory and written fragments into a coherent and celebratory text.

Epoch: The Life of Steele MacKaye, Genius of the Theatre: In Relation to His Times and Contemporaries appeared in 1927, some thirty-three years after the death of its subject. Steele MacKaye (1842–94) became a significant figure on the American theatrical scene in the

1870s, and in the course of his career was an actor, producer, director, playwright, designer, and theatrical inventor. His circle of acquaintances may well have overlapped with that of Elizabeth Buffum Chace; in 1878, the biography reports, he was giving lectures at the Boston University School of Oratory, whose faculty list and Board of Visitors included Ralph Waldo Emerson, Bronson Alcott, and Phillips Brooks. MacKaye's finest moment as an actor came early in his career, when he became the first American to perform the part of Hamlet on the London stage in 1873. The production was enthusiastically received by the London press: *The Spectator* praised it as "by far the best Hamlet of our time," while other reviews noted MacKaye's "radical departure from old-school traditions," and a "new naturalism" that replaced the rant, "stentorian howls" and "rampant puffs" of previous productions.[37] Percy MacKaye quotes at length from the review in *The Critic* that drew attention to the "startling new methods of naturalness in acting and production" and concluded with a burst of eloquence looking forward to "that happy consummation when histrionic art shall be a true exposition of human character, and when human nature shall be presented shorn of conventionality and theatrical mannerism" (1:214).

One can imagine Percy MacKaye reading and rereading these words (which were published shortly before his birth) and associating his father with Hamlet throughout his life. So, evidently, did others of his age; MacKaye concludes his moving description of his father's final days with the words Henry Irving inscribed on his funeral wreath: "Good night, sweet Prince." Not long before his death, Steele had written a long letter to Percy, then a freshman at Harvard, setting forth his aesthetic philosophy, as if exhorting his son to carry on the flame into the twentieth century. The letter is reprinted in full, after which Percy observes that "the keen sensibilities of aesthetics and ethics were indissolubly blended" in his father's life. This letter, and other remarks like it, were Steele MacKaye's "Remember me!" to his son. Rather like Hamlet, Percy MacKaye set out to reconstruct his father's life and death, inspired by a felt sense of sacred obligation to measure up to the legacy of that "dynamic personality, whose still living ideals are peculiarly kindred to those of forward visionary leaders in our time," as he described Steele MacKaye in his preface (1:viii). The parallel is inexact, of course; whereas Hamlet's whole being is consumed by the process of eliciting information, judging, and punishing, until he ceases to have a life apart from the enormous enterprise of remembering and avenging his father, Percy MacKaye went on to write thirty-one plays and operas and several books of poetry and essays. But the ghostly presence of the father clearly haunted him just as vividly as it haunted Hamlet: so, at least, he implies in the final words of *Epoch*:

Once more I am there in that autumnal hour, toward sunset. . . . Once again, my father silently leads me with my brothers—now strangely a mystic host with brotherly faces! —guiding us, through cluttered debris, to a grim iron stairway. . . . Once again my father seems neither to see, or to hear. But now I know I am mistaken. —He hears; he sees. His eyes are focussed far off— beyond—on the clear contours of vast imagined to-morrows . . . alluring us to follow his vision. . . . (2:485)

One has only an occasional glimpse of the darker side of the Hamlet story in *Epoch*. Persistent illness plagued and shortened Steele MacKaye's life, while bribery and graft cheated him of his final great project, the Chicago Spectatorium, a technically innovative theatrical enterprise that was eclipsed by the World's Fair. Percy MacKaye's involvement in the short-lived American Pageant Theatre movement, which ended in 1918, was, he wrote, an effort to perpetuate the "theatrical aims and social motive which imbued the Spectatorium concepts of my father" (2:479). The "Claudius" in Steele MacKaye's life was a theatre-going public incapable of supporting a visionary philosopher/entrepreneur and his equally idealistic son. Since their goal had been nothing less than the "drama of democracy," it was not simply an artistic venture that had died in its youth but an expression of the American dream.

"The Drama of Democracy" is the title of an address Percy MacKaye wrote in 1908 and subsequently reprinted in his collection *The Playhouse and the Play and Other Addresses* (1909). For several years, MacKaye had been touring the country delivering public addresses setting forth his philosophy of the theatre, arguing for an "emancipation from Broadway commercialism" and proposing instead a nationwide network of little theatres, university theatres, and stadium theatres (2:478). He envisioned "dramas of democracy" to be written by poets,

for in the very nature of its ideal the drama of democracy will be a poetic drama. Not a revival of old forms, not an emulation of Elizabethan blank verse, but a fresh imagining and an original utterance of modern motives which are as yet unimagined and unexpressed. Not a revival, but a new birth; not a restoration, but a renascence of poetic drama.[38]

MacKaye's first published play, *The Canterbury Pilgrims*, appeared in 1903; during the next few years, he went on to write "some seven or eight 'dramas of democracy,' or communal plays," massive spectaculars performed in stadiums and involving large numbers of amateur and professional actors. Of the great "St. Louis: A Civic Masque," Vachel Lindsay wrote that "the fiery spirit of Percy MacKaye—like his father before him—knew how to turn men of clay into archangels for a day."[39]

MacKaye estimates that eight thousand to ten thousand citizen actors took part in this masque, which was seen by nearly five hundred thousand spectators during a five-day run in 1914.[40]

Percy MacKaye's most spectacular masque, *Caliban*, was produced in 1916 at Lewisohn Stadium in New York for the tercentenary of Shakespeare's death and then performed again the following year at Harvard Stadium, with a cast of five thousand citizen actors (*Epoch*, 2:480). As subsequent transformations of *The Tempest* would do, MacKaye's work expands upon the glimpses Shakespeare gives us of Caliban, his mother Sycorax, and Setebos their "half-toad, half-tiger" god of primeval force.[41] In the opening Prolog, Prospero delivers Ariel from the jaws of Setebos and declares that he will "transform" and educate Caliban. The subsequent pageantry, performed before the cell of Caliban, enacts this education, beginning with scenes from Egyptian history and art and proceeding to the Greek and Roman eras. These three "actions" have served as instruction for Ariel as well, and with the beginning of act 1, Ariel and his spirits assume responsibility for the education of Caliban, through a sequence of plays within plays. The masque contains another cycle of Egyptian, Greek, and Roman visions, consisting of scenes from *Antony and Cleopatra*, *Troilus and Cressida*, and *Julius Caesar*. These are followed by a medieval Germanic Ur-Faust performed on a pageant wagon, a French and English joust, and an Italian commedia. Act 2 consists of the Ghost scene from *Hamlet*, scenes from *Romeo and Juliet*, *The Merchant of Venice*, and *The Winter's Tale*, culminating in an eight-part sequence of seasonal rituals, May Day festivities, and morris dances. More scenes from Shakespeare's plays follow, as Caliban woos Miranda and summons the spirits of Lust, War, and Death to overpower Prospero and Ariel. MacKaye allows Caliban to triumph momentarily at the end of act 3. But true to its didactic purpose, the masque ends happily: In the Epilog, Caliban yields to the "female Spirit of Time," who speaks of "Unconquered Art" and ushers in "two hundred community actors representing the world's greatest actors, playwrights, and directors," with Shakespeare among them. *Caliban* concludes with a grand gesture of reconciliation, as Caliban turns to the assembled actors and calls out to them to bow to Shakespeare, at which the assembled choirs burst into song, culminating in "The Star Spangled Banner."[42] This, clearly, was encyclopedic form on a grand scale.

MacKaye believed that Civic Theatre could recapture the spirit of the medieval mystery plays and offer citizens of all classes an opportunity to uphold the moral and social values of the nation through art; eventually, he suggested, the "natural impulses for self-development and competition" would be channeled into a cooperative and democratic "substitute for war."[43] Some thirty years later, writing in Littleton, Massachusetts while the Second World War raged throughout the rest of the world, MacKaye's optimism would become subdued, though it asserts itself in the face of treachery and self-betrayal throughout *The Mystery of Hamlet*.

MacKaye viewed the tetralogy as part of a life work that began in 1896 with his sonnet cycle "A Garland for Sylvia," written for his beloved wife Marion Morse MacKaye, whose sudden death in 1939 cut short a creative collaboration that he describes in his Afterword to the tetralogy as "two sensitive human beings in touch with supersensible beings."[44] Finishing the great work after her death was "a sacred task imposed on me . . . [by] the will of powers far greater than my own." The divinity that shapes our ends, which he credits with "revealing" the tetralogy ("this work was experienced rather than 'written'. . . ."), prevented him from completing his task, however; his planned sequel to *Hamlet* remained unwritten at his death in 1956.

MacKaye shares with Wyman a keen awareness of the incompleteness of Shakespeare's text. Derived from a legend that spanned many years and that was retold in countless forms, Shakespeare's *Hamlet* frustrates the reader—particularly the nineteenth- and early twentieth-century reader—by confining itself to the last few months of its characters' lives. To rewrite *Hamlet* in the age of the novel almost inevitably entails novelistic strategies. MacKaye's insistence upon creating a poetic drama that revitalizes sixteenth-century conventions does not prevent him from adopting the novelist's vantage point and starting at "the beginning." The Prologue that begins the first play, *The Ghost of Elsinore*, deliberately echoes Shakespeare's opening scene, a strategy, often bordering on parody, that MacKaye will use throughout his work. On the castle ramparts at Elsinore, just before dawn, a guard calls "Stand there!" The voice that responds belongs to Gertrude, whom MacKaye endows with some of the same solicitude Wyman's Gertrude had possessed, here directed toward her beloved husband. King Hamlet is torn between his desire to remain with his pregnant wife and his duty to "go forth to fight with Fortinbras" (8). A dreamlike sequence follows, with the sleepwalking Hamlet surrounded by Voices and the "Wraith of Gertrude," chanting in counterpoint:

> *Voices:* Kill, kill
> > *Wraith:* Be kind!
> > > *Voices:* Go forth!
> > > > *Wraith:* Remain! (11)

"Voices of the Invisible" join in, heralding the Cock Gallucinius, a spiritual presence who serves as the carrier of much of the four plays' Christian symbolism. The Cock announces itself to be a recurring figure throughout history, from Pharaoh's Tomb to the hill at Golgotha. After a masquelike "eerie Pageant" Gallucinius approaches King Hamlet and announces: "My aim, at Elsinore, King Hamlet, is to show thee to thyself" (13). Excerpts from act 1, scenes 1 and 5 of *Hamlet* follow, which the King views as if in the "Crystal" of the future that Gallucinius holds before him. The audience hears the familiar words of the Ghost telling Hamlet how he was murdered, ending with Hamlet's vow, "Remember thee? Ay, thou poor ghost, while memory holds a seat / In this distracted globe . . ." (21).

Act 1 takes place in daylight on the day when Hamlet must leave. Gertrude attempts to hold him with talk of love, the "all-begetting, all conceiving / Executive and servant. There's none other / Than love." King Hamlet responds, "There's war," and adds, a few lines later, "You are a woman, Gertrude, / And woman's mind is frail" (29). Here then, is an Antonylike tragic hero, confronted with the conflicting claims of private love and public duty, who goes forth to war without any illusions about its grandeur: "Mortals must feed on mortals, till the residue / Is dung, for states to bloom in" (35). The King's trusted younger brother offers to stay behind, "to guard the Queen" in Hamlet's absence, even though "To go is glorious" (39–40). This first act ends with Hamlet rushing off to fetch his armor.

> *Gertrude:* [*crying after him, poignantly*] No, no, no
> [*Then slowly fixing her stare upon Claudius, she speaks in a dull, raw tone.*] No.
> *Claudius:* [*Kneeling to her.*] My Queen! (41)

So begins a tragedy of temptation, vacillation, treachery, and guilt, in which Gertrude, though never the central figure she was in Wyman's text, plays a large and complex role. MacKaye seems to see her as a Clytaemnestra-figure, the woman left behind while her warrior husband immerses himself in the absorbing business of war. As Clytaemnestra tells Orestes in *The Libation Bearers*, "It hurts women, being kept from men, my son."[45] Just as Aigisthos succeeds in supplanting his cousin, Claudius is able to break down Gertrude's resistance over the thirty years covered by the tetralogy.

Mingled with the tragic elements are long sections of festive romance, replete with masquelike interludes and comic characters whom MacKaye has added to Shakespeare's cast, using *Hamlet* and other plays for inspiration. The most memorable of these are Moll

Cowslip, the midwife who delivers Hamlet, and Yorick, a major figure
in the first two plays, and a wonderfully witty and musical version of
the Shakespearean Fool. Topas the Gravedigger describes Yorick as
one who'll "twiddle a psalm-tune on his funny-bone / Will make the
pixies scamper to churn the cream / They's come to steal" (245). The
scenes in which Yorick figures exhibit MacKaye's strategy of repeat-
ing and refracting patterns and incidents from *Hamlet*. Yorick's four-
teen-year-old daughter Angela, a charming, innocent creature associated with St. Agnes, dies on the day Hamlet is born, the first victim of
Claudius's jealousy. She is poisoned by the hebenon he intended for the
infant. The father who loses his child thus anticipates the child who
will lose his father, rather as *The Spanish Tragedy* mirrors *Hamlet*.
Yorick will later present the hebenon to Claudius, urging him to pour
it out and save his soul.

   The Fool in Eden Garden, the second play in the tetralogy, takes place
on Hamlet's seventh birthday. Yorick is master of ceremonies throughout this festive play, which is filled with Halloween lore, and which features a complete performance of the *Norwich Grocer's Play*, presented
by a company of traveling players as part of the birthday celebration.
At the play's end, young Hamlet unmasks the actor who had played the
serpent in Eden and discovers him to be none other than Claudius.
Claudius had left Elsinore abruptly after the birth of Hamlet and death
of Angela and has now returned, serpentlike, to seduce Gertrude/Eve.
But to say that Claudius "seduces" Gertrude is to oversimplify, for in
this complex exploration of the varieties of love, Gertrude offers
Claudius kindness and forgiveness, and knowing of his "secret lust" for
her, nevertheless asks him to "protect" her son with his serpent's wisdom (221, 223).

   MacKaye views love as a sacred and redemptive element in the
human and spiritual realm. The principal advocate of divine love and
forgiveness in *The Fool in Eden Garden* is Padre Celestino, an entirely
invented character who serves as the prince's tutor and a spiritual
adviser to the other characters. Rather like Yorick, he is a spokesman
for the ethos of trust and affirmation. At the birthday celebration, he
gives young Hamlet a blank tablet of Memory, with the words, *"Remember only the true! / Then thou'lt be loving."* When older, he must write
"anew, what's writ / Already there, unseen, and wipe away / All trivial
fond records" (150). King Hamlet bids his son and Horatio to "swear"
upon a child's wooden lath sword the sacred "mandate": *"Love and
Memory . . . And Verity!"* The theme of remembering is rooted in the
very logic of the plays, as they echo *Hamlet*, remembering and recast-
ing its most memorable phrases. MacKaye's transformation compels
us to return to the Ghost's "Remember me!" with a heightened sense

of its significance. Remembering mingles with anticipating and prophesying the future in *The Mystery of Hamlet*, through flash forwards consisting of interpolated excerpts from Shakespeare's play. The characters live in a mysterious realm of present and future time, glimpsing their impending tragedies but unable to understand, much less prevent, them. The audience participates in this sense of complicity of present and future, for example, by watching the seven-year-old Hamlet and Laertes engage in a half-playful, half-angry sword fight during the birthday party, while shadows of two other figures duel on the wall above, accompanied by the words of act 5, scene 2 of *Hamlet.*

After the children have gone to bed, Padre Celestino reads aloud to Gertrude, Hamlet, and Claudius from *The Divine Comedy*. Once again text plays off text, as Claudius questions the Padre about Beatrice, who "hath something of a mother's sorrow / For her wandered child's mishaps" (193). Celestino tries to convince him to believe in the all-consuming power of Love, adding that we "are not the serfs but masters of our errors / To make our passions slave to truth" (199). In a scene that clearly parallels the prayer scene in *Hamlet*, Claudius tries to pray but can think only of Angela, the "budding elf, with hair of candleshine / Whose flame of life I quenched" (204). If she is the Beatrice he prays to for forgiveness, so is Gertrude, whom he feels an uncontrollable desire to possess.

Twenty-two years pass between the end of *The Fool in Eden's Garden* and the beginning of *Odin Against Christus*. Once again MacKaye begins by dramatizing the conflict between Love and War, this time by contrasting the Nordic religion of "Odin, the One-Eyed, the wise All-Father of battle-sons and breed o'master-men" with the worship of the Virgin, bringer of peace (301). As before, the division poses the masculine principle against the feminine one; for the charcoal burner Erik, at whose hut the opening scene takes place, the Virgin Mary his wife Isbel prays to is a false god. As he threatens to break the shrine and replace it with wassail, a deep voice interrupts from offstage. Into this scene strides King Hamlet, armed for battle. He hears the two sides of the argument and recasts it as the conflict within himself. Moments later Voltimand arrives from Elsinore, bearing a letter that reads "Hamlet—come home—Gertrude—a kiss" (312). From the exchange that follows, the reader understands better than Hamlet does the desperation of a wife longing for her absent husband, a husband who blindly assumes that his brother will "divert her / From any pain of overthought on me" (314). By the time he reaches Elsinore, some sixty-four pages later, Valentine's Day festivities are in full swing. Claudius has been wooing Gertrude with poetry, masques, and an aphrodisiac obtained during a descent into the hellish wine cellars, where Gallucinius, posing as a cellarer, assumes the role of Claudius's other self. Just as Gallucinius had offered Claudius the choice between love and hatred in *The Ghost of Elsinore*, and when Claudius chose hatred, supplied him with the vial of hebenon that killed Angela, so now he provides the wine of Tiberius, "most witching-succulent / For orgy of Elsinore" (346). MacKaye's method, here and elsewhere in the tetralogy, is to borrow freely from a number of Renaissance plays; hence Claudius bears a resemblance to Macbeth, Doctor Faustus, and other characters who succumb to a supernatural solicitation that serves as the outward manifestation of their inmost self-destructive desires.

The plays also engage in an ongoing dialogue with nondramatic texts. *Odin Against Christus* returns to the mystery of earthly and heavenly love as depicted by Dante. When Hamlet and Gertrude are finally alone together in the mirrored Hall of Shrines (a location that will provide the play with its dominant image), they remember the words of Padre Celestino twenty-two years earlier and reaffirm their love for one another. As husband and wife stand before the mirror, gazing at themselves, Hamlet prays:

> So let our souls
> Stand mirror'd in our own serenity,
> Reflecting what we are—eternal mates,
> Surface and spirit substance. Were we else,
> The glass itself would crack in twain, and warp
> Apart, in shiver'd splinters.
>
> (407)

A few pages later, the mirror offers Hamlet a covert glimpse of Gertrude and Claudius gesturing to one another. Symbolic object that it is, the mirror now reveals a rift in the finely polished glass. In the next scene a saddened Gertrude tells Claudius that "the glass hath crack'd which shall reflect / All Elsinore in ruin, ere it shivers" (431), and we sense that the inexorable progress toward tragedy has begun.

The theme of doomed love is played out on another level in *Odin Against Christus* in acts 3 and 4, when the twenty-two-year-old Hamlet returns from Wittenberg to see Ophelia, to whom he gives a betrothal ring during a tender love scene. He treasures this brief day with her, for he anticipates the "dark mischance" of future times (448). The King proposes sending his son as an envoy to England in place of Claudius, who had volunteered to go, but leaves the final decision to Gertrude. She agrees to let her son undertake the voyage and later tells Claudius that she suspects the King of having trapped them by exposing her "yearning choice to hold thee here." This is Gertrude's first admission in the tetralogy of her tormented, adulterous love. Painfully, she acknowledges that she has sent her son away "to destroy myself with thee." When Claudius responds "Destroy thyself ? Surely, thou mean'st—enjoy!" she answers "It is all the same. All's one, when joy doth feed / Itself on infidelity" (487). The play ends shortly thereafter, with King Hamlet, alone in the Hall of Mirrors, speaking a melancholy soliloquy that ends with a vow of revenge.

Despite the obvious differences between Wyman's and MacKaye's transformations of *Hamlet*, the two works exhibit a common interest in the older generation—Gertrude, Claudius, and for MacKaye in particular, King Hamlet. Each gives us a play without the prince, a text that replaces political power and ambition with the complexities of personal relationships. MacKaye's encyclopedic scope and inability to resist any opportunity to embellish his tale with intertextual allusions and borrowings prevent Gertrude from being the major focus of attention she was for Wyman. Yet the tetralogy does attempt to dramatize the dilemma of the isolated, tempted wife, whose ambivalent love, riddled with mother-guilt, for her rather distant and self-absorbed son sets her apart from the plays' other, more idealized women. (Angela, her dead mother Mariana, Ophelia, her dead mother Cornelia, and Moll Cowslip are all variations on the recurring figure of the beloved mother-wife-daughter, her life cut short by death while giving birth or assisting in the birth of a child/creation and as such are clear allusions to MacKaye's wife Marion, the "mother" of these plays.) Ultimately, though, whatever psychological realism MacKaye achieves in his portrait of Gertrude is undermined by the melodramatic, fantastic, mixed-media effect of the work as a whole.

MacKaye's tendency to stage allegorical action is especially evident in the opening scene of the fourth play, *The Serpent in the Orchard*. Claudius, hidden in an apple tree, watches unseen as a trio of musical rustics observe a poisonous asp disappear into its 'mound' beneath the tree. The stage is thus set for the climactic event of the play, in which Claudius will reassume his role as the scheming, villainous serpent. MacKaye transforms the Hamlet legend in a startling way, however. The King's death occurs only after a terrible descent into madness that begins with a sleepwalking incident, for which MacKaye borrows freely from Lady Macbeth's sleepwalking scene, Ophelia's bawdy songs, and most improbably, Othello's handkerchief. Prince Hamlet observes to Horatio that "my father's thoughts seem poison'd / Even at the source"; as in *Othello*, the poison of words and suspicious appearances that "corrupt" a once-great military hero are far more destructive than any chemical poison. The maddened King has very little of Prince Hamlet's witty melancholy in Shakespeare's play. Instead, he raves and hurls books around his study, "once Lord of sweet words," he now utters "raw spew" (560).

From the very beginning of *The Mystery of Hamlet*, MacKaye has suggested that King Hamlet placed temptation in Claudius's way, and so bears partial responsibility for his brother's monstrous villainy. Like Wyman, he is drawn to one of the most conspicuous gaps in Shakespeare's play, the relationship between the two brothers, a relationship that, if understood, might somehow make the fratricide believable in human terms. Now, in a daring reassignment of roles, MacKaye transforms his warrior-king into a madman intent upon revenge. The two brothers meet during the sleepwalking scene, and the King, not recognizing Claudius, mutters aloud about hunting for poison with which to "damn" his brother, that "adulterous, incestuous beast" (565). Claudius draws him out, asking how he will administer the poison. Hamlet replies, "Pour in the porches of his ears" (566). MacKaye thus implies that the maddened King has invited his own destruction and described the means by which it will occur. Prince Hamlet, meanwhile, is closeted with Gertrude in the library, hoping "to work this out to some good end / For our beloved one" (570). Gertrude's self-protecting, and perhaps self-deceiving instincts cause her to mislead her son; she tells him that the source of the King's madness is the "filth / In dirty minds; of stench from scandal breath . . . In wedlock calumny." Hamlet vows to become "the scavenger of Elsinore" and "exonerate . . . All three of you" (571–72). MacKaye is ambiguous about Gertrude at this crucial juncture. It is impossible to know how much guilt she feels about her actions, or how calculating she is when she insists on the King's madness and asks her son to become regent, knowing that he will refuse and nominate Claudius instead. For Hamlet wishes to be "free from vow of regency, or royal heirdom, / To serve—first, last— as son; and in some happy / Sequel, as lover of my trusting mate, / Heavenly Ophelia!" (585). Gertrude promises from the depth of her heart to help him. As the curtain falls on act 3, we are left wondering about the motivation of this strangely divided woman, who seems to love her husband and son and yet is tragically driven to act in such a way as to destroy them.

The fourth act depicts King Hamlet donning his armor and going off to take his nap in the orchard. Once again Claudius hides in the orchard, as father and son enter and speak their final words to one another. Then, believing himself alone, the King launches into a long and violent soliloquy, vowing revenge and describing his cruel plan to have Gertrude, "my unsuspecting queen of guilelessness," administer the poison to Claudius through the porches of the ears. The King is resigned to his own damnation, and he resists the efforts of Gallucinius, who makes his final appearance in an attempt to persuade Hamlet that "Seeing clear / Is love. Revenge is love reversed" (605). As King Hamlet continues to insist upon revenge, Gallucinius describes what lies ahead: "thy murder's sequel. . . . Murder shall cry, through Elsinore, upon / Thyself—all thou lovest, and most of all—thy son; / 'Revenge! Remember me!'" (606). Remembering the vision in the crystal so many years earlier, the King answers "I've known—I know" but does not change his mind. Rather like the fall in Milton's Eden, this is a tragedy that has been predestined and foreknown.

The final act of the tetralogy prepared the way for the beginning of *Hamlet*. Prince Hamlet's opening soliloquy, a tortured plea to "the God of terrible silences," yields to a scene of brotherly devotion with Horatio (625). Suspicious though he is of Claudius, Hamlet is overjoyed to hear that his uncle has been proclaimed king by the council, for this means that he is "free" to marry Ophelia. Gertrude arrives to tell him that the Council has "solemnly adjured" her to share the throne with Claudius. She calls this course of action a "sever[ing of] the obstacles, which otherwise / Might stand between you and your happiness" and reminds him of her promise to "free thee / From the immense responsibilities / Of state" (637). MacKaye has wrought an intriguing variation on Wyman's self-sacrificing mother; this Gertrude, who agrees to marry again in order to further her plans for her son, seems suspiciously self-serving, or perhaps self-deluding, in her insistence on her son's happiness. After an intense debate between mother and son, Gertrude departs, giving Hamlet a letter "writ in love"(640). The letter states simply that she will wed Claudius after the funeral feast and prays that he give the enclosed ring—her wedding ring—to Ophelia, with these words: "I am night. May thou and Ophelia be ever of the morning" (643).

As so often is the case in the works we call tragedies, these plays weave a complex pattern of causality and culpability through which the divided sympathies of the audience move in an intricate dance. We may feel, at this moment, that King Hamlet and Gertrude, Hamlet and Ophelia, have all been blasted by tragic circumstances and their own human vulnerability, and that even Claudius, villain though he is, has been a victim of the powerful emotions of jealousy and desire. True to his epistolary motif, MacKaye concludes with a letter from Hamlet to Ophelia, urging her to "Return to thy nunnery" and asking "Wherefore didst thou emerge to freshen this desert world? The wells are dried up here" (645). There follow shouts and huzzahs for the new King of Denmark, as "King Claudius and Queen Gertrude, standing aloft, smiling in their splendid crowns," receive homage and then, the familiar lines of act 1, scene 2 of *Hamlet*:

> Though yet of Hamlet our dear brother's death
> The memory be green . . .

The final words of the tetralogy are "But break my heart; for I must hold my tongue," accompanied by a "heart-moaned cry" from out of the darkness: "Hamlet! . . . Remember me! . . ."

When MacKaye and Wyman talk back to Shakespeare, they do so with a fierce determination to present their agendas to the public. There is no single argument in *The Mystery of Hamlet* that corresponds to Wyman's insistent defense of Gertrude against her detractors; rather, MacKaye seems to have several interrelated objectives. The unresolvable conflict between Nordic vengeance and Christian forgiveness, so central to almost any experience of *Hamlet*, led MacKaye to an ambitious assertion of his belief in love as a force capable of reversing destructive human impulses. Gallucinius, as the psychologist Erlo van Waveren observes in his Commentary at the end of the tetralogy, represents the voice of wisdom that Claudius and King Hamlet are sufficiently elevated in consciousness to hear, but unable to follow:

> Neither can take advantage of his counsel, as the primitive forces in them are too powerful. The Christian virtues—of love, humility, sacrifice—although recognized, are not sufficiently developed in the characters of Hamlet and Claudius to counterbalance their instinctive impulses. This is the chief reason for their ultimate doom. (666)

Although the festive comic side of the plays can celebrate and affirm the conciliatory power of love, for the principal characters there can only be tragedy. MacKaye ends where Shakespeare does, leaving unchanged the final events at Elsinore. Yet he arrives at these events via a route that suggests the culpability of father and son in ways that have no counterpart in Shakespeare's play. The mad, vengeful King, obsessed with poisoning his brother, and the Prince who rejects the public responsibilities of kingship in preference for a life given over to romantic love and so encourages his uncle's diabolical ambitions are sad commentaries on human frailty.

Both Wyman and MacKaye were products of cultures that revered Shakespeare, and that knew his works almost as well as they knew Scripture, with the same familiarity born of repetition. Their way of talking back to Shakespeare also reflects the fact that they were writing late in their own lives. They speak of and to him in a very different voice from the young voices of the 1960s who will be the subject of the next chapter. And original as their respective texts are, neither is as sweeping in its re-visioning of Shakespeare's work as many of the other transformations I discuss later. Indeed, MacKaye was, if anything, more reluctant than Wyman to transform the essential cirumstances and destinies of Shakespeare's characters. His decision to compose his epic as a prologue to Shakespeare's play gives it the same supplementary role that Cowden Clarke's "girlhoods" have; however much seems possible in the new text, its outcome is predetermined by the known text to which it is implicitly subordinated. The tetralogy is thus a very different kind of transformation from a sequel such as Lewisohn's *The Last Days of Shylock*, which is free to imagine an entirely different "ending" for its main character.

It may seem surprising that, despite all of the authority our age confers on Shakespeare and the consequent attention to virtually everything related to his life and works, MacKaye's tetralogy has gone virtually unnoticed since its first and only performance in 1949. Had it been written a century earlier, it might have been afforded the status Cowden Clarke's work has attained, as an intriguing literary curiosity that tells us more about the audience for which it was written and whose values it reflects than it tells us about the plays themselves. MacKaye's encyclopedic tetralogy is such a literary curiosity, I think, precisely because it is so very un-Shakespearean. There is something audacious about the way MacKaye appropriates Shakespeare's characters and places them in a symbolic landscape and philosophical scheme so remote from Shakespeare's own. Epics—and this tetralogy certainly aspires to epic proportions—have usually been the products of a self-conscious nationalism or sense of national destiny. Strangely enough, there is something intrinsically American about *The Mystery of Hamlet*, even though it contains no specifically American borrowings; it is as if MacKaye, like Spenser and Milton before him, set out to forge a national epic out of the myths and literature his country shared with Western Europe, an epic that would in some way speak to a people at war, urging them to replace hate and war and betrayal and revenge with a transcendantal, all-encompassing doctrine of Love, a love that is as inclusive and eclectic as American culture itself.

4

Shakespeare in the Sixties

Every historical period, said Jan Kott in 1964, finds in Shakespeare what it is looking for and what it wants to see. A mid–twentieth-century reader or spectator, he continues, "cannot do otherwise" than to interpret the plays through his or her own experiences.[1] *Shakespeare Our Contemporary* has been called the most influential single piece of Shakespeare criticism of our times, partly, no doubt, because it has sparked so much controversy. At a public seminar conducted by the International Association of Theatre Critics to celebrate the book's twenty-fifth anniversary, an extraordinary collection of directors, theatre critics, translators, and writers from around the world met in London to consider the ways in which Shakespeare remains contemporary. Kott's opening statement was characteristically provocative: he remarked that the special "relationship" between "the time on the stage and the other off of it" that existed in the sixties seems to have changed, so that Shakespeare "is not so much of a contemporary today."[2]

Shakespeare Our Contemporary served as a catalyst for certain aspects of the representation of Shakespeare in the sixties, some of which have become important landmarks in the annals of Shakespeare production. It is best known for the influence the essay "King Lear or Endgame" had on Peter Brook's celebrated and controversial 1962 production and subsequent film of *King Lear*, which, with its radical cutting and rearrangements of the text, qualifies as a transformation. Brook's preface to the English translation of *Shakespeare Our Contemporary* evokes the highly charged atmosphere of the sixties:

> I first met Jan Kott in a night club in Warsaw: it was midnight: he was squashed between a wildly excited group of students: we became friends at once: a beautiful girl was arrested by mistake under our eyes: Jan Kott leaped to her defense and an evening of high adventure followed. . . . .

It is clearly important to Brook that "Kott is undoubtedly the only writer on Elizabethan matters who assumes without question that every one of his readers will at some point or other have been woken by the police in the middle of the night."[3] Not surprisingly, the last chapter of *Shakespeare Our Contemporary* ends on a distinctly sixtieslike note as well. Speaking of the line "And my ending is despair" in Prospero's final monologue, Kott notes that "despair" does not mean resignation. The clue to Shakespeare's meaning, he concludes, can be found in Cleopatra's line in act 5, scene 2 of *Antony and Cleopatra*: "My desolation does begin to make / A better life." Martin Esslin remarks in his introduction to *Shakespeare Our Contemporary* that it was essential for Kott and his generation of East Europeans to find in "great autonomous works of art . . . the strength and consolation that must spring from a sense of communion with kindred spirits who have faced similarly extreme situations" if they were to forge a better life in the future.[4]

The better life envisioned by the key players of the sixties brought with it a sense of freedom and possibility that lasted until about 1973, when a worldwide economic crisis touched off by the Yom Kippur War brought the epoch to an end.[5] The legacy of this period, it has been suggested, is less political than it is "the encouragement of a wide-ranging questioning of cultural norms and institutional authority."[6] The eight plays to be discussed in this chapter were first performed between January 1965 and January 1972; each, in its own way, captures that particular conjunction of desolation and despair, freedom and possibility, anger and outrage, questioning and asserting, irreverence and mockery, that characterizes the decade. Some of these emerged from the Kott-Brook-Marowitz nexus, which was influenced by both the Theatre of the Absurd and the Theatre of Cruelty of Antonin Artaud (whose book, *Le Théâtre et son double* was reprinted in 1964).[7] Kott, for example, questioned humanistic theories about Shakespearean tragedy and tragic character in his opening chapter on the history plays. "History," he says, is a "cruel mechanism, from which there is no escape, but which one cannot accept." Thus Lady Anne in *Richard III* "goes into Richard's bed to be destroyed" for "history is no more than a gigantic slaughter. . . . In Shakespeare's royal histories, there is only hate, lust and violence; the Grand Mechanism which transforms the executioner into a victim, and the victim into an executioner." He contrasts Shakespeare's heroes with Corneille's, who are stronger than the world: "In Shakespeare all human values are brittle and the world is stronger than men. The implacable steam-roller of history crushes everybody and everything."[8]

Or almost everybody and everything. Falstaff, Kott observes, "will not let history take him in. He scoffs at it."[9] It would be interesting to

know whether Kott knew of Orson Welles's *Chimes at Midnight*, produced as a play in 1960 in Ireland and subsequently transformed into a
film. Welles talks back both to unsympathetic portrayals of Falstaff
and to Laurence Olivier's *Henry V*, which was filmed during the Second World War. Welles's rendition of the battle of Shrewsbury "reflects
the changed perspective of the 1960s," says Bridget Gellert Lyons; it
becomes "more and more inglorious, fragmented and difficult to follow," in deliberate contrast with Olivier's representation of the battle
of Agincourt and in so doing confirms Falstaff's cynical view of the
meaninglessness of honor. The moment in *1 Henry IV* that so bothered
my students (see Chapter 1) is described by Lyons as follows: After the
death of Hotspur Falstaff's *"breath is visible through the vents in his
visor"* as Hal says "Poor Jack, farewell! I could have better spared a
better man." The Prince *"shows by his expression that he realizes Falstaff is alive"* and says *"emphatically"* "Emboweled will I see thee by-
and-by," as he exits. Falstaff speaks his next lines lying down; then
two men enter, and help him to his feet as he says "It was time to coun-
terfeit" Later, when the Prince says, "Why Percy I killed and saw thee
dead," Falstaff answers starkly, "Lord, Lord, how this world is given
to lying," and the camera cuts to the Prince before Falstaff goes on with
his speech. Welles scoffs at the "heroic" Hal by implying that if Falstaff is a liar, so, indeed, is Hal.[10]

In much the same spirit, the playwrights of the sixties scoffed at
Shakespeare—or rather, at the tradition-encrusted versions of Shakespeare that held sway in classrooms and theatres and libraries around
the world. The Marowitz *Hamlet*, first performed in Berlin in January
1965, expresses much of the iconoclastic outrageousness we have come
to associate with the sixties. Marowitz had no doubt read Kott's book,
and like Kott, he attached much more importance to the role of Fortinbras than conventional Hamlet-centered criticism and productions were
prone to do. "Let us imagine a modern director starting analytical
rehearsals of *Hamlet*," Kott proposes. An actor asks, "Is *Hamlet* a political play?" The director thinks for a while and then says quietly to himself, "Perhaps it depends on who our Fortinbras will be." Fortinbras is
important, for "he speaks the final words of this cruel drama. . . . What
does he represent? Blind fate, absurdity of the world, or victory of justice?" Instead of offering an answer, Kott ends his chapter cryptically:

> The producer has to decide. Shakespeare has only told us his name. But the
> name is significant: Fortinbras—*forte braccio*. Fortinbras, the man of the
> strong arm. A young and strong fellow. He comes and says: "Take away
> these corpses. Hamlet was a good boy, but he is dead. Now I shall be your
> king. I have just remembered that I happen to have certain rights to this
> crown." Then he smiles and is very pleased with himself.

A great drama has been concluded. People fought, plotted, killed one another, committed crimes for love, and went mad for love. . . .They all stood for something. Even their crimes had a certain greatness. And then a vigorous young lad comes, and says with a charming smile: "Take away these corpses. Now I shall be your king."[11]

"I despise Hamlet," Charles Marowitz proclaimed in the 1968 introduction to *The Marowitz Hamlet*. "He is a slob, / A talker, an analyser, a rationalizer." Fortinbras, on the other hand, "is a kind of wish-fulfillment conjured up by Hamlet; a marvelously wrought figment who soldiers where Hamlet shirks and who reigns after Hamlet disappears."[12] This, the observant reader will recall, sounds very much like the judgments set forth by first readers in Chapter 1. Marowitz later described his collage as an experiment that would enable audiences to understand *Hamlet* differently, by seeing it from "a new vantage-point." In keeping with the spirit of the sixties, he set out to "indict the values" Hamlet had come to represent: "misdirected moral concern, intellectual analyses as action-substitute, etc." To "assault" the character of Hamlet became a way of "deriding the supreme prototype of the conscience-stricken but paralyzed liberal: one of the most lethal and obnoxious characters in modern times."[13]

Marowitz begins his *Hamlet* collage with a fragment from act 4, scene 4 that immediately establishes Fortinbras as a major character. Fortinbras speaks his opening speech ("Go, Captain, from me greet the Danish King. . . .") while Hamlet watches. The Captain's important lines about the "little patch of ground" and Hamlet's subsequent speech about aggression as "the imposthume of much wealth and peace" are omitted, however, and Marowitz cuts directly to the soliloquy. As Hamlet speaks the words "that capability and god-like reason," Fortinbras interrupts (*accusingly*) to finish his sentence: "To rust in us unused." The scene then shifts abruptly to a seven-line fragment from act 1, scene 4, and then to fragments from act 1, scene 2. Hamlet is surrounded by the Ghost, the King, the Queen, Ophelia, and the Clown/Polonius, all of them questioning, instructing, demanding responses. The King's words "Think of us as a father" are echoed by Fortinbras and the Clown; the Queen joins in with "Thou hast thy father much offended," then Laertes with "And so have I a noble father lost," and the Ghost with "If thou didst ever thy dear father love . . . ," while Hamlet's responses are repeatedly interrupted.[14]

As the play continues, Hamlet's weakness in contrast with Laertes' passion becomes more and more evident. In marked contrast with Shakespeare's play, Hamlet is never alone on stage, and the rapid cuts from one scene to another make him seem overwhelmed, embattled, harassed. After a wickedly funny version of Polonius's advice speech, transposed to a schoolroom where the Queen ("as teacher") leads a class consisting of Hamlet, Laertes, Ophelia, and the Clown through a sing-song recitation of "these few precepts," Fortinbras returns, rather like a schoolyard bully and *"catches HAMLET before he has a chance to go"* (40). With the Ghost, he reminds Hamlet of his purpose, using Hamlet's own reproachful lines to Gertrude in the closet scene. A few lines later, the stage directions indicate that Fortinbras has usurped Hamlet's place as the son: *"GHOST suddenly enters with his arm around FORTINBRAS as if he were his son and confiding in him."* With prompting from the Clown Hamlet repeatedly tries to remind himself that "Rightly to be great / Is not to stir without great argument / But greatly to find quarrel in a straw / When honor's at the stake" but breaks down, *"exhausted and humiliated"* (42–43). Marowitz seems to have cast Hamlet in the role of the ineffectual student-as-actor, prompted by others to utter his familiar lines but unable to "do it." The fifth act duel is wittily recast as a verbal duel between Hamlet and Laertes, with the court booing at Hamlet's lines and cheering Laertes'. Hamlet's request for a "judgment" at line 280 inspires a *"swiftly arranged"* trial scene, in which Fortinbras serves as counsel and the King as judge. Hamlet is in the dock, and Ophelia gives evidence against him (her speech to Polonius, "My Lord, as I was sewing . . ."). Marowitz's collage technique proceeds from the theoretical premise that speeches contain possibilities independent of their original contexts and speakers. But I suspect that this is a dramaturgy that succeeds best with a limited audience, one capable of the intertextual calculations that work to keep the "old" placement of the speeches in constant juxtaposition with the "new." Consider, for instance, the point at which Fortinbras, mediating between Hamlet and Laertes in the trial scene, says to the "court":

> Was't Hamlet wrong'd Laertes? Never Hamlet
> If Hamlet from himself be ta'en away
> And when he's not himself does wrong Laertes,
> Then Hamlet does it not. Hamlet denies it.
> Who does it then?
> *Clown:* (*Impulsively*) His madness.
> *Fortinbras:* If't be so, Hamlet is of the faction that is wrong'd. His madness is poor Hamlet's enemy.

An audience who does not remember that these lines were originally spoken by Hamlet does not get the point of the appropriation. Marowitz uses and reassigns Shakespeare's lines, rather than making up new ones, precisely so that he can make a statement about the ineffectuality of words in their ordinary contexts. So when Fortinbras, alone with Hamlet at the end of the trial (*"urging direct action"*), uses Hamlet's own words to persuade him ("Rightly to be great . . ."), we are reminded that this Hamlet has failed to live up to his reputation, his role, as traditionally construed. Marowitz does supplement Shakespeare's language, through the stage directions that frame these displaced speeches. Hence this dialogue ends as Fortinbras *"washes his hands"* of Hamlet with a final, damning appropriation of part of Hamlet's "To be or not to be" soliloquy: "Thus conscience doth make cowards of us all . . ." (59–65).

The Marowitz Hamlet ends with all of the characters back on stage, sarcastically chanting phrases from the "What a piece of work is man" speech as they surround Hamlet, who has slowly slumped to the floor. Fortinbras speaks his own lines "Bear Hamlet like a soldier to the stage . . .", but Hamlet isn't dead. He rouses himself with "one last burst of energy," "kills" all of the players with a toy sword, and says, to the accompaniment of their "derisive laughter," "From . . . this . . . time . . . forth . . . . My thoughts be bloody or be nothing worth" (67–69). The implication is that his thoughts—and words—are indeed "nothing worth," since, despite his repeated vows, he has not accomplished the vengeance he promised to his father's ghost. Marowitz's collage is deliberately circular: in its final moments the Ghost is still trying to get Hamlet to "swear" to take revenge, and Hamlet is still vowing to "wipe away . . . all saws of books," although he has tried, ineffectually, to defend himself with now-hackneyed lines such as "The play's the thing" and "There is something rotten in the state of Denmark" (66). The circularity expresses Marowitz's conception of Hamlet as a man who, "like many contemporary intellectuals, equates the taking of a position with the performance of an action"; "he glories in having an important job to do and lashes himself for not being up to it."[15]

Hamlet, Kott said in *Shakespeare Our Contemporary*, "is like a sponge . . . it immediately absorbs all of the problems of our time." For Marowitz, the "problem" was that posed by the "pseudo-adventurousness" of sixties intellectuals, "armchair-commandos" who "trumpet their moral righteousness [while] less demonstrative activists . . . infiltrate southern ghettos and get their heads bashed in, or risk their civilian lives supplying plasma and medicine to the wounded in Vietnam."[16] For Tom Stoppard, whose *Rosencrantz and Guildenstern Are Dead* had its first performance on the "fringe" of the Edinburgh Festival in August 1966, the problem was different, though not entirely so. His Rosencrantz and Guildenstern are passive victims of chance, without memory, or a sense of purpose, or any control over their existences. They too are inactive; the "play" of *Hamlet* comes and goes, while they remain on stage, "caught up" in events that will "play themselves out" if only they "tread warily, follow instructions," with no sense of direction, nothing "to go on" except "Words."[17] Unequal to their mission, to "draw Hamlet on to pleasure" and "glean what afflicts him," they fail miserably at the game of Questions and Answers and do not even attempt to prevent their own deaths.

Rosencrantz and Guildenstern Are Dead is a brilliantly conceived synchronic transformation that turns Hamlet inside out, as the Player remarks: "We keep to our usual stuff, more or less, only inside out. We do on stage the things that are supposed to happen off. Which is a kind of integrity, if you look on every exit being an entrance somewhere else" (28). Shakespeare's language is frequently consigned to the stage directions and to the periphery of scenes. Both Stoppard and Marowitz were in effect objecting to the "centrality" of Hamlet the character. By literally moving him offstage, Stoppard was challenging the authority of standard readings of *Hamlet* and asking his audience why we have always considered Hamlet the play's most honest, intelligent, and interesting character (all problematic terms). Just as Wyman brought Gertrude to center stage and invented some new scenes for her, so Stoppard gives the so-called "minor characters," Rosencrantz and Guildenstern and the Player, the stage time, introspective monologues, and star turns that belong to the protagonist. But at the same time he explicitly denies Rosencrantz and Guildenstern any consciousness of the past; the absence of a prior time before the day of the play's events is clearly a gesture to Ionesco and Beckett, yet it also draws attention to the many questions Shakespeare left unanswered about his characters. In the 1930s and 1950s Ludwig Lewisohn and Percy MacKaye had gone to great lengths to fill in the blanks; Stoppard, in 1966, calls attention to those blanks by refusing to do so.[18]

Rosencrantz and Guildenstern Are Dead participated in a mid-sixties reaction against the way Shakespeare in general and *Hamlet* in particular had been played until that point. Ronald Hayman notes that the Royal Shakespeare Company's Brechtian *The Wars of the Roses* in 1962 transformed the way minor characters were deployed on stage:

> Instead of composing the soldiers and minor courtiers into picturesque groupings around the central heroic figure, Peter Hall and his co-directors found ways of exposing the underside of the supporting characters' theatrical existence. The audience was persuaded to sympathize with the ordinary soldiers in their physical exertions, their boredom, their despondency. In 1965, while Tom Stoppard was reworking his script of *Rosencrantz and Guildenstern*, David Warner was appearing at Stratford-on-Avon in Peter Hall's production of *Hamlet* without a princely prince. Nobility was no longer the keynote. As Ronald Bryden wrote, "He slops ostentatiously through the castle in a

greenish, moth-eaten student's gown, peering owlishly over his spectacles to cheek his elders. He knows his position as heir to the throne protects him, and abuses it as far as he can." Or as David Warner said later in a *Times* interview, "How the hell do I know what princely is? . . .You can be a prince and you can pick you nose because the prince has the freedom to do whatever he wants."[19]

Jan Kott had envisioned a Hamlet "deeply involved in politics, rid of illusions, sarcastic, passionate and brutal . . . a born conspirator."[20] The David Warner Hamlet of 1965 was very clearly a Hamlet of this sort: his was "a youthful modern contempt for the ruling classes who live by lies and govern by intrigue . . . a lanky, seedy, overgrown student" who clearly belonged to the student movement of the sixties and was the first in a series of rebellious, antiestablishment Hamlets on the British stage.[21]

Stoppard had a similar idea in mind when, at the age of twenty-nine, he chose as his protagonists

> these two guys who in Shakespeare's context don't really know what they're doing. The little they are told is mainly lies, and there's no reason to suppose that they ever find out why they are killed. And, probably more in the early 1960s than at any other time, that would strike a young playwright as being a pretty good thing to explore.[22]

But he introduced a counterpoint to Rosencrantz and Guildenstern's naive passivity in the character of the Player, who articulates the anger of the artist-as-working man and who is endowed with a world-weariness and self-consciousness that produce some of the most compelling moments in the play. When Guildenstern complains that "We don't know how to act" and "We only know what we're told," the Player answers sagely, "Everything has to be taken on trust; truth is only that which is taken to be true. It's the currency of living. . . . One acts on assumptions" (66–67). In a mocking gesture to the Shakespearean soliloquy, the Player probes the mysteries of human action and inaction, the assertion of identity and the questioning of identity, invoking characteristic willingness of the sixties to live in an improvised fashion, certain only that "Uncertainty is the normal state." (In a 1974 interview Stoppard confessed that "my distinguishing mark is an absolute lack of certainty about almost anything.")[23]

The Hamlet of *Rosencrantz and Guildenstern Are Dead* seems remarkably uninteresting, perhaps because we know exactly what he is going to say, whereas Rosencrantz and Guildenstern and the Player are constantly surprising us with their meandering mock-philosophical speculations, their non sequiturs, and their witty wordplay. Hamlet, in contrast, seems humorless, intimidating, incomprehensible, a nuisance. When Claudius sends Rosencrantz and Guildenstern to seek out Hamlet after the closet scene they are understandably nervous, since from their perspective he is an unpredictable madman, who, as Rosencrantz cautions, "might be violent" (87). And when Stoppard has them revert to their Shakespearean language in order to communicate with him or Claudius or Gertrude, we know they are playing roles, acting their parts in "a trying episode" that they don't pretend to understand. "What's he doing?" they keep asking one another, as they warily watch Hamlet go through the motions of his role in dumb show. For without Shakespeare's language, Hamlet is no longer the great tragic poet; he is merely "Walking" or "Talking to himself."

Stoppard's final act takes place on shipboard, playfully filling in the gaps left by this offstage scene in *Hamlet*. Rosencrantz and Guildenstern read the letter to the King of England and discover that they are taking Hamlet to England to be killed; thus, unlike their counterparts in *Hamlet*, they have an opportunity to examine the ethical implications of their position. But they are players, their parts are "written" and cannot be changed:

> *Guil (broken):* We've travelled too far, and our momentum has taken over; we move idly towards eternity, without possibility of reprieve or hope of explanation. (121)

Moments later, they read the second letter, the one that substitutes their names for Hamlet's. Now they know they are going to die, but instead of rising to the occasion like tragic figures, they are paralyzed, resentful, puzzled:

> *Ros:* Who'd have thought that we were so important?
> *Guil:* But why? Was it all for this? Who are we that so much should converge on our little deaths? (*In anguish to the* PLAYER:) Who are we?

This, Stoppard suggests, is the secular modern alternative to Hamlet's serene knowledge that "the readiness is all." It remains for the Player, ever the authoritative voice, to respond "You are Rosencrantz and Guildenstern. That's enough" (122). But it isn't, at least not for Guildenstern, who finally asserts himself and turns on the Player, in an effective variation on the "To be or not to be" speech.

> I'm talking about death—and you've never experienced that. And you cannot act it. You die a thousand casual deaths—with none of that intensity which squeezes out life . . . and no blood runs cold anywhere. Because even as you

die you know that you will come back in a different hat. But no one gets up after death—there is no applause—there is only silence and some second-hand clothes, and that's death— (123)

The players play at death, enacting the deaths of Rosencrantz and Guildenstern in England; the Player dies *"tragically; romantically."* Whereas Rosencrantz enjoys and applauds the show, Guildenstern continues to struggle with language that is unequal to the reality it attempts to grasp:

No . . . no . . . not for us, not like that. Dying is not romantic, and death is not a game which will soon be over. . . . Death is not anything . . . death is not. . . . It's the absence of presence, nothing more . . . the endless time of never coming back . . . a gap you can't see, and when the wind blows through it, it makes no sound. . . . (124)

For Rosencrantz, death is a relief; his last words, before he disappears, are "I don't care. I've had enough." Guildenstern, however, is still wondering about causality in life: "There must have been a moment, at the beginning, where we could have said—no. But somehow we missed it." Then he, too, is gone, with a philosophical, "Well, we'll know better next time," and the play reverts to Shakespeare's language, with the Ambassador announcing that Rosencrantz and Guildenstern are dead. The last lines are Horatio's speech offering to explain "how these things came about" (125–26). But Stoppard's talking back has all along questioned the assumption that events can be explained, have meanings, make sense. From the mysterious suspension of the laws of probability in the coin-flipping sequence to the arbitrariness of Rosencrantz and Guildenstern's deaths, he has challenged the "special providence" that explains and somehow justifies the fall of a sparrow in Hamlet. Hamlet died confident that Horatio could report him and his cause aright. Stoppard's Rosencrantz and Guildenstern inhabit a world that renders such reports impossible.[24]

The enormous critical acclaim that followed from Ronald Bryden's rave review in the *Observer* of the hastily assembled Edinburgh Festival performance launched Stoppard as a successful playwright. The National Theatre production of 1967 was a huge success, and Stoppard found himself among the ranks of Britain's best-known playwrights virtually overnight. Stoppard was surprised; he had expected that his novel, *Lord Malquist and Mr Moon*, published the same week as the 1966 performance, "would make my reputation and that the play would be of little consequence either way."[25] Nothing Stoppard has written since *Rosencrantz and Guildenstern Are Dead* has been as widely read or well-known, and it is tempting to attribute the play's enduring popularity to its Shakespeare connection, at least in part. Despite its flaws (more evident in the recent film version, directed by Stoppard), *Rosencrantz and Guildenstern Are Dead* works, and works brilliantly, because of the way it exploits the "Hamlet-mystique"—the popular image of *Hamlet* as a repository of wisdom—with a brittle, intellectual cleverness and a genuine seriousness that were to characterize the rest of the sixties.

The Rosencrantz and Guildenstern of Marowitz's *Hamlet* enter "as a vaudeville team . . . linked together by a long rope that connects one to the other," a slapstick version of Stoppard's subsequent use of English music hall conventions for the back-and-forth banter that constitutes his play's dominant rhythm. Joseph Papp's *"Naked" Hamlet*, first performed at the New York Shakespeare Festival in 1968, uses vaudeville strategies throughout: As Papp explained in an introduction that is a splendid example of sixties-style rhetoric, "distraction is the norm . . . the psychological questioning—the why's—become totally irrelevant . . . truth is unbearable. . . . And so we devised burlesque skits, song and dance routines, familiar vaudeville tricks . . . to reveal the truth in easy doses."[26] Papp briefly assumes the role of social critic, using Shakespeare's phrases as the starting point for a quick circuit through the twentieth century, not unlike a documentary collage:

> We are tearing ourselves to tatters, to very rags, and we are capable of nothing but inexplicable dumbshows and noise. Discretion is no tutor, and the modesty of nature is stepped over. If we hold, as 'twere, the mirror up to nature, it would be a distorted mirror and a spookhouse of a carnival. . . . What a piece of work is a man—sprawled in the dirt of Vietnam—on the beaches of Iwo Jima—in the trenches of Verdun—on 125th Street in Harlem—on the streets of Detroit, Newark, Cleveland—in a grave in Alabama that held the remains of Andrew Goodman, civil rights worker—the death of Roosevelt, of Einstein, Marilyn Monroe, and a fourteen-year-old boy in the Bedford-Stuyvesant section of Brooklyn. How noble in reason, infinite in faculty. What is this quintessence of dust? (27)

This verbal riff, a free association unwinding from Shakespeare's familiar words, goes on for another couple of paragraphs, concluding with a series of oracular pronouncements that must have sounded rather like clichés even in 1969:

> Words take on new meanings. Words change as ideas change. . . . Words have power. Words must be spoken. Words left unsaid are a form of destruction, of death, of nihilism. . . . The world has changed through words. The world will change again through words. (28)

Hamlet, Papp concludes, is "a play on words," one "so richly endowed" that "it is possible in this time to rearrange the words, to shatter them, to blow them at the moon and watch them float down into the lives of the characters like so many fragments of living matter and begin to form into new shapes." He continues a paragraph later, "The play, unloosed from its moorings, requires the viewer to be free-floating, to give himself to space, to go with it, to dig it, to fly fearlessly through the air and turn and twist and stand on his head and his arms and let his hair blow in the wind" (28–29). Flying imagery pervades the introductory essay, which, curiously enough, makes no reference to the word "naked," nor has it any of the language of stripping away and exposing one might expect, apart from a brief reference to the program notes, which described the production as " 'gamma-ray shadowgraphing' the play, to detect the real *Hamlet* beneath the layers of nineteenth-century lacquer" (40). *Rosencrantz and Guildenstern Are Dead,* with its empty stage and isolated and vulnerable title characters, cut off from an idealized past they can hardly recall (*Ros.:* "I can remember when there were no questions. . . . There were answers to everything" [38]) gives a stronger impression of nakedness than Papp's *Hamlet,* which has an abundance of costumes, props, music, and visual effects.

Whereas Stoppard's play takes its production values from *Waiting for Godot,* Papp's borrows his from the American rock musicals of the sixties. The printed text is "an arbitrary interruption" of an ongoing process of revisions and performances, which Papp invites the reader to continue in "your production" (31). It bears a passing resemblance to Marowitz's collage technique but is less radical because the basic sequence of the play remains Shakespeare's, and there are only a few reassignments of lines. At least 50 percent of the text consists of stage directions, notes, and arch subtitles, often as many as four or five to the page, which have the effect of dividing the play into a series of rapid-fire gags, or "bits." They make it difficult to imagine the play as continuous action; the reader is constantly aware of Papp's presence, identifying and organizing the audience's response to the various bits, with titles like "The I'm-A-Big-Boy-Now Bit" (52) or "The Terrible Discovery Bit" (66). The note-writer lectures and advises the reader: "The audience will applaud and cheer three times out of four if the actor playing the Ghost [as "something of an orator, an old-time vaudevillian"] is doing his job," or "Remember that Hamlet makes the jokes. . . the other characters must let Hamlet play the jokes on them. If they are funny they must not know it" (58, 55, 68).

The "Naked" Hamlet is less obviously a "statement" about Shakespeare and the cultural values we assign to him than either *The Marowitz Hamlet* or *Rosencrantz and Guildenstern Are Dead.* Papp appears to be talking back to the elitist high culture appropriations of *Hamlet* by having his Hamlet disguise himself as Ramon the Puerto Rican Janitor (this follows Claudius's line to Rosencrantz and Guildenstern "Something you have heard of Hamlet's transformation" [76]). The "Ramon Routine" consists of Ramon speaking Spanish ("Eighth joke: language barrier repeat" [78]), ignoring the other characters, and carrying around a long broom and a garbage can. When the original Hamlet, Martin Sheen, was replaced by Cleavon Little, Ramon became Rastus, the Negro Janitor. While Hamlet is in his Ramon disguise, he does not seem to be recognized by the others. The disguise comes and goes, very much like the "antic behavior" of Shakespeare's Hamlet; for instance, when he speaks the "To be or not to be" soliloquy with a Puerto Rican accent, the Note observes that the audience will laugh at the accent but gradually become very quiet as he removes his wig and begins speaking more carefully (145). At the beginning of the final scene he is still wearing his janitor's attire and standing apart from the other formally dressed characters. The stage direction indicates that he strips off the last of his Ramon clothes and resumes his normal voice just as he says, "This is I, Hamlet the Dane" (148–49). Claudius then calls for a pistol, as the duel scene is transformed into a game of Russian roulette. The deaths are all playful; Claudius, for example, refuses to die until Hamlet shows him the text, at which he throws down his hat in disgust and lies down. After everyone, including Horatio, is dead, Hamlet offers the gun to someone in the audience ("Sociological Note: Someone will always accept the role of Hamlet's murderer . . ." [115]). When the spectator pulls the trigger we hear an empty click; stage directions call for loud cheering and clapping over the loudspeakers, and then Hamlet *speaks triumphantly*: "You that look pale and tremble at this chance, that are but mutes or audience to this act, had I but time, O I could tell you. . . ." Waving to the audience, he runs up a circular staircase on stage, trips, and the gun goes off. The cheering stops, he staggers back on stage, picks up the text and reads, "the rest is silence" (156).[27] Then the lights go out.

The Cleavon Little version of the *"Naked" Hamlet* toured the neighborhoods of New York City during the summer of 1968 and also played in public schools, according to the photo captions. The Preface, which consists mainly of excerpts from reviews, letters, and audience surveys, suggests a strong and mixed audience response. Papp clearly relished the talking back his show provoked. Here is a sample from a whole page of expressions of outrage:

> One furious lady in her seventies accused the production of contributing to the "defiance of teenagers who are already blatantly defiant." She called it "wild-

ly languaged buffoonery for kids who already clown and scoff at any sem-
blance of authority and order." Not to be left out, the superintendent of education called it "a gross distortion of Shakespeare unsuited to the maturity of
high school students." Someone else said that "it caused the utter disintegra-
tion of regard for constituted authority into which youth eternally erupts" (10).

There are also quite a few excepts from appreciative letters:

> *Miss G.:* "I felt you were faithful to Shakespeare's *Hamlet.* The beauty and
> dynamism, too often lost or overshadowed in the traditional productions . . .
> was retained and made more understandable because it became so relevant."
> *Mrs. S.:* "I felt that your production . . . did something very personal for
> me, in the sense that I feel much closer to the young people who are reacting
> against the institutionalized brutality and hypocrisy of our time—and conse-
> quently much closer to my own son" (11).

The chairman of an English department praised the production,
saying that

> Shakespeare is proved once again to be our contemporary; this is just the sort
> of attitude and presentation which is necessary to convince modern theater-
> goers—particularly the younger ones—that a work of established repute and
> "classic" status does not need to be dead or "textbooky." (15)

Clive Barnes of the *New York Times* disliked the *"Naked" Hamlet,*
but other critics praised it. The distinguished director and teacher
Robert Brustein, for example, called it "pretty courageous," part of an
ongoing effort by the Public Theatre "to discover what theatre can
mean to America in the sixties" (12).

Papp's introduction suggests that the *"Naked" Hamlet* makes a pointed statement about the youth culture of the sixties. The "psychological premise" behind his production is that Hamlet is

> "too much i' the sun" and the son is too much in him . . . [he] chooses to remain
> the eternal son, to hold back the process of nature . . . he refuses to alter his
> role and insists on remaining the son of a father and not the father of a son.
> (20–21)

One wonders whether an audience would arrive at this interpretation
without being told, though, since virtually everyone in the cast takes
part in the play's seemingly childish carnivalesque highjinks. Hamlet,
for example, pelts his mother with peanuts as she protests her innocence
in the closet scene; she picks them up and throws them back at him,
"sometimes playfully, sometimes in earnest" as she cries out, "O speak to

me no more." She is sitting under a table shelling and eating the peanuts as the Ghost enters (117–19). The peanut motif, or "peanut vendor bit," as it is called in the text, appears at several points in the *"Naked" Hamlet*. Papp's staging of the nunnery scene takes Hamlet into the audience, *"wearing a straw hat, carrying several helium-filled balloons on strings and a vendor's tray filled with bags of peanuts."* As Ophelia speaks to him he tries to ignore her, offering balloons to members of the audience, hawking his peanuts and addressing lines such as "We are arrant knaves all; believe none of us" to individual audience members (71). In the next scene, he puts the straps of the vendor's tray around Polonius's neck as he says "Let her not walk i' the sun. Conception is a blessing, but as your daughter may conceive—friend, look to't" (73). All of this stage business is at once playful and suggestive—Hamlet's angry and crazy madness, and the way it affects and infects other characters, comes across with a certain bizarre clarity as the peanuts, at once missiles, fun food, and tokens of exchange, are thrown around the stage. As *The Village Voice* review remarked, "It's a hallucinatory *Hamlet*, with the clashing styles, jagged emotional tone, and image overload of specifically the 1960's" (13). The word "specifically" stands out in this sentence, pointing to the time-bound quality of this particular *Hamlet* transformation. Readers of the nineties may feel that Shakespeare is their contemporary but not Ramon the Puerto Rican Janitor. The same will be the case with the next two transformations.

Papp's irreverent production of *Hamlet* may well have been influenced by two extraordinarily successful Shakespeare transformations which had appeared a year or so earlier. Barbara Garson's *Macbird* opened in January 1967 at the Village Gate in New York with Stacy Keach in the title role and Cleavon Little playing the second witch as *"a Negro with the impeccable grooming and attire of a Muhammed Speaks salesman."* (How often in the history of Shakespeare production has an actor graduated from second witch to Hamlet?) December 1967 brought the previews of *Your Own Thing*, a rock musical version of *Twelfth Night*, which went on to become the first off-Broadway show to win the New York Drama Critics Circle Award and the Outer Critics Circle Award.[28] The many productions of *Your Own Thing* throughout the United States and around the world "have made 'doing your thing' a household phrase," according to Hal Hester, who wrote the music and lyrics with Danny Apolinar. Taken together, *Macbird* and *Your Own Thing* evoke two sides of the sixties: the disillusionment with and rebellion against "establishment" politics during the Vietnam era, and the counterculture "love generation," with its rejection of everything old, "straight," repressive, and responsible in favor of a youth culture that celebrates unabashed self-indulgence (your own thing). Both plays appropriate Shakespeare as a mocking gesture of defiance directed against the high culture that had so entrenched him in the first place; both talk back to authority by parodying the text that authority respects. *Macbird* and *Your Own Thing* aren't really about Shakespeare; rather, they are about modern culture, aesthetics, politics, sexual roles, and the market economy that binds them all together. And unlike Marowitz's or Wesker's more "serious" theatrical transformations, both made a lot of money.

Macbird originated as a slip of the tongue at an August 1965 antiwar rally in Berkeley, California, in the heyday of the student protest movement that gave the sixties many of its most memorable images and phrases. Once Lady Bird Johnson had become Lady Macbird, everything else started to fall into place. The play begins at the 1960 Democratic Convention, where the three witches (the other two are "*a student demonstrator, a beatnik stereotype,*" and "*an old leftist, wearing a worker's cap and overalls*")[29] predict that Macbird (Lyndon Johnson), already the leader of the Senate, will become Vice-President and President hereafter. Lady Macbird, reading her husband's letter, fears that he is "not direct enough"; able to "swindle if the act were vague enough / And yet you'd never swipe it clean and clear, / For lack of means to mystify the deed" (19–20). The 1963 assassination of President John "Ken-O'Dunc" occurs shortly thereafter, staged as if viewed by a crowd of onlookers, with a back-wall projection depicting the famous diagrams of the scene in Dallas. The audience's familiarity with *Macbeth* would lead them to conclude that Lyndon Johnson was the assassin, an audacious accusation that Garson stops short of making explicit. Just as Macbeth admits to killing the grooms offstage in act 2, scene 3 of *Macbeth*, so in the corresponding scene in *Macbird*, Macbird strides to center stage and, echoing Shakespeare's lines, announces the death of the just-captured suspect: "Who could refrain when Ken O'Dunc lies dead? / Who could be calm that saw that scoundrel grin? / Who could be loyal yet neutral?" (36). Robert and Ted Ken O'Dunc are now cast in the roles of Malcolm and Donalbain but instead of fleeing Robert says he will stay and observe Macbird's next move (36).

Garson digresses from the *Macbeth* parallels in her second act, much of which borrows speeches from other Shakespeare plays. Interrogated by Robert about Macbird's motives, Lord (Adlai) Stevenson, the Egg of Head, expostulates "To see or not to see? That is the question." Should statesmen ignore what goes on around them or "speak out against a reign of evil?" The speech works beautifully in its new context, ending with a confession that politics "makes us rather bear those ills we have / Than fly to others that we know not of / Security makes cowards of us all" (41–43). The elements of burlesque and satire are foremost, and famous bits from other plays are used opportunistically. *Macbird* appropriates Bullingbrook's line from *Richard II* to ask "Have I no friends will rid me of this living fear?" (50) and Johnson's Great Society becomes the "Smooth Society," in which the land will be "carefully pruned" and "lofty branches will be lopped off," as in the garden scene in *Richard II* (54). Stevenson is likened to Cicero from *Julius Caesar* when the conspiratorial congressmen and senators wonder if they can trust him, and when the Earl of Warren is asked to conduct an investigation of the assassination he responds "O cursèd spite / That ever I was born to set things right" (48).

Garson returns to *Macbeth* in her third act, with the witches dancing around their cauldron (called first a "protest pot" and later a "melting pot") chanting the refrain "Burn baby burn and cauldron bubble," as they sing a series of verses filled with topical references. Once the witches have delivered their two prophecies, the scene shifts to a saloon, the location for the banquet scene, where the entertainment consists of a star turn by Cleavon Little and his two fellow witches in minstrel attire, doing a soft shoe and "walk-around steps" to the tune of "Massa's in de Cold, Cold Ground" (Kennedy is the "dere old Massa"). This is a classic American vaudeville routine of songs interspersed with jokes at the expense of "de Macky Bird." Singing witches, interestingly enough, were a popular feature in the touring company *Macbeth*s that were regularly performed in San Francisco and other western cities and towns during the nineteenth century. A recent study called *How Shakespeare Won the West* documents the popularity of Shakespeare during the Gold Rush period (1849–65). *Macbeth* and *Hamlet* were among the favorites; the plays were heavily revised and embellished by actors who interpolated bits of comedy and topical jokes to cover for lapses of memory. Some of these, one critic complained, "have been so long indulged in as to have acquired a kind of prescriptive right to keep their places." A farcical "afterpiece" followed each play, in a tradition that goes back to the seventeenth century and continued until World War I.[30] Garson, writing her play in the California of the mid-sixties, belonged to a venerable American frontier tradition of popular and populist Shakespeare transformations, whether she realized it or not.

In the seventies and eighties, the witches continued to be singled out and afforded star treatment. Terry Eagleton, for instance, begins his 1986 "exercise in political semiotics" by calling the witches

> the heroines of the piece. . . . It is they who, by releasing ambitious thoughts in Macbeth, expose a reverence for hierarchal social order for what it is, as the pious self-deception of a society based on routine oppression and incessant

warfare. The witches are exiles from that violent order, inhabiting their own sisterly community on its shadowy borderlands, refusing all truck with its tribal bickerings and military honours.

He goes on to say that "They are poets, prophetesses and devotees of female cult," whom "official society" can only imagine "as chaos rather than creativity."[31] The only major difference between Eagleton in 1986 and Garson in 1966—and it is an important one—is that Garson preceded the feminist consciousness-raising that grew out of the student radicalism and civil rights movement of the sixties. She indicates that her beatnik first witch is female (the third witch calls her "sister" [7]) but doesn't make much of the gender mix. Eagleton, writing with all of the confidence of a successful male academic theorist, can inscribe his witches with the positive female qualities celebrated by post-1970 feminism, while as a Marxist, characterizing them as "radical separatists who scorn male power." Garson, by contrast, deliberately made her witches both male and female, perhaps to avoid the negative stereotypes of witches-as-women. Here, as elsewhere, the Shakespeare transformations of the sixties seem to belong to a past that, paradoxically, is more remote for being so recent.

When Macbird, echoing Claudius from *Hamlet*, interrupts the witches' song in the banquet scene, the stage darkens, and the Ghost of Ken O'Dunc appears. Robert, now a Macduff character, watches the spectacle and says, to the accompaniment of "High Noon" music, "Mark me, Macbird / Tomorrow we shall meet" (96). As the stage empties, the witches are left to comment on Macbird's failing popularity and Robert's ambition: "He's just like all the rest." The third witch, the old leftist, advises the impatient black activist to keep a few precepts in his memory: "Be thou militant but by no means adventurist.... But this above all: to thine own cause be true." He exhorts the first and second witches to "Behold the great rebellions of the past," holding up his lantern, an emblematic object he has carried throughout the play, but they are impatient and refuse to listen. As *"flames shoot up and spread throughout the theatre,"* we hear the voice of the second witch chanting "I'm through with you, whitey—so burn, baby burn!" (98–100).

The final scene of *Macbird* takes place on the convention floor in 1964. Despite a great deal of vote-switching, Macbird confidently relies on the witches' prophecies that "No man of heart and blood shall touch your throne" and "Macbird shall never be undone / Till burning wood doth come to Washington" (81). Macbeth's Crony reports that he has seen the cherry trees burning from the hotel roof, and "savage blacks rampaging down below" (an allusion to the Watts riots during the summer of 1965). Macbird begins to "fear the equivocation of those fiends" but vows he'll "die with harness on my back." Robert's forces, with trumpets, drums, and banners, advance across the convention floor, and Robert confronts Macbird with "Turn, tyrant, turn." Macduff-like, he explains the secret of his birth: his father, "to free his sons from paralyzing scruples," replaced their human hearts with steel and plastic apparatus at birth, "thus steeling us to rule as more than men." As Robert raises his spear, Macbird clutches his heart, and speaks his last words: "thus cracks a noble heart." Robert proclaims himself President and vows to follow his "great predecessor" in "hewing out the Smooth Society." The message clearly, as the second witch said in the banquet scene, is that white politicians all look alike. The final image is of Macbird and Ken O'Dunc banners waving side by side as the procession carries Macbird's body offstage (105–9).

There are moments in *Macbird* that vividly illustrate the timeliness, the contemporaneity, of Shakespeare. Just as Hamlet's observations about Fortinbras's invasion of "a little patch of ground / That hath in it no profit but the name" became extraordinarily relevant during the Falkland invasion, so the line "Each morn new widows wail, new orphan cries / Howl up to heaven" (64) uttered by the Wayne of Morse evokes the horror of Vietnam. Nevertheless, of all the Shakespeare transformations of the sixties, this one may strike the reader as the most dated. Garson's burlesque implies that Johnson wanted Kennedy out of the way, benefited from his death, and eventually fell from power because of a coalition of liberals, blacks, and antiwar activists manipulated by the Kennedy clan and their henchmen. She could not know, in December 1966, that eighteen months later Robert Kennedy would die in a horrific reenactment of his brother's assassination, a recapitulation of the 1963 tragedy that could have been plotted by a playwright with a penchant for iterative action. *Macbird* was thus, in a very real sense, obsolete by June 1968; its cynical portrayal of RFK would no doubt have been viewed as being in poor taste by Americans who looked back on the assassinations of the Kennedys and Martin Luther King as one of the least funny episodes in our political history.

Stewart Benedict's 1970 introduction to the Dell edition of *Your Own Thing* (which also contains the complete text of *Twelfth Night*) informs the reader that "there are respects in which Shakespeare is not our contemporary." He is thinking first of Shakespeare's language but adds that while Elizabethans would have found Feste's tormenting of Malvolio "hilarious," we find it "slightly sadistic." Similarly, "the idea that a woman must necessarily be a physical coward strikes us either as quaint or condescending, but hardly uproarious."[32] These considerations and others led the authors of *Your Own Thing* to omit Sir Toby, Sir

Andrew, Maria, and Feste from their musical, substituting a "gallery" of characters that includes Everett Dirksen, John Wayne, Queen Elizabeth, Shirley Temple, Humphrey Bogart, the pope, and Buddha, all of whom appear as projections on a cyclorama. Mixed media collages employing slides, film, comic strip balloon writing, and psychedelic kaleidoscope effects are an important dimension of the show, only imperfectly communicated through the written text. Shakespeare's language makes infrequent appearances among the sixties slang and rock music lyrics.

The idea for *Your Own Thing* occurred to Hester when he came across a synopsis of *Twelfth Night* shortly after reading an article by Marshall McLuhan about "the youth of today" and their rejection of "the Establishment's standards of masculinity and femininity" (9). He became convinced that *Twelfth Night* "communicates very directly with members of the 'love generation'" and that it depicts a society which reassures the apparent outcast "that he has not actually been excluded, for their love encompasses all their fellow beings, even those who are constitutionally unable to understand their spirit of fun and games"(12). This would no doubt strike many readers as a rather dubious interpretation of *Twelfth Night*, and, indeed, the authors of *Your Own Thing* may have thought so, too, for they gave their Malvolio a very small role with only two brief appearances. No one reassures him that he has not been excluded; indeed, he is virtually ignored by the other characters. Instead, Orson is the character who fears that he is excluded from Illyria's idyllic youth culture, "where the pursuit of happiness is the principal vocation, avocation and religion" (13). He is a "square" theatrical agent who manages the successful rock group Apocalypse, which will be appearing at Olivia's trendy discotheque. Orson tries and fails to emulate the "now generation"; his desire to be accepted as "one of them" and so win the love of the fashionably youth-oriented Olivia is juxtaposed with the nonconformist "your own thing" ethos in a song that contains such stirring affirmations as "I've got to be what I've got to be," "I'm not afraid of me," and "I like the feeling of feeling free" (137–39).[33]

The only character to sympathize with Orson is Viola, who arrives in Illyria after the shipwreck just as one of the four members of Apocalypse is drafted. She answers an ad for a replacement (and a few scenes later, Sebastian, after an encounter with a nurse who scolds him about his long hair, answers the same ad). When Orson confides his fear of being "square" to Viola, now Charlie, she assures him that "Just the right square can be groovy" (142). The play switches to Shakespeare's language as Orson employs Viola/Charlie to plead his case with Olivia, and much of the subsequent action consists of skillfully choreographed running back and forth on ramps between Orson's and

Olivia's houses, as Orson sends messages via both Viola and Sebastian. The staging is reminiscent of *A Comedy of Errors*, with the two Dromios being sent interchangeably on errands. Unlike Shakespeare's Viola and Sebastian, these twins are seldom disturbed by or even aware of the confusion they cause; in *Your Own Thing*, the phrase "let it be" resolves all difficulties. One wonders if it occurred to members of the sixties' audiences that the "let it be" and "do your own thing" philosophy coexists uneasily with the contempt the play's "love generation" feels for Olivia's humorless stage manager (the Malvolio counterpart) and the square Orson, whose main problem seems to be that he lacks the boundless self-confidence displayed by the youthful rock stars. Being free in this society means that it is okay for the twenty-year-old Sebastian and the thirty-year-old Olivia to be lovers; it does not mean that the testy stage manager is free to take seriously the business of filling out W2 forms.

The confusion caused by the twins merges with Orson's confusion about his sexuality. Attracted to Viola/Charlie, he begins to speculate anxiously about latent homosexuality, in a long monologue accompanied by slides depicting everything from Greek lovers to wry commentary from John Wayne and Humphrey Bogart. When Viola tries to explain that she has not told the truth about herself, he assumes that Charlie is a closet homosexual, too. After much singing and chasing about the stage, the couples finally get themselves straightened out when Viola whips off her shirt to reveal a *"feminine bra."* At this point Olivia gets to deliver her *Twelfth Night* line, "Alas, poor fool, how have they baffled thee," here directed to Orson instead of Malvolio. "Who's baffled," he responds, and tells Viola, "I . . . thought you were to be loved no matter what you were" (187–88). In a parallel development, Olivia's decision to love a twenty-year-old causes her some anxious moments (it doesn't seem to bother Shakespeare's Olivia a bit), but in a soliloquy she decides that "Rules, labels, slots, categories / Lead the way to lonely purgatories / What does it matter? / I finally made it! I shook myself free!" (167). Her willingness, once this hurdle is passed, to accept whichever twin is available, an aspect of the play my eighties undergraduates had trouble with, makes more sense in *Your Own Thing* than it did in Shakespeare's play, for neither twin has exchanged very many words with her; the attraction is unabashedly physical.

When all four lovers embrace at the end as Apocalypse sings "Do your own thing / Pay no attention to people who look down on you" a slide of Shakespeare appears, saying "I had the same trouble with the ending" (189). Hester and Apolinar's decision to end on this note is revealing, for it draws attention to the way the neat heterosexual couplings suppress a confrontation with the issue of homosexuality that both *Your Own Thing* and *Twelfth Night* seem to edge toward, only to back quickly away. Orson would be a clearer embodiment of the principles embodied in the "I'm not afraid to be me" song if he did, in fact, discover and affirm his own homosexuality and if the others accepted him as he was (or if they didn't, revealing the shallowness of their rhetoric!). But the authors were not about to change the ending in this respect; to do so would have required changing the beginning—making both twins male, for example.

If they were writing the play in the eighties they might have considered making such a change; their transformation would then have become a statement about gay rights. In 1989 I received a student transformation entitled "Romeo and Julio"; in it, Julio Sanchez, a community college student "from a lower class traditional Spanish family" falls in love with Romeo, an intelligent and cunning "player in the game of life," who "always felt there was something wrong" with his heterosexual relationship with Lisa. The play ends with Romeo and Julio being violently beaten by a group led by Lisa's jealous former boyfriend, who discovers a note revealing Romeo and Julio's love for one another. After Romeo's death Julio decides to die with his beloved and so "pulls the tubes out of his arms." The murderers are arrested and convicted of murder. The young woman who wrote the play said that she wrote it to comment on increased violence against homosexuals brought on by AIDS. The play has an interesting sixties reference in it: Romeo's parents, who run a health food store, are "reformed flower children" who have an easygoing, open relationship with their son, in contrast with the traditional and religious Sanchez family.

It's unlikely that such a play would have been written (and submitted for a grade) by a college student in 1967. Despite all its rhetoric about doing your own thing, the sixties were not ready for this kind of open discussion of gay rights. One "trouble" contemporary readers might have with the ending of *Your Own Thing* is that Orson's courageous decision to love Viola "no matter what you were" turns out to be unnecessary, just as Shakespeare's Viola's readiness to die for Orsino does. Viola and Apocalypse have a song with the refrain "We are the now generation":

> We're revolting from the age when lines were drawn
> To separate the sexes
> We're revolting from the age when all the men
> Came from the state of Texas. . . .
> Let your hair down and shake out all your curls
> What's the difference, the boys all look like girls.

(165–66)

Their cry of protest has very little to do with gay pride, sexual preference, and gender-as-a-social-construct; it is largely about the "unisex
look." "Stuff your crew cuts and prim morality / Up your stone-age conventionality," they proclaim. But the crew cuts are not a symbol of
something bigger; it really is hair styles that are at issue here. (As a
rock musical, *Your Own Thing* has been eclipsed by the more enduring
Hair, which takes its theme from the sixties phenomenon of hair as a
form of rebellion, in a similar vein.) That does not necessarily mean
that the play trivializes the issue of challenging "stone-age conventionality"; what it does mean is that, less than twenty-five years later,
we are reading *Your Own Thing* very differently and that a cultural and
ideological gap separates us from this play just as much as it does from
Shakespeare's. Perhaps even more so—the questions about love at
first sight, gender confusion, and rapid shifts of allegiance that troubled the first readers who talked back to Shakespeare in my writing–
intensive class in the mid-1980s may seem even more problematic in
Your Own Thing than they did in Shakespeare's version of the story.

Much of the appeal of *Twelfth Night*, for Hester and Apolinar, as for
other directors and adapters, has been the idea that people can become
indistinguishable, interchangeable, confused about their identities and
confusing to others. The replication and blurring of identity or indi-
viduality suggested by twinning exerted a powerful attraction on playwrights of the sixties, perhaps because these offered a means of commenting on the confusion and fragmentation of identity in the machine
age. Stoppard acted on a cue from Shakespeare, whose Rosencrantz
and Guildenstern appear to be inseparable and indistinguishable,
while at the same time he was clearly alluding to the extraordinary
world-wide appeal of Beckett's Vladimir and Estragon, two characters,
says Esslin, who "have been seen as so complementary that they might
be two halves of a single personality."[34] Twinning, as Beckett and Stoppard used it, is a mocking variant of doubling; instead of having one
actor play two parts, two actors play what seems to be one part, but in
the process raises questions about what constitutes a part, or separate
dramatic identity. Marowitz had used Shakespearean doubling ironically to create a twinning effect in his *Hamlet*: the actor who played the
Clown/Polonius wore a grey glove that he held up to his chin to suggest
Polonius's beard as he slipped from one role to the other. Knowledgeable spectators at a performance of the *"Naked" Hamlet* would have
been confronted with a different kind of twinning in the graveyard
scene, in which the Ghost speaks Hamlet's lines and Hamlet (with his
Ramon accent) speaks the Gravediggers'. Another kind of twin-
ning/doubling occurs when Papp uses what he calls "The Dummy Bit"

for the "How all occasions do inform against me" soliloquy, with Hamlet sitting on the Ghost's lap like a ventriloquist's dummy as the two speakers alternate lines.

In *A Macbeth*, first performed in May 1969 in Wiesbaden, Marowitz carries this twinning/doubling technique much farther. The streamlined cast consists of eleven actors: Duncan, Banquo, Malcolm, Macduff, three witches, Lady Macbeth, and three Macbeths. The second and third Macbeth have a variety of functions; at first they seem like Macbeth's shadows, *"whispering the words MACBETH speaks"* as he delivers the first ten lines of the "If it were done, when 'tis done, then 'twere well / It were done quickly" soliloquy of act 1, scene 7. Sometimes, they represent an inner dialogue taking place within Macbeth's divided mind, as when Macbeth says "I dare do all that may become a man" and the second Macbeth answers, appropriating Lady Macbeth's speech beginning: "What beast was't then / That made you break this enterprise to me?"[35] Later, there is a long sequence in which all three Macbeths participate by turns, juxtaposing the rest of the act 1, scene 7 soliloquy, Malcolm's speech from act 4, scene 3 in which he tests Macduff by describing what a brutal king he'd be, and more of Lady Macbeth's lines from act 1, scene 7 (95–97). The second and third Macbeths also play the messengers, the grooms, the murderers, and, with the witches, the banquet guests, an economical solution to the problems posed by Shakespeare's large cast. But unlike conventional doubling, they are presumably always recognizable as Macbeth's alter egos. There is hardly a page in the text that does not include either the extra Macbeths or the three witches or some combination thereof.

Lady Macbeth, Marowitz implies, is in league with the witches. The play begins with the following stage direction:

> *Lights come up on effigy of MACBETH. In front of it, back to audience, stands LADY MACBETH. On a signal, the three WITCHES enter and surround the effigy. Each adds bits to it until it clearly resembles MACBETH. After a pause, LADY MACBETH begins to intone an incantation. (81)*

This effigy reappears a few pages later, and again in the spectacular final moments of the play. As Macduff

> *raises his sword over* [Macbeth, who has been beaten to death by all the characters with broomsticks] *LADY MACBETH raises her instrument over the effigy's head. As MACDUFF strikes, LADY MACBETH dashes off the head of the effigy.* (131)

The effigy becomes, in effect, a fourth Macbeth, dehumanized and without any vestiges of volition. There is also an effigy of Lady Macbeth, around which the witches chant "Double double, toil, and trouble" as they stab and tear at it just before the sleepwalking scene (121). The witches are present throughout this scene, their cauldron incantations superimposed on Lady Macbeth's monologue. Marowitz does not explain how Lady Macbeth, who dies and is laid on her bier at the end of the sleepwalking scene, happens to be alive and embracing Macbeth three pages later; however, the stage direction indicates that as he goes to kiss her she "*Transforms*," announces "The queen, my lord, is dead," and "becomes immobile." The witches suddenly appear and remove her body (129). In this transformation Marowitz seems to be probing the slippery and elusive boundaries between discrete identities and states of existence.

The witches also double as other characters, most interestingly, in masks as Lady Macduff and her children. In a visual echo of an earlier scene, where the second and third Macbeths had "*placed two daggers into* MACBETH'S *hands, and . . . usher[ed] him over to the sleeping* DUNCAN" (99–100), so here they thrust daggers into Macbeth's hands and force him to stab Lady Macduff and her son. After excerpts from Malcolm and Macduff's scene in act 4, scene 3, "LADY MACBETH *discovers* WITCHES *removing* LADY MACDUFF *gear*" and scolds them, using the Hecate speech from act 3, scene 5: "Saucy and overbold, how did you dare / To trade and traffick with Macbeth" (120). This metatheatrical awareness of disguise and role-playing within the play is a device Ionesco will also use in his transformation of *Macbeth*.

The repeated doubling and twinning in *A Macbeth* effects a morality-playlike fragmentation of Macbeth's character into warring impulses that interact as distinct personalities onstage. As elsewhere in *The Marowitz Shakespeare*, stage directions are important aspects of the text:

> 2nd Macbeth: (*Snide*). . . .
> 3rd Macbeth: (*Exhorting*). . . .
> Macbeth: (*Lamely rationalizing*). . . .
> 2nd Macbeth: (*Washing hands of him*). . . .
> 3rd Macbeth: (*Reasoning*). . . .
>
> (96–97)

These occur during the long three-way monologue that precedes the murder of Duncan, a deed Macbeth does not finally accomplish until "LADY MACBETH *appears, takes hold of* MACBETH'S *hands and drives the daggers into* DUNCAN'S *heart*" (100). This Macbeth seems to share some of the Marowitz Hamlet's paralysis, and the contempt the second and third Macbeths display toward him may be a reflection of the author's. Rather as in *Macbird*, the witches seem to be the characters who mediate between the audience and the rest of the cast, if such a concept can be used in connection with Marowitz's surreal dramaturgy. At the very end of the play, after the death of Macbeth and the beheading of the effigy, the witches *"take off their stocking masks"* as the first Witch says *"simply, conversationally,"* "When shall we three meet again? / In thunder, lightning, or in rain?" (131). By placing the spotlight on them, rather than on Malcolm and Macduff, Marowitz is suggesting an unbreakable recurring cycle of disorder and brutality, very much as Ionesco will in his *Macbett*.

Ionesco's *Macbett* was first performed in January 1972 in Paris; a year later, Grove Press published an English translation by Charles Marowitz and Donald Watson. Ionesco thought of *Macbett* as a farcical comedy that "leans more toward Jarry's *Ubu Roi* [than toward *Macbeth*]": "I hope that people will laugh," he remarked in a 1972 interview. According to Ruby Cohn, the play implies that "the power drive converts life into a sinister farce."[36] The twinning/doubling effect is evident from the outset, although it takes a rather different form than in Marowitz's *A Macbeth*. The opening scene consists of Glamiss and Candor, who *"come on without acknowledging each other and stand center stage, facing the audience"*:

> *Glamiss (turning toward CANDOR):* Good morning, Baron Candor.
> *Candor (turning toward GLAMISS):* Good morning, Baron Glamiss.
> *Glamiss:* Listen, Candor.
> *Candor:* Listen, Glamiss.[37]

The conversation continues in this fashion as they become increasingly angry toward the Archduke Duncan, who is "sucking [them] dry." They proceed to plot a rebellion:

> *Candor:* Down with Duncan.
> *Glamiss:* He's no better than we are.
> *Candor:* Worse, if anything.
> *Glamiss:* Much worse.
> *Candor:* Much, much worse.

(5)

Very much like Shakespeare's and Stoppard's Rosencrantz and Guildenstern, Macbett and Banco share a similar confused identity; when Lady Duncan rides out to the battlefield to see who has won, she says "Rise my dear Macbett" to Banco and he responds "I'm not Macbett, I'm Banco" (24). Earlier in the play, after the battle against Glamiss and Candor, Macbett and Banco had delivered identical prose soliloquies describing the horrors of war in rather matter-of-fact terms, marked by the same kinds of clichés that characterize their speeches elsewhere: "I thrashed about a bit too hard. My wrist aches. Luckily it's nothing serious. It's been quite a pleasant day. Feeling quite bucked" (16). The flatness of the language seems to be a deliberate affront to Shakespeare's rhetorical complexity, and in its own way is as parodic a send-up of *Macbeth* as *Macbird* is.

The play doubles back on itself after about thirty pages as Glamiss escapes, and Duncan sends Macbett and Banco off to "start all over again." "What a disaster," they each remark twice (37). The stage darkens, the stage direction indicates *"wind and storm,"* and the First and Second Witches appear; they hail Macbett as Thane of Glamiss and prophesy that he will be Archduke and rule the country. A little later they hail Banco, "who won't be Thane of Glamiss," and in a repetition / variation of the scene with Macbett, provoke a rivalry between the two generals (37–41).

Ionesco's re-vision of Macbeth's character parallels other sixties transformations that reduce whatever is heroic in Shakespeare's protagonists to an ordinary, contemptible passivity. Macbett is stolidly, stubbornly loyal to the Archduke Duncan (himself a foolish and cowardly leader); when he meets with the witches again to find out more, he tells them that he wants only to serve his sovereign. They laugh derisively at his willingness to be used and urge him to "Be your own master." To the accompaniment of music, their false noses, chins, hairpieces, and old clothes are stripped away to reveal Lady Duncan and her maid. "I'll be your mistress," Lady Duncan says to Macbett; "Madam, I have certain scruples . . . ," he stammers; "Pull yourself together," she commands and delivers the famous equivocating prophecies (57).

Some twenty pages later, the coronation and wedding feast take place, and then Lady Duncan (now Lady Macbett) and her Lady in Waiting enact a reversal of their earlier unmasking by divesting themselves of crown, cross, and royal clothes and open a suitcase from which they remove the various components of their witches' costumes. The metamorphosis takes place in full view of the audience, with stage directions indicating that Lady Macbett *"puts on her smelly old dress, her apron covered in vomit, her dirty gray hair, takes out her teeth, shows the plate to the audience, puts on her pointed nose, etc."* "A job well done," the Second Witch says smugly. The First Witch exults, "The boss will be pleased. . . . He'll be waiting to send us on another mission." With that they sit astride the suitcase and appear to fly away (85–86).

When Duncan's Ghost appears in the banquet scene, he informs Macbett that "there is one thing you haven't got quite right. You didn't steal my wife." A rather rumpled and different looking Lady Macbett ("*or rather LADY DUNCAN*," says the stage direction) enters and announces herself to be "the faithful widow of your rightful king, the Archduke Duncan." She denounces Macbett as a murderer and usurper (97–98). Duncan's son Macol arrives, and the forest "*lumbers*" forward to encircle Macbett, whose death is as ordinary and unheroic as his life: his last word as Macol stabs him in the back is "merde." The people rejoice, praising Macol and denouncing Macbett for about thirty lines. Then Macol tells them to "shut up," a stage direction indicates that "*a forest of guillotines appears upstage as in the first scene*," and finally, for the first time, Ionesco shifts to Shakespeare's language. With devastating irony, he has Macol deliver Malcolm's speech to Macduff to the "*discontent, amazement [and] despair*" of the crowd, who leave the stage as the long speech continues to unwind:

> In me I know
> All the particulars of vice so grafted
> That, when they shall be opened, black
> Macbett will seem as pure as snow and the poor state
> Esteem him as a lamb, being compared
> With my confineless harms. . . .
>
> (101–4)

Despite the farcical tone of the play as a whole, there is something terrible, maybe even bordering on the "tragic" in Kott's sense of the word, about Macol's deadly serious rendition of Malcolm's testing-speech. In *Macbeth*, the audience has the consolation of knowing that this shocking confession of the would-be tyrant is only a ruse; Macol, however, really intends to be the diabolical ruler Shakespeare's powerfully evocative language describes. At the very end of the play, he says "I shall / Uproar the universal peace, confound / All unity on earth" (105). This indeed is the Grand Mechanism, from which there is no escape. Ionesco's *Macbett*, arguably, is a tragedy for the "poor country" over which the tyrant will rule; as such, it shares with the other transformations of the sixties the distinction of being a serio-comic tragedy without a tragic protagonist.

Ionesco's adaptation of the Shakespearean disguise motif, to which he adds the *deus ex machina* surprise appearance of the "real" Lady Duncan, constitutes a mockery of the many neat resolutions in literature that spring a crucial piece of information on the audience or reader in the final scene or pages. Like Garson and Marowitz, in a tradition reaching back to Davenant's Restoration adaptation of *Macbeth*, he gives the witches larger and more active roles than Shakespeare had done, thus transforming Macbeth into a comic dupe, a gull, sexually manipulated by a fairy-tale witch concealed beneath the outward guise of a beautiful, seductive woman. "Almost all modern offshoots are hostile to Lady Macbeth," Cohn remarks in a chapter that ranges widely through the many modern offshoots of "this preponderantly masculine tragedy," Today's Lady Macbeth, she concluded in 1976, "needs Women's Liberation."[38]

The Shakespeare appropriations I have been discussing tend to invert or reverse some of the accepted moral categories used to "place" or rank characters. Nowhere is this more evident than in the talking back that *The Tempest* has provoked among writers for whom the island Prospero "stole" from Sycorax is a microcosm of colonialism throughout the world. Aimé Césaire's *Une Tempête*, written in 1969 (translated by Richard Miller in 1985 as *A Tempest*), belongs to an interrelated collection of *Tempest* offshoots that interrogate and complicate the relationship between Caliban and Prospero. Fredric Jameson, in "Periodizing the 60s," proposes that we "mark the beginnings of what will come to be called the 60s in the third world with the great movement of decolonization in British and French Africa. . . . Indeed," he continues, "a first world 60s owed much to third-worldism in terms of politicocultural models, as in a symbolic Maoism, and moreover, found its mission in resistance to wars aimed precisely at stemming the new revolutionary forces in the third world." The sixties was the period in which millions of " 'natives' became human beings, and this internally as well as externally: those inner colonized of the first world—'minorities,' marginals, and women—fully as much as its external subjects and official 'natives.' "[39] Caliban, for generations of Shakespeare audiences, had been a fanciful and comfortingly domesticated representation of the "native"; at once brutish and naive, he resents and plots to overthrow the firm, just authority of his colonial overlord, until the fifth act resolution when he acknowledges his folly and vows to "be wise hereafter, / And seek for grace" (5. 1. 295–96). It is difficult, now, to imagine the part being played in this way.

The Tempest became a vehicle for resistance to a politics of domination and repression as early as 1848, a year of revolutions and social upheaval in Europe. William and Robert Brough's satirical *The Enchanted Isle* depicts Caliban as "an hereditary bondsman" who is "determin[ed] to be free"; he voices antislavery sentiments, appealing to the "sons of freedom" in the audience. The authors adapt Prospero's request to be released "with the help of your good hands" in *The Tempest* as a corresponding final speech delivered by Caliban, who, having completed his "lawless acts," requests a demonstration "not with arms—no, only with the *hand*," in an apparent repudiation of his earlier revolutionary fervor.[40] Ernest Renan's 1877 philosophical drama *Caliban* is similarly ambivalent in its portrayal of Caliban. This diachronic transformation continues the story after the characters return to Milan, rather like the *Merchant of Venice* transformations discussed in Chapter 2. Restored to his dukedom, Prospero has once again begun to neglect his duties, prompting Caliban to lead a successful people's revolt and take control of the government. As Cohn describes it, "the pardoning spirit of Shakespeare's Prospero is inherited by Renan's Caliban."[41] He rises above his "bend of nature," outgrows his cursing, and adopts Gonzalo as his adviser; moreover, he refuses to deliver Prospero to the Inquisition and permits him to "work at his ease along with all the philosophers and artists under my patronage."[42] "Despite or because of his antidemocratic bias," Annabel Patterson has observed more recently, "Renan provides remarkable insight both into *The Tempest* and into the critical tradition, which has deeply invested in the play's projection of idealisms—neoplatonism, providentialism, benevolent rule, the redemptive power of forgiveness."[43] Renan's own idealism is evident in a sequel to Caliban, entitled *l'Eau de Jouvence* (1989), in which Caliban weds Ariel, now a beautiful maiden representing the purity of the soul.[44] An even more unabashed idealism was attached to Caliban forty years later in Percy MacKaye's masque *Caliban*, described in Chapter 3.

The impact of Darwin's theory of evolution created a new role for Caliban, that of the missing link between beasts and men. Daniel Wilson's *Caliban: The Missing Link* (1873) was the first of a series of ideological treatises that appropriated Caliban's name, much as Shylock's name has been appropriated in discussions of usury. Wilson argued that "the moral instincts of man have no part" in Caliban, yet he is in need of (and thus capable of benefiting from?) tutoring and development, like the natives subject to Europe's "civilising mission" in its colonies.[45] In 1931, with the publication of Leonard Barnes's *Caliban in Africa*, subtitled *An Impression of Colour-Madness*, Caliban was explicitly identified with a specific racial or ethnic group, in this case, the South African blacks who were oppressed and persecuted by the Boers.[46] The Nicaraguan journalist-poet Rubén Darío associated him with everything vicious, bestial, and acquisitive in North America in his 1898 "The Triumph of Caliban"; similarly, José Enrique Rodó's 1938 *Ariel* used Ariel and Caliban to represent complementary qualities, the best and worst of Spanish-American culture.[47] More sociopsychological and political treatises followed during the next three decades. D. O. Mannoni, in *Prospero and Caliban: The Psychology of Colonization* (1950), inspired by the 1947–48 uprising against the French in Madagascar, attached Caliban's and Prospero's names to two complexes the author claimed to have identified in colo-nialism, the Prospero-complex, which drives the white man to seek out uncompetitive situations in which he can dominate, and the Caliban-complex, a dependency on authority experienced by people "forced out of a secure 'tribal' society and into the less stable, competitively edged hierarchies of semi-westernized existence."[48] Mannoni's theories pro-voked a good deal of talking back from British writers ambivalent about colonialism, such as Philip Mason, in *Prospero's Magic* (1962) and D. G. James in *The Dream of Prospero* (1967), and more immedi-ately, from two Martiniquean writers, Frantz Fanon, and then Aimé Césaire, whose *Discours sur Le colonialisme* was an angry rebuttal of Mannoni's thesis.[49]

The opening chapter of Fanon's *Black Skin, White Masks* (1952) looked at the role of language in the relationship between colonizer and colonized, taking off from Caliban's famous line in *The Tempest*: "You taught me language, and my profit on't / Is, I know how to curse" (1.2.363–64). Other writers who focused on Caliban's two languages are the Nigerian John Pepper Clark in "The Legacy of Caliban" (1970) and the West Indian George Lamming in his 1960 book *The Pleasures of Exile* (Lamming's later novel, *Water with Berries* [1971] takes up another theme from *The Tempest*, that is, Caliban as would-be rapist). Clark and Lamming are less optimistic about Caliban's ability to tran-scend both his native tongue and the repressive language of the colo-nizer than the German scholar Janheinz Jahn is in his *History of Neo-African Literature* (1968), which exhibits "an unlimited faith in Caliban."[50] Jahn perceived Caliban as a poet analogous to the fran-cophone writers in the Négritude movement, one whose "emancipa-tion, his break-out from the prison of Prospero's language, gives Pros-pero too a chance of freedom." Prospero, Jahn affirms, can turn "from a tyrant into a humane person" by asking Caliban questions and aban-doning his colonialist arrogance by showing that he is willing to be instructed.[51]

Caliban, Ariel, and Prospero function largely as "metaphors" (to use the Vaughans' term) in these sociopolitical treatises, metaphors that assign the names of characters to ideological constructs or sets of char-acteristics. This form of appropriation is quite different from adapting or transforming the structure of events and relationships in which the characters originated. A poem by Michael Hamburger entitled "The Tempest: An Alternative" (1944) envisions a sequel to the events of the play, in which Caliban controls the island and Prospero is left behind, "an old man with a bent back," to "bear logs for Caliban."[52] Hamburg-er's inversion of roles may have been inspired by the dislocations of lives caused by the war. But among the ideological critics who used *The Tem-pest* to depict the respective roles of colonizer and colonized, only Aimé

Césaire talked back to Shakespeare from within the confines of the play's action, drawing on the creative anger of the sixties as well as the long history of *Tempest* appropriations. *A Tempest* shares certain features with the other transformations of the sixties, although the others discussed in this chapter were written by much younger writers. Césaire's adaptation of *The Tempest* for a black cast came at the end of a long and remarkable career. He had left Martinique in 1931 at the age of eighteen to study in Paris, where he and the Senegalese writer Léopold Sédar Senghor founded the Négritude movement with their review *L'Etudiant Noir.* He later returned to Martinique and served as mayor of Fort de France for many years. A distinguished poet, he began in 1956 and devoted the last ten years of his life to a third-world theatre group based in Paris until his death in 1973.[53]

A Tempest follows the sequence of scenes in Shakespeare's play more closely than any of the other transformations of the sixties. Césaire has added only one new character, Eshu, a black devil-god, who disrupts the masque by mocking the goddesses and singing an irreverent and bawdy song. He is the embodiment of disorder, as the song indicates:

> Eshu can play many tricks,
> Give him twenty dogs! You will see his dirty tricks.
> ·
> Eshu can throw a stone yesterday and
> Kill a bird today. He can make a mess out of
> Order and vice-versa. Ah, Eshu is a wonderful bad joke.[54]

Caliban's "insubordination," Prospero tells Ariel, "call[s] into question the whole order of the world" (55). This theme continues in the play's final moments, when Prospero, surprised at Caliban's articulateness, remarks, "Well, the world is really upside down" (70). He offers to make peace with Caliban, who refuses in a stirring speech in which he prophesies that "one day my bare fist, just that, will be enough to crush your world. The old world is falling apart!" (71).

The only new scene—that is, a scene without a counterpart in Shakespeare's play—is a dialectical encounter between Caliban, "a black slave," according to the cast list, and Ariel, "a mulatto slave." This occurs at the beginning of act 2, right after a scene that corresponds to act 1, scene 2, in which the dialogue between Caliban and Prospero has been expanded significantly. Caliban rejects "the name given me by hatred" and choses to be called X instead (following a Black Muslim practice), to draw attention to the way his name "has been stolen" (18). His first word in the text, repeated throughout, is "Uhuru!" (Swahili for independence), a word that Prospero does not understand. When Caliban and the obedient servant Ariel are alone together, Ariel tells

his "brother" that "we both want our freedom—only our methods are
different." He has come "on my own" to warn Caliban that Prospero
"is planning horrible acts of revenge" and to convince him that "you
aren't the stronger, you'll never be the stronger" (24). Caliban's contempt for what he calls Ariel's "Uncle Tom patience" is transparent;
Ariel responds that he does not believe in violence, which meets with
more scorn. Césaire used Ariel to represent an optimistic belief that
the oppressor can and will change and "acquire a conscience" through
the power of patience, love, will power, and dreams. Caliban, by contrast, says he would choose death over humiliation and injustice (26).
Interestingly, the Ubu Repertory Theater's New York revival of *A Tempest* in October 1991 had an all-black cast. Ariel was played by an actor
with lighter skin, which had the effect of setting Ariel apart from the
other characters and making him less obviously Caliban's "brother"
than he might otherwise have been.[55]

Caliban's subsequent willingness to accept the exploitative Stephano
as king may appear improbable, but it is consistent with his short-
sighted preoccupation with revenge; in the dialogue with Ariel, who
speaks repeatedly of gaining his freedom, Caliban harps on vengeance.
When he meets Stephano and Trinculo, he tells them "I'm perfectly
willing to give you my right to [the island], but you'll have to fight Prospero for it" (49). The scene ends with Caliban's "Freedom hi-day" song
("as in Shakespeare," says the stage direction), but it is prefaced by his
rousing declaration "Let's drink, my new-found friends, and let us sing.
Let us sing of winning the day and of an end to tyranny" (49). Césaire's
Caliban has clearly mastered the oppressor's language and speaks it
eloquently. Not surprisingly, when he becomes disillusioned with
Stephano and Trinculo after they are distracted by the gaudy clothing,
he says to himself: "Oh well! History won't blame me for not having
been able to win my freedom all by myself. It's you and me, Prospero!"
and advances on Prospero alone, weapon in hand. (63)

Césaire's reworking of the final scene of *The Tempest* explicitly
questions the psychological validity of Shakespeare's comic resolutions in which characters leave the "green world" behind and return to
"civilization" to resume their former lives. Ignoring Gonzalo's warn-
ing that Caliban is "a hardened criminal," Prospero says expansively,
"Draw near, Caliban. What say you in your own defense? Take advan-
tage of my good humor. Today, I feel in a forgiving mood" (69). Caliban angrily rejects his overture, but Prospero persists: "In spite of
everything I'm fond of you, Caliban. Come, let's make peace. We've
lived together for ten years and worked side by side. . . . We've ended
up by becoming compatriots!" (70). Caliban understands his master
better than Prospero understands himself: he predicts that Prospero
won't go back to Europe because, "You're just an old colonial addict,

that's what you are!" (72). Prospero experiences a characteristically Shakespearean moment of recognition: "For it is you who have made me doubt myself for the first time." He turns to the nobles and tells them that he will remain on the island: "My fate is here: I shall not run from it." When everyone else has left the stage he turns to Caliban and says

> And now Caliban, it's you and me!
> What I have to tell you will be brief:
> Ten times, a hundred times, I've tried to save you,
> above all from yourself.
> But you have always answered me with wrath and venom,
> like the opossum that pulls itself up by its own tail
> the better to bite the hand that tears it from the darkness.
> Well, my boy, I shall set aside my indulgent nature
> and henceforth I will answer your violence
> with violence!
> *(Time passes, symbolized by the curtain's being lowered halfway and reraised. In semi-darkness Prospero appears, aged and weary. His gestures are jerky and automatic, his speech weak, toneless.)*
> PROSPERO: Odd, but for some time now we seem to be overrun with opossums. Peccarys, wild boar, all of the unpleasant animals! But mainly opossums. With those eyes! And the vile grin they have! It's as though the jungle was laying siege to the cave . . . .But I shall stand firm . . . I shall not let my work perish! *(Shouting.)* I shall protect civilization! *(He fires in all directions.)* They're done for! Now, this way I'll be able to have some peace and calm for a while. But it's cold. Odd how the climate's changed. Cold on this island . . . Have to think about making a fire . . . Well, Caliban, old fellow, it's just us two now, here on the island . . . only you and me. You-me . . . me-you! What in the hell is he up to? *(Shouting.)* Caliban! *(In the distance, above the sound of the surf and the chirping of birds, we hear snatches of Caliban's song.)*
> FREEDOM HI-DAY, FREEDOM HI-DAY!! (74–75)

And on this note Césaire's *A Tempest* ends, its Caliban unvanquished and still aspiring to freedom, its Prospero locked in a self-destructive embrace with an other who has become part of himself. It is not at all clear that Caliban has triumphed; nor, however, has he been defeated. The colonialist stalemate persists.

In the years since *A Tempest* was first performed in 1969, appropriations of Shakespeare's two major characters have continued to appear. Roberto Fernández Retamar, a postrevolutionary Cuban writer, viewed

Caliban as a representative of the Carribean *mestizos* enslaved by white settlers, in a 1971 essay entitled "Caliban: Notes Towards a Discussion of Culture in Our America."[56] For Retamar, the issue is one of class rather than race; "the lofty Ariel is representative of the intellectual who must choose between collaborating with Prospero and deliberately allying himself with Caliban, the exploited proletarian who is to advance revolutionary change."[57] Other uses of Caliban's name and its cumulative associations include Lemuel Johnson's poetry collection, *highlife for caliban* (1973), David Wallace's *Do You Love Me, Master?* (1977), about a Zambian houseboy who breaks the stick of his boss, Prospero, and drives him away, and the Barbadian Edward Braithwaite's poem "Caliban," which celebrates the Cuban revolution with the refrain "Ban, Ban, Ca-Caliban."[58] French Canadian writers identify with Caliban as a "cultural mulatto caught between two cultures," as in Pierre Sequin's 1977 novel *Caliban*, which in turn was influenced by the Haitian-born Max Dorsinville's *Caliban without Prospero: Essay in Québec and Black Literature* (1974). Among the English Canadian literary community, however, Miranda became a symbol of their subservience to Prospero's "despotic tutelage"; "she will always be Prospero's progeny and may never rebel against [his] authority."[59] The Nigerian Nkem Nwankwo in the poem "Caliban to Miranda" sees the collapse of the West prefigured in *The Tempest*: "We Calibans will inherit the earth."[60] As Chantel Zabus concludes in his survey of *Tempest* offshoots, "Caliban has become the inexhaustible symbol of the colonized insurgent."[61]

When did the sixties-inspired talking back to Shakespeare end? Perhaps with Edward Bond's misogynistic and nihilistic *Lear* (1971), which Bond describes as an appropriation "for our time":

> I'm afraid that we use the play in the wrong way; as a society we use the play in a wrong way. And it's for that reason I would like to rewrite it so that we now have to use the play for ourselves, for our society, for our time, for our problems.[62]

"Violence," he says elsewhere in the interview, is our "consuming problem."[63] Guido Almansi characterizes Bond, along with Ionesco and other European playwrights, as the "thumb-screwers," who "tend to reestablish a Shakespeare who is more Elizabethan than the Elizabethan age could allow . . . whose language is in chaotic upheaval and whose characters rant and rage."[64] Bond's Lear is shot in the back at the play's end, by a soldier drafted into the victorious Cordelia's army. Bond rewrites Shakespeare's Cordelia in a way that anticipates Jane

Smiley's Cordelia character in *A Thousand Acres*; "she's a very dangerous type of person," he said in the interview, while "the other daughters, though I'm not excusing them, were very unfairly treated and misunderstood."[65] Like so much else that happened in the sixties, this re-vision of Lear's daughters proceeds aggressively and provocatively to invert and interrogate the unexamined value judgments of an Anglo-American cultural heritage that had relied on Shakespeare for eloquently-inscribed words of comfort and wisdom. By dismantling, fracturing, ignoring, and parodying those words, the playwrights of the sixties recreated Shakespeare in the image of their own time.

5
What Happy Endings?

"What happy endings?" demanded British actress Fiona Shaw, when asked about the roles that she and four other actresses had played for the Royal Shakespeare Company. "You can't celebrate the outcome for Kate and Bianca," she continued. "Bianca plays by the rules and loses her soul. Kate breaks the rules and wins—Elizabethan marriage."[1] Defending his decision to stage *Hamlet* with an abundance of antic humor, Joseph Papp commented that "We must take a new look at these old sturdy classifications." "We are confused when Shakespeare labels *The Merchant of Venice* a comedy," he noted, adding, "Are *Measure for Measure, The Tempest, All's Well That Ends Well* comedies?"[2] This chapter begins by focusing on three of Shakespeare's women characters, Imogen in *Cymbeline*, Isabella in *Measure for Measure,* and Helena in *All's Well That Ends Well*, each the assertive heroine of a play that by its very nature raises questions about comedy and tragedy as genres. Imogen, Helena, and Isabella attracted the clamorous nineteenth-century voices of Mary Cowden Clarke, Mary Lamb, Edith Nesbit, and Helen Faucit, women who did not hesitate to rewrite Shakespeare in accordance with the expectations and sentiments of their female readers. Their renegotiations of Shakespeare's problematic texts offer striking insights into the way women writers have talked back to the gaps, dissonances, and invitations to revise inherent both in Shakespeare's portrayal of women and in his assumptions about comic endings. Brecht's and Marowitz's *Measure for Measure* transformations also interrogate the play's status as a comedy, by pursuing the political issues it raises, in a spirit much closer to that of the plays of the sixties.

More recently, Shakespeare's tragic women have also invited revisions that challenge the rules of genre. Ann-Marie MacDonald's *Goodnight Desdemona (Good Morning Juliet)* and Jane Smiley's *A*

Thousand Acres, two very recent transformations, raise the question "What unhappy endings?" that is the logical corollary to "What happy endings?" Who says that Juliet, Desdemona, Cordelia, Goneril, and Regan have to die—and die in these particularly violent ways—at the ends of their respective plays? How might we begin to reinvent the lives of women characters who are so much a part of our literary (and popular) culture according to less rigid notions about tragic causality and closure?

The five actresses interviewed in *Clamorous Voices: Shakespeare's Women Today* saw Shakespeare's comic endings as open rather than closed. "There isn't a fixed end to a play," said Juliet Stevenson as she talked about her performances as Isabella in Adrian Noble's 1983 production of *Measure for Measure.* The ending is "something that has to be renegotiated every performance."[3] George Bernard Shaw's "*Cymbeline* Refinished" came into existence in just this way, as a renegotiated fifth act commissioned for a 1937 London production. Shaw explains in his 1945 Preface that he set out to "rewrite the act as Shakespear [*sic*] might have written it if he had been post-Ibsen and post-Shaw instead of post-Marlowe." As Marowitz later did, he justifies "*Cymbeline* Refinished" by asking rhetorically whether Shakespeare had the "right to refashion Hamlet?" Shaw goes on to speak of the many successful variations created by composers, concluding that "I stand in the same time relation to Shakespear as Mozart to Handel, or Wagner to Beethoven." With typically Shavian self-regard, he announces "I have luxuriated in variations."[4]

Shaw reduces Shakespeare's last five scenes, nearly one thousand lines in total, to a single long scene, omitting the masquelike vision that appears to the imprisoned Posthumus, the soothsayer, the identifying mole, and a good deal of the explaining. Posthumus's long guilt-stricken soliloquy remains (5.1.1–33), after which Shaw brings all of the major characters onstage within a dozen lines or so. Iachimo has not yet begun his confession when Imogen recognizes Posthumus's voice and rushes forward to reveal her own identity. Shaw's stage direction indicates that she "*puts her hand on his face*" (793), a gesture that presumably takes him by surprise. As in Shakespeare's text, he strikes her, and a few lines later, Pisanio cries out "O my Lord Posthumus, / You never kill'd Imogen till now!" (5.5.230 –31; Shaw, 793). To the despair, no doubt, of many directors, Shakespeare had derailed the couple's reunion with a twenty-five line digression on Cornelius's role in substituting the sleeping potion for the poison the Queen thought she gave to Pisanio. During these speeches, Imogen and Posthumus are presumably standing impatiently onstage waiting for a chance to retrieve the dramatic moment. Finally Imogen embraces Posthumus, saying "Why did you throw your wedded lady [from] you? / Think that you are upon a rock, and now / Throw me again" (5.5.261– 63). Shaw eliminated the digression and had his Imogen respond immediately after Pisanio's line with

> Oh, let me die. I heard my husband's voice
> Whom I thought dead; and in my ecstasy,
> The wildest I shall ever feel again,
> He met me with a blow.
>
> (793)

There is reproach and sorrow in her voice; a moment of "wildest ecstasy" has passed, never to return, and she can feel only an indignant skepticism ("You dare pretend you love me") when he loudly proclaims his "joy." The tension intensifies as Iachimo tells the story of his night in the chest and offers payment as recompense for the ring and the bracelet. The twentieth-century Imogen's indignation toward her husband continues to assert itself: "You made this wager! And I'm married to you!" (794) she exclaims to Posthumus during Iachimo's account, and then, after he ends his tale, "And this, you think, signors, makes good to me / All you have done, you and my husband there!" Iachimo remarks, realistically, that

> It remedies what can be remedied.
> As for the rest, it cannot be undone.
> We are a pitiable pair. For all that
> You may go further and fare worse; for men
> Will do such things to women.
>
> (795)

Shaw is obviously interrogating the comic logic of Shakespearean happy endings, endings in which it often seems that all can be undone. He does so in ways that anticipate subsequent feminist readings of *Much Ado*, *All's Well*, and *Measure for Measure*, all problematic comedies in which a badly treated woman is seemingly consigned without protest to a "happy ending" of love and marriage with a man who has deceived, belied, or betrayed her. Imogen's desperate isolation is intensified a hundred lines later, after her two brothers' identities have been revealed (both, ironically, decline the privilege of being crown prince, preferring their former life in Wales). When she and Posthumus once more become the focus of attention for the large cast assembled onstage, Cymbeline says waspishly to Posthumus:

God's patience, man, take your wife home to bed.
You're man and wife: nothing can alter that.
Are there more plots to unravel? Each one here,
It seems, is someone else. [To Imogen] Go change your dress
For one becoming to your sex and rank.
Have you no shame?

The dialogue continues with Imogen's defiant response:

Imogen: None.
Cymbeline: How? None!
Imogen.   All is lost.
Shame, husband, happiness, and faith in Man.
He's not even sorry.
Posthumus.   I'm too happy.
Iachimo: Lady, a word. When you arrived just now
I, as you saw, was hot on killing him.
Let him bear witness that I drew on him
To avenge your death.
Imogen: Oh, do not make me laugh.
Laughter dissolves too many just resentments,
Pardons too many sins.

(798–99)

Imogen's resistance here grows out of her refusal to accept the kind of "happy ending" the play's patriarchal scheme affords her. To laugh would be an act of assent, of complicity in the "comedy"; it would constitute a relinquishing of the righteous, self-affirming rage, the "just resentment" that she wants to preserve. Her final words are

I will not laugh.
I must go home and make the best of it
As other women must.

Posthumus replies: "That's all I ask." and *"clasps her"* (799). The stage directions do not indicate her response to his gesture of affection/possession, and *"Cymbeline* Refinished" ends, with biting irony, by reverting to Shakespeare's Cymbeline's final speech about justice and peace between Romans and Britons.

When I discussed this renegotiated ending with students, some of them wished that Shaw had gone one step farther and allowed Imogen to leave her husband and father (rather like Ibsen's Nora) and go off on her own—to negotiate a new ending for herself, in effect. After talking about the text for a while, though, they decided that Shaw's ending makes a more compelling point. Imogen has become a representative of the great mass of unhappy wives who must "make the best of it"; the return to an idyllic bucolic life in the Welsh cave may be possible for her brothers, but it is a luxury society does not extend to married women. She, alas, is her husband's possession, and she must shed her liberating boy's clothes and "go home." Some of my students believed that Shaw's ending was not entirely without hope: perhaps, they said, she and Posthumus would negotiate a stronger, more equal marriage in the aftermath of their respective ordeals. Curiously, Iachimo "pleads" for Posthumus in these final moments of "*Cymbeline* Refinished":

> Let me plead for him.
> He has his faults; but he must suffer yours.
> You are, I swear, a very worthy lady;
> But still, not quite an angel.

(799)

Shaw is refuting the view of woman as angelic and idealized, a view that endeared *Cymbeline* to nineteenth-century readers like Swinburne. In place of the woman-on-the-pedestal, Shaw gives us a feisty, assertive and perhaps not altogether appealing Imogen, rather like his own heroines, a character who has to resign herself to the supposedly happy ending of conventional comedy. She has been transformed by her journey, her disguise, her suffering, and her new allegiances in ways that make her a very different woman than she was at the play's beginning, but Shakespearean comic structure cannot accommodate the character she has become. Shaw's ending is thus much more than a structural solution to an overly long and lumbering fifth act; it is a penetrating critique of comic resolutions.

In an essay that reviews the history of *Cymbeline* adaptations, Ann Thompson juxtaposes Shaw's transformation of the play's fifth act with another ending for Imogen, invented approximately fifty years earlier. The nineteenth-century actress Helen Faucit was motivated by the same kind of novelistic impulse to extend a character's life backward or forward from the play's time scheme as that which inspired Mary Cowden Clarke's "girlhoods." Faucit, however, imagines a future for Imogen, whom she called "Shakespeare's masterpiece." She views Imogen as a "delicate creature" whose "terrible ordeal" and "heart-sickness" cannot be as easily dismissed as Shakespeare's reunion scene would seem to suggest. Happiness comes to her "too late" and despite the efforts of the physician Cornelius, "the hurt [is] too deep for mortal leech-craft to heal. The 'piece of tender air' very gently, but very surely, will fade out like an exhalation of the dawn."[5] Faucit talks back from a perspective that is somewhat akin to Lillie Wyman's, in an appeal to female readers who would recognize the sensitivity of a woman who is strong and nurturing enough to help her brothers learn how to behave at court but unable to save herself from the pain inflicted by a male-dominated world. Like Shaw, she asks her readers whether they can accept an Imogen who can so quickly forgive her husband after all that has happened, and return to her former life unscathed.

Still another effort to imagine an expanded life for Imogen is proposed by Harriet Walter, one of the five actresses interviewed in *Clamorous Voices*. The actresses, reports Carol Rutter, "all construct past scenarios for their characters and even sometimes imagine their futures." Harriet Walter, for instance, explains that "the scenario I adopted to explain what had happened just before [*Cymbeline*] begins—the clandestine marriage—was that Imogen and Posthumus, in quite an arrogant way, saw themselves as representing everything that is good about Britain." She saw Imogen as a "rebel" who has "defied her King" and "taken the law into her own hands," a "very courageous, certain person . . . a decision maker."[6] What sort of future, one wonders, would Walter envision for her Imogen?

Changing attitudes toward marriage as the "happy ending" to which young women aspire have made it increasingly difficult to think of the ending of *Measure for Measure* in conventionally comic terms. We are more and more likely to feel that Isabella cannot possibly agree to marry the Duke—the silence Shakespeare gives her in act 5 almost certainly signifies a rejection of his proposal. When she does accept him, as in the 1989 New York production directed by Mark Lamos, she does so with an aggressiveness that, in its own way, threatens to undermine conventional assumptions about Shakespearean romantic comedy.[7] Shakespeare remains equally silent concerning Isabella's relationship to the sisterhood of St. Clare. In a scene dominated by various acts of closure, Isabella's future is left uncertain, and the contemporary reader may be quite inclined to feel that marriage—either to the Duke or to the church—would be unacceptable and inappropriate for the person she has become. Talking back to Shakespeare frequently takes the form of asking questions: What, we would like to ask him, did he expect us to make of Isabella's silence at the end of the play? Is her relief at seeing her brother alive overshadowed by her sense of having been cruelly and unnecessarily gulled? And is she consenting to marry the Duke, knowing that she will never entirely forgive him for his manipulative stage-managing, which is motivated, it would seem, by his assumption that he had the right to test and temper her virtue by exposing her to extreme grief and rage, casting her in the role of the Patient Grissell who endures all?

When I discussed these questions during rehearsals with an actress playing the role of Isabella in a student production,[8] she proposed a staging of the last scene that was radically different from the one the director finally decided upon. The director chose to have Isabella quietly leave the stage while the Duke was disposing of Lucio, after bidding a silent farewell to her brother and Mariana. The actress, however, wanted very much to talk back to Shakespeare by altering the blocking of the final scene. She envisioned an Isabella who defiantly and contemptuously rejects the Duke by walking away from him and allies herself with Lucio and his companions. This could have been a nihilistic *Measure for Measure* indeed; the chaste and high-principled would-be nun transformed into a cynical outlaw, rejecting not only the Duke who manipulated her and exposed her to needless suffering as the price of saving her brother's life, but also the church that had once seemed a place of refuge from the compromises of life in the world. This imagined Isabella has suffered a psychological rape more damaging than the physical rape from which she was rescued and, like many rape victims, will never again be able to regard men with respect and trust. So she opts for life among the comically carefree exploiters and exploited, the liars, prostitutes, and tricksters, transformed as she is by her role in the Duke's experiment. Moreover, she recognizes that Lucio, though a compulsive slanderer and boaster, was at least capable of sympathizing with her in her moment of greatest desperation ("O pretty Isabella, I am pale at mine heart to see thine eyes so red. . . ." [4.3.151–2]), and it is to him, finally, that she turns for fellowship.[9] The Duke Vincentio of this hypothetical production had his chance to gain freedom from his role as an authority figure and, disguised, engage in the courtship ritual unhampered by the trappings of power, as romance heroes and heroines so often do. But he misused that freedom, and as a result, finds himself publicly rejected as a suitor in the play's final moments.

Another way of staging the last scene would be to place Francesca the nun prominently onstage for the final scene and have Isabella leave the stage with her after silently rejecting the Duke's proposals. The Isabella I envision would be a young woman who, judging from her exchange with Francesca in act 1, scene 4, has sought out the cloister, with its highly regulated restrictions on speaking with men, as a way of bringing external controls to bear on this human frailty. Mary Cowden Clarke's portrait of Isabella's girlhood, entitled "The Votaress," suggests such a reading of Isabella's character. Her child Isabella is an orphan drawn to the convent where she has been adopted by a kind and sympathetic nun. Sister Aloysia tells Isabella that "I have frequently warned you against a warmth of indignation in your disposition which exists beneath your calm exterior—and which, if not watched and checked betimes, will become a serious evil." Cowden Clarke's prequel attempts to explain Isabella's choice by depicting the convent as a very positive place, emphasizing its intellectual and communicative side; Isabella describes Sister Aloysia to Claudio as

> never weary of answering my questions; never finding fault with me when I am stupid, and can't perceive her meaning at once; never caring how often she repeats an explanation, or in how many ways she re-words a sentence, if I am unable to make it out. And then she tells me such curious things, and so many of them, and encourages me to consider them with her, and to tell her, in return, if there is anything I don't understand in what she speaks of, that I could wish our three hours were twelve.[10]

Interestingly, this representation of the convent is similar to the actresses' image of it in *Clamorous Voices*. Both Paola Dionisotti, the Isabella in Barry Kyle's 1978 production, and Juliet Stevenson envision the convent as a place of fulfillment; Isabella, they feel, made a "positive choice," not to flee the world but to "avoid becoming its slave."[11] If Isabella cannot return to this all-female "place of fulfillment" at the end of her experiences in the corrupt world of the court, then her ending is arguably more tragic than comic.

Charles Marowitz's *Measure for Measure* collage, which was first performed in 1976, raises questions about the play that correspond, in intriguing ways, to the reactions of the graduate student actress and the freshman whose letter to Escalus was discussed in Chapter 2 (neither of whom had read or heard of Marowitz's play). As in his other collages, Marowitz proceeds by compression, reassignment of lines, and very explicit stage directions; for example, early in his play, the Duke drinks from a bottle he keeps in the arm of his throne as he describes his plan to the Bishop, a character who assumes parts of the roles of Friar Thomas and the Duke himself. Marowitz merges Isabella, Mariana, and the Juliet whom the Duke chides in act 2, scene 3 to create a complex victimized woman who sins with Angelo partly out of a desire to save her unworthy brother (stage directions indicate that Claudio tries to grab her in a *"lecherous embrace"* as he asks her to "save a brother's life")[12] but also because she seems attracted to him. Perhaps she momentarily believes Angelo when he says "Plainly conceive, I love you." Marowitz implies this by giving her Juliet's lines about her love for Claudio and herself. The play reaches a climax in a surreal sequence in which Isabella and Claudio *"desperately embrace,"* after which he leads her to Angelo's bed, from which she later arises, alone, to find Claudio's severed head staring at her from the desk (214–16).

If there is a "good" character in Marowitz's play it is Lucio, who calls himself "a looker-on here in Vienna" and is given other lines that originally belonged to the Duke as well as Friar Peter's role in act 4, scene 6. When he is bid to hold his peace at the end, it is because he is the only character who sympathizes with and tries to defend Isabella. This Lucio is akin to the one imagined by David Margolies in his critique of "Shakespeare as a hegemonic instrument": In challenging the way the Duke's authority is "mystified" and presented as "right" by a teaching establishment that uses Shakespeare to uphold "received wisdom," Margolies proclaims his sympathy with Lucio, who "has a warmth of friendship not shown elsewhere in the play," and who, by challenging authority and mocking the Duke, gives *Measure for Measure* a "subversive character."[13] It is this same subversiveness that appealed, I suspect, to the graduate student actress in her proposed staging of Isabella's final choice.

In Marowitz's version of act 5 everyone except Lucio—the Provost, Escalus, and the Bishop—is controlled by the Duke and they all silently assent to Angelo's denial of guilt. After the Duke condemns Isabella and sends her to prison (Shakespeare's lines 5.1.121) while delivering Angelo's speech (2.2.90–99) about how the law is now "awake," Angelo approaches Isabella and whispers the Duke's lines "I have a motion much imparts your good. . . ." She expressionlessly shoves away his hand and goes offstage conducted by the Provost, unwilling to negotiate further with a male conspiracy designed to corrupt and exploit her. Marowitz adds a final, festive scene in which the Duke, Angelo, and Escalus are drinking, laughing, and mimicking the lower classes. Angelo speaks some of Pompey's and Lucio's lines from earlier in the play, to which Escalus responds with Abhorson's line, "Fie upon him, he will discredit our mystery" (224). Marowitz's cynical appropriation of the word "mystery," which Abhorson had used to denote the elaborate art of executing prisoners in early modern England, talks back to Shakespeare's own appropriation of a word normally associated with religious belief or ritual practices. The "mystery," or art of these three, Marowitz makes quite clear, is corrupt politics of the most profligate and irresponsible variety, but the word carries with it a set of associations that slyly points to the way the ruling classes—then as now—mystify their practices and in so doing prevent public scrutiny.

Marowitz's transformation is bitterly satirical rather than potentially tragic in the way that a performance of Shakespeare's text could conceivably be. Peter Zadek's "notorious production" of *Measure for Measure*, performed in Bremen in 1967, was even more violent and cynical; clearly, it belonged very much to the sixties in its outrageous iconoclasm and utter rejection of the traditional image of Shakespeare as a champion of human dignity. Zadek recast the play so that

> the Duke was murdered by the people, Mistress Overdone took his place, [and] she had Angelo and Mariana executed and Isabella sent to a brothel. Zadek distrusted Shakespeare's justice. He also distrusted fine language and controlled gesture. Both were abandoned. For example, Isabella says to her brother Claudio: "If I hop into bed with Angelo, you're free, Claudyboy. You make me vomit, you're a beast, utter dirt."[14]

Translating the play into German freed Zadek to update the language in radical ways. Marowitz, by explicitly rejecting this option, may seem to be "vandalizing" or "trashing" Shakespeare to a lesser degree. His collages are in some ways more provocative, though, because they serve as reminders of the arbitrary connections between words and what they have come to signify.

Marowitz's comment on corrupt politics at the end of his *Measure for Measure* is no doubt an allusion to the final scene of Brecht's play *Roundheads and Peakheads*, which began as an adaptation of *Measure for Measure* and then evolved into a very different work. Written in the early 1930s, it is both more and less than an adaptation; as the title suggests, Brecht intended it to be a sardonic allegory about Jews and Aryans in Hitler's Germany. At times, it seems to have more in common with Charlie Chaplin's film *The Great Dictator* than it does with *Measure for Measure*.

Inspired by Shakespeare, Brecht begins *Roundheads and Peakheads* with the departure of an ineffectual Regent who, on the advice of his privy counselor, appoints a "dictator" to solve the pressing economic problems confronting the country of Yahoo and repress an incipient revolt by the Sickle party of disaffected peasants. Angelo Iberin is a man with a vision: He has recast the struggle between landlord and peasant as a conflict between crafty, foreign "hearth-profaning" peakheads and noble, worthy roundheads, the Czichs and Czuchs respectively.[15] The Claudio role is assigned to Emanuele De Guzman, a rich landlord who had seduced the peasant girl Nanna and then refused to give her the two horses he had promised her tenant farmer father, Callas. De Guzman's sister Isabella, who is about to enter a convent, provides Brecht with the opportunity for some savage anticlerical satire; his transformation of the exchange between Shakespeare's Isabella and the sister of St. Clare depicts the De Guzman family lawyer and the Mother Superior bickering over how much valuable property will accompany the young lady into the "sanctuary." Whereas lives hang in the balance in *Measure for Measure*, the two horses become the principal object of contention in *Roundheads and Peakheads*. As Isabella remarks to the

Mother Superior, "In all this business of the horses, we forgot my brother" (249). Arrested because he is a peakhead, and only incidentally because of his mistreatment of the peasants, De Guzman asks his sister to save him; and so the assignation with Angelo Iberin is arranged through an intermediary. Since Isabella and Iberin have never met onstage, this development seems rather arbitrarily imposed on the play. As one might expect, the substitution occurs: Nanna, now a prostitute, is ordered to take Isabella's place by Madame Cornamontis, her unscrupulous employer, who presides over the plot in lieu of Shakespeare's Duke and keeps most of the money. When the Regent returns in the final scene, he finds a trial in progress, with Callas disguised as De Guzman ("I was promised exemption from two years' rent if I would do this. I was told that the landlord would never be hung" [273]) and his daughter Nanna disguised as Isabella. The characters are unmasked, and the Regent releases De Guzman and orders Callas to return the horses and pay his rents. He then calls for dinner to be served to Iberin and the other rich landlords, both roundheads and peakheads, using the judge's bench as the dinner table. As the Regent offers a toast to "things as they are" (279) and declares that the scheme of Czuch and Czich is no longer necessary since the rebellious peasants have been put down, Brecht leaves the audience with the final image of a newly painted red sickle on a whitewashed wall.

Brecht's transformation of *Measure for Measure* is less a "counterplay" or refutation of Shakespeare's play than it is an appropriation of the plot elements for a rather different purpose.[16] Brecht is not talking back to Shakespeare in the way that Marowitz does; rather, he is incorporating traces of *Measure for Measure* into his own independent drama, after the fashion of other writers who use Shakespeare allusions throughout their works. It is not necessary to know *Measure for Measure* in order to read *Roundheads and Peakheads*, and were it not for the names Angelo and Isabella, the Shakespeare connection could conceivably go unnoticed. And yet, like Marowitz, Brecht has altered our reading of *Measure for Measure* by intensifying our uneasiness about the distribution of justice. He thus invites some questions concerning Shakespeare's intentions that might not have otherwise arisen: What *about* the role of class in the unfolding of events? Will Pompey and Mistress Overdone and the prostitutes remain in prison while Claudio and Angelo go free? Has the Duke made any significant or lasting change in the social-sexual-economic environment that produced the bawdy houses? Does Brecht's merging of Juliet and Mariana into the much larger Nanna role suggest a pointed mockery of Shakespeare's shadowy characterization of these two potentially interesting women? Or perhaps, do these transformations imply that young unmarried women in Juliet's and Mariana's situations are more likely to end up like Nanna than they are to marry gentlemen and live happily ever after?

Brecht's appropriation of *Measure for Measure* seizes upon Isabella's words "Hark how I'll bribe you" (in her first conversation with Angelo in act 2, scene 2). These, one could argue, represent a recklessness with language on her part that contributes to the play's abrupt shift into the realm of corruption and manipulation. Characters repeatedly offer and accept bribes in *Roundheads and Peakheads*, for this is a cynical world filled with calculating and manipulative people, none of whom exhibit the self-awareness one senses in Angelo and Isabella. Brecht is finally less interested in the individual characters than he is in the larger social and political forces at play in his allegorical drama. He viewed *Measure for Measure* as Shakespeare's most "progressive" play, one that required those in power to be measured as they measure.[17] In his version, the rebellion, presumably, will continue, and the temporarily repressed peasants will eventually triumph, an event that is of far greater significance than the futures of Isabella and Nanna.

The ironically titled *All's Well That Ends Well* has long been perceived as a 'difficult' play, one that presents exceedingly mixed signals to readers, directors, and audiences, particularly in the way it ends. After centuries of relative obscurity, *All's Well That Ends Well* is attracting attention among Shakespeareans—the play J. L. Styan, writing in 1984, said "has had no theatrical history worth mentioning until a few years ago."[18] *All's Well's* curious status in the canon can be attributed, at least in part, to Helena's character, and the way her role runs counter to long-held comic expectations. Trevor Nunn, director of the Royal Shakespeare Company's 1981 *All's Well*, believed that its legendary unpopularity "stemmed from the fact that Helena is a woman who gets what she is after"; so reported Harriet Walker, as she spoke about her performance as Helena in that production. Walter observed that while Helena "has a wonderful capacity almost instantly to win the hearts of other people," such as the Countess, the King, the Widow, and Diana, she is also "manipulative," "very intense," " obsessive," "not someone you'd like to have at a dinner party" (unlike, say, Rosalind or Beatrice).[19]

Helena has been likened by an unsympathetic critic to two of Shakespeare's more ambiguous male characters, Duke Vincentio and Prospero;[20] Susan Snyder, rather more sympathetically, remarks that Helena "acts as her own Oberon to bring about her own order."[21] But without Oberon's magic, she lacks the ability to transform people as thoroughly and neatly as he can: the magical "cure" the King experiences is ironically juxtaposed with Bertram's stubborn refusal to be transformed into the admiring and devoted lover. And unlike these male counterparts, Helena frequently seems to be "driven by Venus," to use Susan Snyder's phrase, in ways that set her apart from her cooler and more delightfully virginal companions in the roster of Shakespearean heroines.[22]

Helena's decision to use her father's prescriptions to accomplish her goal seems like a comic device, the assertive action of an intelligent heroine, but in retrospect, it may look more like a tragic mistake. This mistake is compounded by that of the King, who, according to one line of interpretation, may have been violating Bertram's rights as a ward. In his study of the *All's Well* story from Boccaccio to Shakespeare, Howard Cole suggests that Elizabethan and Jacobean audiences would have felt that the King violates Bertram's rights as a ward by marrying him against his will to Helena. Cole begins by quoting from an "Apology of the House of Commons" dated 20 June 1604, which deals with wards and complains of the "great grievance and damage of the subject, to the decay of many houses and disabling of them to serve their prince and country" resulting from the "great mischief" occasioned by "forced and ill-suited marriages"; the document calls for "the restitution of this original right in disposing of our children."[23] Bertram's opening lines, "now in ward, evermore in subjection" (1.1.5), Cole adds, "would have suggested nothing good to the Elizabethan audience," accustomed as they were to seeing guardianships bought and sold for quick profits. Other contemporary documents, such as the 1607 tract "The Miseries of Inforst Marriage," attest to the topicality of this aspect of *All's Well*. Cole suspects that Shakespeare's audience might have found the King's sentiments on true nobility (2.3.117ff) unconvincing, inasmuch as these are customarily invoked by lovers to justify their own choices, not "enforced choice."[24]

Thus, when Bertram insists that he "cannot love [Helena] nor will strive to do't" (2.3.145), his refusal might initially inspire a certain amount of sympathy. Hearing this, Helena immediately attempts to withdraw from the bargain she has struck with the King: "That you are well restored, my lord, I'm glad. / Let the rest go" (note the emphatic four-beat line). But the King refuses to let go: "My honor's at the stake, which to defeat, I must produce my power." (2.3.48–50). Helena has unwittingly unleashed the dangerous forces of masculine pride—and in a monarch, no less. Harriet Walter described this moment in the 1981 *All's Well* quite vividly:

> I left the ballroom and had to be dragged back in. When the King brings us together I want the ground to open up; it has gone desperately wrong, and this

is not what I want. But now male pride has taken over: the King's honour is at stake. He has been defied, so he forces the marriage through. At that moment both Helena and Bertram are victims of his power and hate it.[25]

Bertram, as Janet Adelman remarks, is in an "impossible dilemma: he must leave his family to become a man, and yet he can take his full place as a man in this society only insofar as he can be reconciled with his mother and the king."[26]

The idea that an irreversible "mistake" occurs early in the play, cutting off all hope of an unambiguous happy ending, is at odds with *All's Well's* folklore origins. In a sense, *All's Well* enacts a sustained and ironic interrogation of the conventional situation in which a Clever Wench is given a riddling quest, successfully accomplishes it, and wins the prize. With its dark, bawdy humor, its unwieldy, belabored subplot, and its dependence on the bedtrick, this play would seem an unlikely candidate for popular adaptation for young readers, particularly in eras when standards of decorum were high. And yet it is one of the fascinating features of *All's Well*'s afterlife that it attracted the attention of three nineteenth-century British women writers, who used the principal creative outlet available to them—the production of accessible prose Shakespeare variations for children and/or "young ladies"—in order to render the play more acceptable and understandable as a romantic comedy. Charles and Mary Lamb's *Tales from Shakespeare* (1807) introduced Shakespeare's plays to generations of children and continues to be widely available in bookstores and libraries. Charles had first pick of the plays, leaving his sister to adapt some of the less well-known ones, including *All's Well*. Nearly a century later, Edith Nesbit published her *Twenty Beautiful Stories from Shakespeare.* Cowden Clarke seems to have been initially attracted to Shakespeare's most assertive heroines: "Helena: The Physician's Orphan" was the third of her fifteen separately published tales, later collected as the three volume *The Girlhood of Shakespeare's Heroines.* Taken together, these three texts constitute a brief cultural history of the adaptability of Shakespeare's plots and characters to the social agendas of a century that took seriously its responsibility to edify and provide models of behavior for youthful readers while introducing them to the classics.

The Lambs' *Tales from Shakespeare* was intended primarily for "young ladies" who had been denied access to Shakespeare's "manly book." Susan Wolfson observes that by 1809 the second edition of the *Tales from Shakespeare* was "being marketed as a conduct manual" designed for "young ladies advancing to the state of womanhood."[27] Lamb suppresses all mention of getting a child in her version of Bertram's letter to Helena, so that the ring becomes the sole object of the quest (here she

is following a stage tradition begun by John Philip Kemble in 1794).[28]
Accordingly, when Helena spends the night with Bertram in Diana's
chamber, it is a night of "conversation" rather than the strict silence
demanded by Shakespeare's Diana. Bertram is "delighted" by Helena's
conversation, as Lamb describes the offstage event.

> Bertram never knew how sensible a lady Helena was, else perhaps he would
> not have been so regardless of her; and seeing her every day, he had entirely
> overlooked her beauty; a face we are accustomed to see constantly losing the
> effect which is caused by the first sight either of beauty or of plainness; and
> of her understanding it was impossible he should judge, because she felt such
> reverence, mixed with her love for him, that she was always silent in his pres-
> ence; but now that her future fate and the happy ending of all her love pro-
> jects, seemed to depend upon her leaving a favorable impression on the mind
> of Bertram from this night's interview, she exerted all her wit to please him;
> and the simple graces of her lively conversation and the endearing sweetness
> of her manners so charmed Bertram that he vowed she should be his wife.[29]

The message to young ladies, apparently, is that young gentlemen are
won over by conversational skills, a form of attractiveness that can be
acquired through study and effort. But the message to the prospective
reader of Shakespeare's *All's Well* goes deeper, implying that a marriage
founded on communication, companionship, and respect is indeed possible between Bertram and Helena. The bed trick acquires a far more
important consequence than getting Helena with child: it frees her
from the repressive silence her gender and social status have imposed
by explicitly and completely transforming the imagined scene from a
wordless coupling to an opportunity for Helena to find her voice. As
Wolfson concludes in the final sentence of her essay, Lamb's narratives
"anticipate, and in some cases correspond to, modern feminist explanations" of the aspirations, resourcefulness, and self-images of Shakespeare's heroines.[30]

The feminist explanation is somewhat qualified by Lamb's final pronouncement, however. After describing the fifth act events at Rousillion, Lamb's narrative voice concludes:

> Thus Helena at last found that her father's legacy was indeed sanctified by
> the luckiest stars in heaven; for she was now the beloved wife of her dear
> Bertram, the daughter–in–law of her noble mistress, and herself the Count-
> ess of Rousillon.[31]

Lamb has highlighted Helena's orphic couplets in act 2, scene 1,
advising the King that

Inspired merit so by breath is barr'd.
It is not so with Him that all things knows
As 'tis with us that square our guess by shows;
But most it is presumption in us when
The help of heaven we count the act of men.
Dear sir, to my endeavors give consent,
Of heaven, not me, make an experiment.

(149–54)

The "luckiest stars in heaven" (Lamb avoids mentioning God directly), to which the heroine's ingenuity is discreetly subordinated, have brought about a happy ending, with no hint of discord.

Edith Nesbit, like Lamb, edited the text of Bertram's letter so that it reads, "When you can get the ring from my finger you can call me husband, but against that 'when' I write 'never.'"[32] Her version of the bed trick in *Twenty Beautiful Stories from Shakespeare* substitutes the cutting of a lock of hair for the getting of a child. This bowdlerized act of violation/appropriation takes place in "a dark room"; Helena does not "speak a single word" as Bertram

> came with a sharp knife and felt a sweet face touch his as he cut off the lock of hair, and he left the room satisfied, like a man who is filled with renown, and on his finger was a ring which the girl in the dark room had given him. (280)

The language is tinged with sexual suggestion and draws, perhaps unwittingly, on folklore traditions that equate cuttings of hair with the very essence of a person's being. Nesbit's version of the play's final moments frames Betram's and Helena's dialogue with a moralizing narrative gloss. Helen "held up the ancestral ring. 'Now that I have this, said she, will you love me, Bertram?' 'To the end of my life,' cried he" (285). The narrator's final sentence begins "His pride was now in shreds. . . ." This version of the happy ending implies a submissiveness on Betram's part that is reminiscent of the woman's role as exemplified by Kate in *The Taming of the Shrew*. In a comment on the juxtaposed plots (Nesbit, unlike Lamb, retains the comic subplots in her adaptations), the narrator had observed earlier that Parolles's behavior had "taught Bertram that the soldier who had been impudent enought to call Helena his "kicky-wicky" was far less courageous than a wife" (280). The chastened Bertram, whose blindness to Helena's virtues had its parodic counterpart in Parolles's blindfold, now has the ability to *see* his wife as others have seen her. Without committing herself to this interpretation, Nesbit leaves open the possible reading that the pride that had confined him has fallen away in shreds so that he can grow. The narrator finishes the last sentence with "and it is believed he made a husband of some sort after all" (285).

It is difficult to know how to read Nesbit's casual qualifier, "a husband of some sort." Perhaps she could not resist the temptation to reveal her own skepticism about husbands and marriage; an independent and resourceful professional writer whose popular and highly regarded children's books supported her ever-growing family and large household, she (and her husband) held a "modern" view of marriage. Through the Fabian society she met George Bernard Shaw, who became one of her lovers and a lifelong friend.[33] Were she unconstrained by commercial considerations and the sensibilities of a youthful readership, Nesbit's heroine might have been closer to the Helena whom Shaw likened to Nora in *A Doll's House*,[34] a woman who would presumably either leave Bertram at the end of act 5 or else make it clear that she will live with him very much on her own terms.

Because Mary Cowden Clarke's "girlhood" narratives are "prequels" rather than adaptations, she was able to avoid the task of reconciling Helena's arguably unladylike strategies with nineteenth-century sensibilities. After the fashion of the nineteenth-century novelist, Cowden Clarke develops her tales slowly and with much attention to pictorial detail and character description, in sharp contrast to the stripped-down narratives of Lamb and Nesbit. As she does in her story of Lady Macbeth (Chapter 3), Cowden Clarke reaches back into the previous generation, devoting much of her tale to Helena's mother Gabrielle, an idealized farmer's daughter, who attracts the attention of Gerard, a banker's son. Their courtship flourishes in secret, until he defies class distinctions and breaks with his parents in order to marry her. Theirs is a beautifully romanticized union, accompanied by revealing narrative comments about the wife as a man's "bosom-friend" and "the crown of his existence," the inspiration and "anchor" responsible for his successes:

> In the clear mind of such a wife, a man secures aid in forming his own judgments; in the natural good sense of such a woman, a man finds support and encouragement in taking enlarged views of life; he rises superior to petty evils; he gains strength of mind, and moral courage; he learns to eschew prejudice, to avoid enmities, to conquer difficulties, to achieve fame, to win honor and consideration, to earn independence; she at once induces and graces his advancement. (I:203)

This perfect marriage gradually withers, however; for as Gerard devotes himself more and more singlemindedly to his profession, Gabrielle weakens and suffers from neglect in Narbonne, longing for the "purity and peace" of the rustic farm where the couple first met.

Meanwhile, the child Helena shows early signs of the stubborn determination that will later distinguish her in her adulthood.

> Helena was singularly given to persist in any point that she had once resolved upon; and without being either obstinate or wilful, she was remarkable for perseverance, and unswerving pursuit of that upon which she had once set her heart. (230)

This quality is illustrated by a little episode in which she brings nosegays from the market each day to the crusty old doctor who had taught Gerard his craft, gradually breaking down his solitary indifference and winning his friendship. Cowden Clarke remarks in a brief preface that her intention was "to place the heroines in such situations as should naturally lead up to, and account for, the known conclusion of their subsequent character and after-fate" (iv). Accordingly, each fictional incident is designed to exhibit the main characters' distinctive traits; Cowden Clarke operates on the assumption that such characteristics evidence themselves in early childhood, determining, rather than being determined by, youthful experiences.

Helena and Bertram are brought together as childhood playmates, and it is immediately evident that he is "rough and selfish," as described by his "Bonne," who makes an important distinction between the "indulgence" which does not "spoil" a "good heart" and "grateful disposition" and the unfortunate outcome that results when "too much power entrusted to childish hands is injudiciously fostering native haughtiness, caprice, and selfishness, and encouraging tyranny" (237). Cowden Clarke is clearly using her tales to advise parents on the upbringing of children, a preoccupation of the Victorian era that had no counterpart in Shakespeare's time. A telling incident occurs during Helena's stay at Rousillon when the young Maudlin Lafeu comes to visit. Cowden Clarke seems to have been trying to make sense of Lafew's unexpected request for Bertram as a husband for his daughter in the fifth act of *All's Well*. She also found a good use for another young woman to contrast with Helena. Maudlin asks to go fishing and Bertram is vexed that he had carelessly broken and lost his new fishing rod a few days earlier. Unbeknownst to him, Helena had pursued the fishing rod down the stream and with much persistence and at some risk had contrived to rescue it. She repaired the rod and kept it until Maudlin's request provided an opportunity for her to present it to him. But the more Maudlin praises Helena's resourcefulness, the more hostile Bertram becomes:

> "If you go on praising it so, you'll make me detest it, instead of teaching me to feel grateful for it;" said he. "I hate things or people that are belauded and

cried up by every one. My mother tells me so much of Helena's good behaviour that I'm rather sick of it; and now you are doing the same, and giving me a downright surfeit of her merits. She's well enough, but she's no such paragon, as you'd all make her out to be."

Maudlin replies, "You are a spoilt young man" and offers to "reform him"—a characteristically female posture in Victorian fiction (262–63).

If Helena were simply the perfect child of modest origins in contrast to the spoiled, upper-class Bertram, the narrative would not accomplish its avowed purpose—to account for her 'subsequent character' in Shakespeare's play. Using the dying father's parting words as her vehicle, Cowden Clarke articulates the positive and negative potential in Helena's distinctive personality, with one eye on her young readers to make sure they absorb the lesson.

"You possess firmness, steadfastness, constancy, my child," said he; "beware that they become not hardness, unrelentingness, obstinacy. You have perseverance, indefatigable and indomitable courage in pursuing an object that you conceive to be right; be well assured that the object you seek is right, lest your perseverance involve you in evil, and your courage be but rash encounter of peril and ultimate wrong. Your spirit of persistence may be productive of the highest good, so that you let it not degenerate into obstinacy, wilfulness, or headstrong, irrational inflexibility. Be sure that your motives are pure, your means innocent, and your aim a hallowed one, and then give full scope to your native disposition; then let nothing abate your courage, then pursue the dictates of your own resolved heart unswervingly, unflinchingly, invincibly. I have that faith in your nature,—which is essentially loving and generous, as well as persistive,—that gives me confidence, you will secure your own welfare, win your own happiness." (274)

Gerard's speech is an especially interesting passage, for it briefly opens up the possibility of an unsympathetic reading of Helena's plotting, one concluding that her "persistive" nature does indeed "degenerate into obstinacy, wilfulness, or headstrong, irrational inflexibility." At a time when Shakespeare criticism frequently consisted of extravagant praise of the master's artistry, this effort to explore, at least tentatively, the ambiguities and contradictions with which Shakespeare endowed a character reveals a critical mind at work, using an unconventional vehicle for her analysis of the character. These speculations about Helena's persistence, especially when juxtaposed with the narrator's earlier description of her as "stable in resolve; faithful in duty; invincible in attachment; and . . . as full of womanly sweetness and gentleness, as if her character were not compounded of such firm elements" (264), invite comparison with Susan Snyder's remark that Helena confuses us with her "shifts between assertion and self-abnegation." These shifts open "a gap which prevents full understanding" for the reader to "fill in with your own assumptions and needs, as you like it."[35] Good Victorian that she was, Cowden Clarke would never have acknowledged gaps of this sort in Shakespeare, even though her tales do in a sense constitute acts of filling in.

Were a contemporary feminist writer for young people to take liberties with Shakespeare comparable to those taken by Lamb, Nesbit, and Cowden Clarke, we might have available to us a different version of the play, with a very provocative variation on the comic happy ending. It is worth noting that while children's versions of Shakespeare abound, they are essentially conservative in nature. Although the writers will alter the text to achieve brevity and attempt to make sense of the action in acceptable ways (Bernard Miles's children's version of *Macbeth*, for instance, attributes as much of the unpleasantness as possible to the witches[36]), they are less likely to appropriate the plays for their own purposes, or to construct re-visions that function overtly as interpretations. Moreover, our modern egalitarian avoidance of gender distinctions has caused us to pay less attention to the way young girls encountering *All's Well* for the first time might respond to it. These three nineteenth-century *All's Well* variations, while admittedly naive and old-fashioned in certain respects, are strikingly contemporary in another: they proceed from the assumption that a male-authored text requires some revision before it can speak convincingly to female readers.

The 1981 Moshinsky film of *All's Well* for the BBC series brought the play to the attention of a larger audience than had ever seen it before. In keeping with the series' stated intention of presenting the plays virtually uncut and with few departures from the text, the film made a fairly explicit commitment to a happy ending for Helena and Bertram. Kenneth Rothwell's *Shakespeare Quarterly* review observed that,

> Angela Down plays Helena as if she were possessed, a witch in fact. The plain, spinsterish, puritanical face with the unruly strands of hair conceals a volcanic disposition, a point nicely punctuated when Down's Helena exchanges an erotic kiss with the King of France.[37]

When I showed this film to my students in 1990, many were surprisingly hostile toward Helena. A few students—some, but not all of them male—loudly proclaimed Helena to be a "bitch" in fact; in their opinion, she should never have pursued the unresponsive Bertram, for she succeeded only in bringing about a miserable marriage for them both. Preoccupied as they undoubtedly were with their own courtship experiences and the unspoken conventions of American university culture, these students seemed to feel threatened, somehow, by what they saw as Helena's self-destructive aggressiveness and unwillingness to "take no for an answer."

When I taught the play in an introductory Shakespeare course a year or so later, many students seemed troubled by what they viewed as Helena's devious scheming. Several response journals (written before I discussed the play in class) spoke disapprovingly of the way she "trapped" Bertram, and one student commented that this was "the wrong thing to do." Another proclaimed that "two wrongs do not make a right: Bertram shouldn't have left Helena abruptly, but tricking him into fathering a child isn't right either." Three or four used the phrase "the end justifies the means," a corollary, they seemed to think, to "all's well that ends well." And for some, this "message" was clearly a questionable one. A male student who said "Helena's love becomes tainted with pure obsession" felt that by the end she had become "a calculating countess out to claim her trophy." Several other journals described Helena as obsessed, and some writers also felt that Helena changed for the worse during the course of the play; as one very thoughtful essay remarked, "Helena turned out to be too scheming for the character I initially took her for." But she liked seeing the woman as "the dominant protagonist for a change" and observed that "the ending is ambiguous; Helena, trying so hard throughout to deserve Bertram, seems to realize at the end that she deserved far more than he had to offer, and that he's not a changed man, just a cornered one." Another wondered if "after Helena turns into a scheming, deceiving woman who resorts to bribing, the audience would have seen her as being punished for her arrogance and aggressiveness." A young woman who admitted that "I'm a bit of a schemer too" said that she "liked the way Helena got what she deserved." Still another said "like Iago, she works to achieve her goals; like Petruchio, she relentlessly pursues and conquers her spouse. I don't like her because she's manipulative, but she interests me."

Many of these writers expressed great indignation in their first readings, in accents reminiscent of the first readers quoted in Chapter 1. "Why didn't Helena realize that forcing herself on Bertram wouldn't make him love her? Has she no pride?" asked one young woman. "I was disgusted by Bertram—he's a wimp and a sucker—and I thought Helena could do better," said another. A young man was bothered by Helena's "utter stupidity": How could she fall for Bertram and then, in the face of his abusiveness and cruelty, "put up with him"? Another said that "I can't believe a woman, even in those times, would act as Helena does. It just seems impossible for me to see how you can be told to your face that you are not wanted and later on forget those words and say All's Well That Ends Well." And another said that when Bertram rejected Helena publicly, "At this point I would have realized that I was not really wanted." The irritation these three young men expressed at Helena's willingness to be mistreated was revealing, I felt; these readers may not be able to recognize her strength of character and devotion, but their reading has something in common with a feminist defense of the woman characters' right to equal and dignified treatment.

A very few students expressed some qualified sympathy for Bertram. "Everyone is dead set against him, even his own mother," a male student exclaimed. Two young women defended Bertram ("Why should he be forced into a marriage because the King wants to return a favor?") and a third, during class discussion, spoke out against "Bertram-bashing." A young man who asked "How unfair can you get?" added, "If he doesn't marry her he is going against the King's word and if he does he has a sad life ahead of him married to a woman he doesn't love." One male writer noted that whereas "Portia finally straightens Bassanio out, Helena, by contrast, is simply making Bertram's life miserable."

Some journals talked back explicitly, offering advice or proposed improved endings. One young man wished that Helena could have let Bertram go, and then "picked another husband," or that, conversely, "Bertram could have tried to make the relationship work." "If I were to write an ending," said another male student, "I'd have both Helena and Diana leave him standing there in his guilt." A young woman said wistfully that "I was hoping that Helena would not end up with Bertram." For many of these writers, starting over was "the normal choice," to appropriate Lillie Wyman's phrase; they inhabit a culture in which no one needs to be paired forever with an unwanted spouse, or indeed, any spouse at all. Another student put it this way, "If this was true and she was around today, I would tell her that looks are only skin deep and to find a new man." The "if"s of this response echo the King's curiously tentative epilogue: "All is well ended, if this suit be won." (This is the fourth occurrence of the word "if" during the last few moments of the play.) A resisting reader might well ask what, if anything, Helena, has "won" and at what price.

Overall, the majority of the class seemed dissatisfied with All's Well and quite willing to comment on what they saw as the play's shortcomings in comparison with the six other plays they had read. "The Epilogue neatly ends a rather messy affair," one student remarked sardonically, and many others said, quite assertively, that all is certainly not well at the end of the play. Their reservations clearly grew, at least in part, out of their own feelings about relationships and self-esteem. One young woman tried to reconcile her own feelings with her interpretation of the play: "Helena is indeed successful at the end, though I personally wouldn't feel that all was well knowing all that had hap-

pened before the end." The Moshinsky film, which ends with a peni-
tent-looking Bertram tenderly kissing Helena, changed a few minds,
but only a few. A majority continued to doubt Bertram's sincerity, and
stuck to their ironic and quite critical readings of the play.

Not long ago a news item announced that Blondie Bumstead, wife of
Dagwood and quintessential cartoon housewife for fifty-eight years,
has taken a job outside the home. Blondie's decision, said King Features Syndicate Group, is "the biggest thing to happen to an American
icon since Superman got married." Blondie "always seems to come up
with the right thing to do," said another cartoonist, speaking of the cartoon strip read by 250 million people around the world.[38] And the right
thing for women to do in the 1980s and 1990s, clearly, has been to go to
work, preferably in challenging, interesting, life-enhancing careers.
All's Well invites us to fill up the gaps in Helena's life by sending her
off to practice medicine as her father did, using his famous "medicine
chest" with the lifetime accumulation of prescriptions and unguents
and distillations Cowden Clarke describes (275). The last "task" of his
life, she writes, was that of "acquainting his daughter with the contents
of the box, and of making her mistress of the numerous valuable secrets
belonging to each." When this is accomplished, he breathes his "parting breath with . . . satisfaction" (276). Freed of the father, and possessed of his knowledge, Helena's life can now truly begin. I can imagine a "subversive" ending to *All's Well* that, as Snyder suggests,
displays the emergence of a "self-confirming female friendship" linking the three strong women who exert control over the final scene[39] but
that concludes by going beyond this to suggest an independent future
for Helena as a doctor. At the end of the last scene she would quite
explicitly reject what Cole calls Bertram's "psychologically and emotionally fraudulent" promise[40] to love her "dearly, ever dearly" and
would pick up the medicine chest, square her shoulders, and go off to
bring about more miraculous cures. If the play were being modernized
and transformed, she might announce her intention to go to medical
school, or join the Peace Corps, leaving a speechless and chastened
Bertram and his mother in charge of the newborn child. Charles
Marowitz, in defending his own Shakespeare transformations, spoke of
the way a play can "cooperate in its own seduction." When this happens, he says, "both director and material are permitted to have their
fling. If the play refuses to play along, obviously, the honorable course
is to desist."[41] Like *Measure for Measure*, *All's Well* does seem to cooperate in its own seduction, for it has already begun the journey away
from comic happy endings and thus is highly susceptible to a firm
directorial shove. Indeed, a transformed *All's Well* might go a step further than the one I have just envisioned: Suppose Helena were to leave

Rousillion to pursue her medical career abroad while pretending to be a pilgrim to the shrine of Saint James, and Bertram, hearing of her eventual fame as a physician, were to attempt to win her back via a modified version of the bed trick? This *All's Well* scenario might lead to the kind of unhappy ending Ervine envisioned for his Portia; Helena would return to Rousillion to take up her responsibilities as wife, mother, and countess, all the while longing for the independent and fulfilling life she had briefly enjoyed as a professional woman. Rather like Césaire's Prospero and Caliban, husband and wife would remain locked in a mutually destructive relationship for the rest of their lives.

The ending I have proposed for *All's Well* would resolve some of the play's ambiguities but in doing so would introduce new questions, new ambiguities, reflecting another culture's most intensely debated social issues. It would also point to the shortcomings inherent in traditional assumptions about comedy and tragedy. Talking back to Shakespeare frequently takes the form of changing—or wanting to change—the ending; often, we can accept a play's peculiar logic, its artifice, its impossible symmetries and coincidences, until we get to the final disposition of the characters' lives, the point at which their "futures" become fixed, unchangeable, or, as in the tragedies, foreclosed.

Goodnight Desdemona (Good Morning Juliet) tackles these issues head-on, from an explicitly feminist perspective. First produced in Toronto in 1988, it was subsequently revised and won Canada's Governor General's Award for Drama in 1990. This Shakespeare offshoot is a time-travel fantasy that pokes fun at the foibles of academia. Its protagonist is Constance Ledbelly, a pathetically unself-confident university lecturer laboring over a thesis entitled "*Romeo and Juliet* and *Othello*: The Seeds of Corruption and Comedy." Constance is not alone in her inclination to see *Romeo and Juliet* as "comedy gone awry, when a host of comic devices is pressed into the blood-soaked service of tragic ends."[42] Like the students quoted in Chapter 1 (albeit in more florid language), she finds herself exclaiming "O Othello, O Tragic Man, stop your ears against the false yapping of that cur, Iago" (16). As Constance sits in her office, reading aloud from her thesis, an ingenious academic argument emerges:

> what if a Fool were to enter the world of both "Othello" and "Romeo and Juliet"? Would he be akin to the Wise Fool in "King Lear"?: a Fool who can comfort and comment . . . the Fool is conspicuous by his very absence, for these two tragedies turn on flimsy mistakes—a lost hanky, a delayed wedding announcement—mistakes too easily concocted and corrected by a Wise Fool. (21)

In a preposterous parody of textual scholarship, Constance announces:

> I postulate that the Gustav Manuscript, when finally decoded, will prove the prior existence of two comedies by an unknown author; comedies that Shakespeare plundered and made over into ersatz tragedies! (21)

Suddenly a "Warp" effect pulls her into her office wastebasket, Alice-in-Wonderland style, and into the *Othello* world; this is MacDonald's adaptation of the time-travel strategy of introducing a traveler from the present into the closed system of a complete text. Unlike the other transformations I have been discussing, *Goodnight* calls attention to and enacts its own interventions, by having as its protagonist the author, or unwitting agent, of change, rather than one of Shakespeare's characters. Thus, when Constance finds herself in the middle of *Othello*, she impulsively interrupts the dialogue and "*plucks the handkerchief from IAGO's hose and hands it to OTHELLO.*" As Othello "*proceeds to bind and threaten IAGO*" she realizes with horror: "I've wrecked a masterpiece. I've ruined the play, / I've turned Shakespeare's 'Othello' to a farce" (30).

When Desdemona enters, it becomes immediately clear that her character has undergone a change. She speaks her lines "That I love my lord to live with him, / my downright violence and storm of fortunes / may trumpet to the world" and then, in MacDonald's re-vision, adds,

> My sole regret—
> that heaven had not made me such a man;
> but next in honour is to be his wife.
> And I love honour more than life!
>
> (32)

A cannon blast sounds, and Desdemona drags the unwilling Constance off to "enjoy the fray" and "acquire a taste for blood" (36–37). "Learn to kill," she advises Constance, "we be women; not mice." Constance has a soliloquy, in which she asks herself "have I permanently changed the text?" (37). Her interference, clearly, has sent the play off in a new direction; the next scene opens with Iago in soliloquy vowing revenge upon "the bookish mouse"; he'll tell Desdemona that Constance is a spy and whore, for she is "of a free and noble nature / that thinks men honest that but seem to be" (39). MacDonald's portrayal of Desdemona makes sense of her scornful refusal to be "left behind, a moth of peace" (1.3.225–26); in this new context, she is indeed a "fair warrior" (2.1.182), one who reacts indignantly when Constance tells her that "Academe / believes that you're a doomed and helpless victim" (41). But she also shares her husband's frailties; these become only too evident when she proves herself to be just as gullible and violent as her husband, once Iago succeeds in convincing Desdemona that Constance is that most transgressive of female knowledge-seekers, a witch, and a seductress, besides.

In the final burst of swordplay and confusion with which the scene ends, Constance narrowly escapes being skewered by Desdemona as the "Warp" effect transports her to Verona. The Constance of act 3, scene 1 has somehow lost her skirt and enters wearing *"long johns, boots and tweed jacket"* as the duel between Tybalt and Mercutio is getting under way. Constance *"tackles"* Romeo just as he *"is about to fatally intervene in the sword fight,"* and together they knock Tybalt and Mercutio apart (52). She thus transforms *Romeo and Juliet* by preventing the action from veering off into tragedy. Predictably, she is mistaken for a "boy"; thinking fast, she rechristens herself Constance. In a burst of asssertive speech-making Constantine does what many readers long to do: she announces that "young Juliet and Romeo have wed . . . and so you fellows should shake hands." Amazingly, they do. In an ironic re-vision of Shakespeare's quintessential love story, Juliet and Romeo have tired of one another after "one hot swift night," and Romeo goes off "to find the lovely Greek boy Constantine" to whom he has taken a fancy (56). Juliet, meanwhile, confesses to her nurse that she's ready to "die of tedium" and prays to the god Hymen to "Make me a maid again!" (59) Comic gender-confusion follows at the Capulets' masked ball (now Romeo and Juliet's wedding party); Juliet, like her husband, is attracted to Constantine, and in a private colloquy with "him" she reveals her conviction that love is inherently tragic: "the readiness to die doth crown true love" (66). Juliet's passion for death, evidently, is her comic obsession, an obsession from which Constance will try to free her.

The play degenerates into silliness and confusion from this point on, and though it would be tempting to see this as MacDonald's comment on the improbable complications and mistaken identities of *Othello* and *Romeo and Juliet*, parody for its own sake threatens to overwhelm the play's feminist agenda. MacDonald regains control of the action at the very end, when Constance finally asserts herself, and delivers a long scolding oration to both Juliet and Desdemona:

I've had it with all the tragic tunnel vision around here. You have no idea what—life is a hell of a lot more complicated than you think! Life—real life— is a big mess . . . Desdemona, I thought you were different: I thought you were my friend, I worshipped you. But you're just like Othello—gullible and violent. Juliet, if you really loved me, you wouldn't want me to die. But you were more in love with death, 'cause death is easier to love. . . .

Because Constance has emerged from the crucible of experience a stronger, more self-confident woman and scholar, she is able to empower Juliet and Desdemona to rewrite their fates, to open up and renegotiate their endings. Through their felt sisterhood with her, they learn to eschew violence and suicide for perseverance in the messiness of life.

> *Desdemona:* Could any fool reveal, how we were wont to err?
> *Juliet:* Or get us to concede, what we will gladly swear?
> *Constance:* What's that?
> *Desdemona:* To live by questions, not by their solution.
> *Juliet:* To trade our certainties, for thy confusion. (85)

This indeterminacy might seem to defy comic convention, despite Constance's insistence on generic labels. Newly emboldened, Constance now realizes that she is both the "Fool" and the "Author" who can "turn tragedy into comedy." In the final tableau, she is alone in her office, a new woman, ready to finish her thesis at last.

Goodnight Desdemona (Good Morning Juliet) ends with every appearance of being a satisfying comedy of the modern sort: its heroine, as Banuta Rubess, director of the 1988 premiere, comments, has a dreamlike experience that "allows her to reconsider her life" (8), or, in the language of current critical parlance, to "reauthorize it." But certain questions remain at the end of the play, and they are questions central to our understanding of comic convention. Now that the principles of comedy have prevailed over those of tragedy, will the transformed Desdemona and Othello and Romeo and Juliet live happily ever after in their respective plays, which Constance, through active intervention rather than sedentary scholarship, has "proven" were comedies after all? The text does not say, although Romeo's and Othello's absence from the final scenes makes us doubt that their wives have much interest in them. Or, will a whole new intertextual ending result, in which Desdemona and Juliet live out the gender-bending fantasies of their respective passions for Constance and enter into an Amazonian union of women that excludes men altogether? (Earlier in the play Desdemona decided that the unmarried Constance was an Amazon virgin.) This alternative would evade the dilemma Shaw confronted head-on with his ending; namely, how can an independent, assertive heroine, tested and disillusioned by experience, negotiate a role for herself in a conventional comic ending? Will scholars like Constance have to go one—or more—steps further and redefine comedy and tragedy altogether in order to make sense of the newly possible roles available for Shakespeare's women? These, surely, are questions for the 1990s, for teachers, scholars, and would-be revisers of Shakespeare's plays.

Jane Smiley's novel *A Thousand Acres* registers a protest against conventional endings in a different medium, the detailed realistic "period" novel, a form that has a far larger potential audience than MacDonald's play. In a sense, *A Thousand Acres* takes up the task begun by Cowden Clarke nearly one hundred fifty years earlier, but with this important difference: Cowden Clarke felt free to reimagine Shakespeare's lives up to the point at which their plays began, but she could not bring herself to change the written text. Hence her heroines, whose girlhoods show so much promise, must step into their comic and tragic roles and live out the endings Shakespeare wrote for them. Smiley also addresses a primarily female readership, women for whom reading is a private experience, fitted in around the other demands of their domestic and working lives, in contrast to theatre-going, which is a public, urban, social event. Once her novel received the Pulitzer Prize, it became a hot property in thousands of public libraries across America, and the paperback edition stayed on the lower end of the bestseller list for about six months in 1992–93. Like other winners of this prestigious award, it may someday be remembered as a popular novel rather than a canonical one—like Alison Lurie's 1985 winner *Foreign Affairs*, or Allen Drury's 1960 *Advise and Consent*. Alternatively, it could be taken up by the academic gatekeepers who preside over the mysterious process that yields lucrative college course adoptions, conference papers, and critical studies, like Saul Bellow's 1976 *Humbolt's Gift* or Toni Morrison's 1988 *Beloved*; indeed, it might be deemed suitable for the public school curriculum, like Hemingway's *The Old Man and the Sea* (1953) or Harper Lee's *To Kill a Mockingbird* (1961).

Set in Iowa farm country in 1979, the novel reenacts Shakespeare's *King Lear*, as narrated by Ginny, the oldest of landowner Larry Cook's three daughters. In translating the *King Lear* story to another time and place, Smiley rewrites our experience of the play and its cultural accretions by inventing a past for her Goneril, Regan, and Cordelia to provide the kinds of explanations for their personalities and behavior that contemporary liberal social theory would endorse. Ginny (Goneril) and Rose (Regan) inhabit a patriarchal culture that permits fathers to abuse their daughters and then channels these young women into early marriages where their success as wives derives from their fertility. In Smiley's transformation of *King Lear*, the perspective of the sympathetically and realistically portrayed older sisters frames and defines the readers' encounters with Larry, Caroline (Cordelia), Harold Clark (Gloucester), Jess Clark (Edmund), Pete (Cornwall), and Tyler (Albany). Smiley adds characters, like Rose's teenage daughters Linda and Pammy, in order to draw attention to Ginny's childlessness and to increase the female population of this women-centered novel about families and family secrets.

Smiley would not have made a point of the alliterative echoes in the names of her four principal characters (but only those four) if she had not wanted her more knowledgeable readers to recognize the intentional *King Lear* connection. But for those who do not recognize it on their own, the novelist is silent; unlike so many of the other texts I have discussed, in this one the explanatory introduction or note or afterwords is conspicuously absent. This absence, more than anything else, signals to the academic reader the author's unwillingness to enter into the intellectual play of theorizing about one's own text, anticipating and preempting the critics' pronouncements. Wesker, Papp, Marowitz, Wyman, MacKaye, Stoppard, Garson, Shaw, and the authors of *Your Own Thing* all included narratives of origin and explication with their Shakespeare transformations, and some, like MacDonald and MacKaye, authorized others to write such narratives on their behalf. The printed text of Howard Barker's 1989 play, *7 Lears*, for instance, begins with an introduction that draws attention to the "significant absence" of the "Mother," whose "extinction can only be interpreted as repression."[43] Barker gives his Lear both a mistress (Prudentia) and a wife (Prudentia's daughter Clarissa), who displays traits that anticipate her daughter Cordelia's insistent honesty. The introduction proclaims that the repressed mother in *King Lear* must have been the subject of a hatred shared by Lear and all his daughters which, "while unjust, may have been necessary." The play differs from *A Thousand Acres* in a number of ways, not the least of which is that its author regards all of his characters, men and women alike, with a cynical detachment reminiscent of Ionesco's in *Macbett*. *7 Lears* is also a prequel, a series of seven scenes organized according to Jaques's seven ages of man, and as such makes no effort to come to terms with Shakespeare's characterization of Goneril, Regan, and Cordelia.

Jane Smiley, by contrast, makes a point of beginning where Shakespeare does in the chronology of her characters' lives, although she does give us a few glimpses of Ginny's childhood memories. And so, when Larry announces his plan to form a corporation among the three daughters and give them the farm to run in order to avoid estate taxes, the obedient daughter Ginny feels an "inner clang" but nevertheless tries to sound agreeable as she says, "It's a good idea." Caroline, raised by Rose and Ginny after their mother's death, and now a twenty-eight-year-old big city lawyer, says abruptly, "I don't know."[44] After some leisurely novelistic flashbacks by Ginny about the fear her father had always inspired, the tense scene resumes. Ginny realizes that

> there was no way to signal her to shut up, just shut up, he'd had too much to drink. He said, "you don't want it, my girl, you're out. It's a simple as that."

Then he pushed himself up from his chair and lumbered past me down the porch steps and into the darkness.

Caroline looked startled, but no one else did. I said, "This is ridiculous. He's drunk." But after that, everyone got up and moved off silently, knowing that something important had just happened, and what it was, too. My father's pride, always touchy, had been injured to the quick. It would be no use telling him that she had only said that she didn't know, that she hadn't turned him down, that she had expressed a perfectly reasonable doubt, perhaps even a doubt a lawyer must express. . . . (21)

With this reimagining of the opening scene of *King Lear*, Smiley tries to make sense of Lear's decision to divide his kingdom and of the two older sisters' efforts to tell their father what he wants to hear, in sharp contrast with the youngest sister's insistence on the precise meaning of words. In doing so, she challenges and demystifies the fairy-tale contrast between the evil and nearly indistinguishable older sisters and the seemingly devoted and principled youngest one. Ginny senses that Caroline is resisting the "trapdoor plunging her into a chute that would deposit her right back on the farm" (21), but that she does not "dare" tell her father this. Nor, however, will she play along and speak her "prescribed part" in the ritual of apology and remorse, as Rose and Ginny are used to doing. Smiley sets up the situation so that her readers sympathize with Caroline's insistence that "It's time we stopped making allowances" but can also understand Ginny when she responds "Are you going to stop him? No! You'll just goad him on!" (34).

The character we don't much sympathize with is Larry; a hard drinking, competitive, humorless man, set in his ways and contemptuous of his less successful neighbors, he emerges through Ginny's descriptions as a patriarch with all of Lear's tyrannical tendencies but none of his eloquence or capacity for self-knowledge. Were it not for the *King Lear* parallels, it would be possible to dismiss Larry as a variation on the masculine villain in consciousness-raising "women's novels" that trace their female protagonist's recognition of and ultimate triumph over social and familial abuse and repression. But the Larry/Lear identification puts the reader—the reader alert to borrowings and departures from *King Lear*, that is—in a curious position. Smiley's project is nothing less than an iconoclastic dismantling of a literary tradition that embraces the flawed but magnificent tragic hero at the expense of the two-dimensional women characters who oppose him. Like so much modern fiction, *A Thousand Acres* rejects a former age's fascination with heroes; Larry is what an unheroic Lear looks like when viewed entirely from the perspective of a daughter whose life he has controlled.

Larry's absent wife, who died when Caroline was six and Ginny fourteen, is a shadowy presence in Ginny's frame of reference, unlike her utterly eclipsed counterpart in *King Lear*. In this respect *A Thousand Acres*, like *7 Lears*, poses a critique of its source-text, but Smiley does so by pointedly reminding her readers that a daughter's life is shaped in essential ways by her mother, and by her mother's and father's relationship. Thinking about her mother, Ginny realizes that "I felt the pressure of my mother and her fears for me like a ballooning, impinging presence. My mother died before I knew her, before I liked her, before I was old enough for her to be herself with me" (93). Ginny resists the impulse to find out more about her mother, to "be drawn into her life," reminding herself that "I was, after all, my father's daughter, and I automatically did believe in the unbroken surface of the unsaid" (94). By the end of *A Thousand Acres*, that unbroken surface will have been shattered again and again, as the unsaid and unremembered erupt into words.

Generations of audiences have been profoundly moved by Lear's speech

> Hear, Nature, hear, dear goddess, hear!
> Suspend thy purpose, if thou didst intend
> To make this creature fruitful.
> Into her womb convey sterility,
> Dry up in her the organs of increase,
> And from her derogate body never spring
> A babe to honor her!

(1.4.275–81)

Smiley weaves a thematic pattern around this curse, by making the hard-won and highly prized farmland, with its network of drainage wells, a source of the cancer-producing toxins that curse the lives of so many of its inhabitants. Ginny, enlightened by Jess, comes to a bitter realization that the fertilizer run-off in the farm's well water is responsible for her several miscarriages. The miscarriages, in turn, give rise to the jealousy that poisons her devotion to Rose and make her marriage barren and unsatisfying, which, in turn, makes her susceptible to Jess's manipulative charm. The water is also responsible for the cancer that killed both Larry's and Harold Clark's wives and required Rose to undergo a mastectomy three months before the events of the novel began. When Smiley attempts to follow Shakespeare closely—by writing the storm scene into her book or paraphrasing Lear's curse ("You'll learn what it means to treat your father like this. I curse you! You'll never have children, Ginny, you haven't got a hope." [183]), she is less convincing that when she uses her own fiction-writing strategies to embark on a large-scale exploration of contemporary topical issues. These include infertility, the relative inattention to breast cancer among medical researchers, and the destruction of the environment in the name of progress. The verbal curses in this novel are far less important than their counterparts in *King Lear*; the real curse is a distinctively male commitment to progress and productivity that poisons the water and ultimately drives the farm families into bankruptcy and early death.

Smiley makes creative use of Lear's curse in ways that are comparable to the uses two modern film makers have made of Lady Macbeth's speech

> I have given suck, and know
> How tender 'tis to love the babe that milks me;
> I would, while it was smiling in my face,
> Have pluck'd my nipple from his boneless gums,
> And dash'd the brains out, had I so sworn as you
> Have done to this.
>
> (1.7.54–59)

Here, too, the maternal imagery is loaded with potential contemporary nuances. Akira Kurosawa's powerful Macbeth transformation, *Throne of Blood*, portrays its Lady Macbeth counterpart as a stern and inflexible wife, older than her husband, who announces that she is pregnant when he seems inclined to appoint the son of the Banquo character as his successor, in accordance with the prophecy. Her child is stillborn in the final, climactic scenes, and her suicide thus becomes the consequence, not only of guilt, but of maternal grief. This plot construction imaginatively expands on the bloody-child imagery in Shakespeare's play, in addition to lending another dimension to Lady Macbeth's character. A more recent Macbeth film transformation, *Men of Respect*, reinvents the play as a power struggle among Italian-American mobsters. This Lady Macbeth confronts her husband with the angry reminder that she knows what it is to kill, for she has undergone an abortion, presumably at his insistence. This accusation gives her an emotional sway over her husband, just as the other Lady Macbeth's pregnancy does, at this crucial moment in the story.

In the films, as in *A Thousand Acres*, the process of transformation involves stretching the plays' themes and characters so as to address contemporary social issues. For readers and viewers prepared to experience the new text intertextually with the old, the ideological slant of the transformation can be seen as a statement about Shakespeare and his presumed ideological stance—and a subversive undermining of the moral and aesthetic assumptions on which the play's critical reputation rests. Knowing what we now know about the mixture of love, hate, and guilt incest victims feel toward their parents could make it difficult for us to go back to Cordelia's crucial line, "I love your Majesty / According to my bond, no more nor less," without thinking of the incestuous Larry beating and forcing himself on the older sisters night after night.

At the end of *King Lear*, all three sisters are dead; at the end of *A Thousand Acres*, Ginny has begun a new life on her own as she and Caroline, now utterly estranged, pay off the last of the farm's debts. Rose has died from a recurrence of breast cancer. As readers we knew from the beginning, of course, that the narrator would live to tell the tale, so we are not surprised that Ginny has moved on in her life to the point where she can look back, assess, and reconstruct the past. This is not exactly a comic ending, but it is, in some respects, as affirmative one. Ginny has freed herself from her repressed existence on the farm and from the shadow cast over her life by her father, her husband, and the patriarchal culture that created them. Smiley is talking back not only to Shakespeare, but more tellingly, to the comic conventions he so invariably adhered to in his fifth acts, even when they seemed uncomfortably inconsistent with the characters he had created. Rather than ending with a marriage and implied promise of future domesticity, *A Thousand Acres* leaves its readers with the unhappy wife's fantasy, 1990s style. Ginny is taking psychology classes at the University of Minnesota, with Pammy and Linda as her "family," in an all-female household where everyone helps with the housework, and Ginny can experience motherhood without the guilt and hostilities that so often accompany it. Her life is something akin to what Wyman's Gertrude could have chosen instead of marrying Claudius, what Wesker's Portia could have done instead of following her father's instructions, or what Marowitz's Isabella could have escaped to after surviving her night with Angelo.

Teaching Shakespeare in the Nineties: An Epilogue

I have before me two recent publications from the National Council on the Teaching of English (NCTE): the April 1993 issue of *English Journal* which contains a series of articles on teaching Shakespeare through performance and a volume of "Practical Approaches and Productive Strategies," entitled *Teaching Shakespeare Today*, which brings together the ideas of thirty-five teachers of Shakespeare, some on the college, and some on the secondary school level. Innovation abounds in the teaching of Shakespeare in the nineties, so much so that Shakespeare seems to be the meeting place for a great deal of the creative thinking about how students are exposed to dramatic literature and poetry. Most of the recent controversy about the canon has passed Shakespeare by, for there seems to be a tacit agreement, among even the most ardent opponents of pedagogies organized around Great Books, that we can banish Milton, banish Chaucer, banish Dryden and Pope and Tennyson, but that we cannot, and will not, banish Falstaff and Hamlet and Macbeth from our syllabi.

Indeed, if anything, Shakespeare assumes a more prominent place in our classrooms precisely because so many other "classics" have disappeared. A 1989 study of the most frequently taught texts in 488 American public, private, and parochial high schools identifies *Romeo and Juliet, Macbeth, Julius Caesar,* and *Hamlet* as four of the top ten texts routinely assigned in English classes. All of the other authors on the list (Steinbeck is in second place, Dickens in third) wrote during the nineteenth or twentieth centuries.[1] Shakespeare is thus not only the oldest author being read by high school students and the only one they return to again and again, he is also our students' primary link with a literary past that reaches back more than a century.

Samuel Crowl's introduction to *Teaching Shakespeare Today* cites similar studies of high school literature courses conducted in 1987 by Diane Ravitch and in 1989 by the Gallup organization. These surveys suggest that students learn and retain more about Shakespeare than they do about any other author or literary period or "cluster." "Why Shakespeare?" Crowl asks, and then proceeds to answer his question by invoking the same kinds of historical arguments Michael Bristol, Lawrence Levine, and others employ to show how indigenously "American" our preoccupation with and deference to Shakespeare has become since the earliest years of the American nation.[2] Harriet Hawkins also asks "Why Shakespeare" in her review of popular Shakespeare appropriations in *Classics and Trash*. Who of us, she asks provocatively, "ultimately has the right to decide whether *King Lear* [or] King Kong . . . should, or should not, be included on or excluded from the syllabus?"[3] The indebtedness to Shakespeare she finds everywhere in American culture, from Cole Porter and Woody Allen to "Dallas" and werewolf movies, serves to break down the presumed distinctions between elitist Shakespeare and popular culture, between classics and trash. Why Shakespeare, then? Because so much in our culture derives from his plays.

As further evidence of the rootedness of Shakespeare in our popular culture, Crowl cites a recent listing of Shakespeare-related films and video adaptations, a total of 747 entries. Interestingly, he accounts for these numbers by drawing an analogy with Shakespeare's own creative environment:

> The immediate popularity of both Renaissance theater and twentieth-century cinema meant that raw material needed to be raided in order to be transformed according to the demands of the new medium. Shakespeare and his contemporaries plundered every available source for plots and materials to be reshaped for the stage. . . . Film faced a similar need for stories to be translated onto the screen. Not surprisingly, Shakespeare was one of the first places it turned to for material.[4]

Just as Shakespeare plundered Hall and Holinshed and Plutarch and Ovid, filmmakers plundered—and popularized—Shakespeare. Thanks to the video revolution of the last decade, this wealth of readily available films has given our students greater access to performances and transformations of Shakespeare than ever before imaginable. And in the not-too-distant future, students and teachers alike will be using computer software to move in and out of different performances and adaptations with ease, setting them side-by-side on screen with written texts and producing their own collages and adaptations.

Another volume on the teaching of Shakespeare appeared recently, *Shakespeare in the Changing Curriculum*, compiled in Britain, where the teaching of Shakespeare is if anything an even bigger business than it is in North America. In an essay devoted to "some utopian thoughts" on teaching through performance, Simon Shepherd identifies the "problems" that students bring with them into his workshops. These sound very similar to the preconceptions of my first readers:

> These attitudes originate in conceptions of dramatic characters as recognizably "real" people, where (a) the text is aiming only for an imitation of "reality," (b) that "realism" is not defined within specific cultures but is a transcendental quality the accuracy of which may be vouched for by students on their experience alone, (c) empathetic engagement with characters is always the first basis for analysis of the text, and (d) characters are not an effect of text but autonomous entities who may sometimes function as mouthpieces for the author.[5]

To "dissolve" these problems Shepherd proposes improvisatory techniques that involve

> an analogous (often modern) situation (*Romeo and Juliet* as gang warfare, *Merchant* as racial harassment); or speeches may be chopped up, rearranged, spoken as unison choral work, split between various performers. All such techniques are (of course) modes of rewriting. . . .[6]

A similar pedagogy of re-vision, or transformation, has started to make an appearance in some of the many study guides the Shakespeare industry has produced. To cite one example: the recent edition of *The Merchant of Venice* in the Longman Study Text series concludes with class exercises and writing assignments which solicit appropriations, transformations, prequels. The editors invite students to "construct a short scene involving these missing characters. 1. Young Shylock receives a turquoise ring from Leah. 2. Portia's father assisted by his cousin Bellario draws up his will." A series of "drama activities" suggests ways to translate "the basic situation of a scene into a present-day context": students are asked to think about whether "justice has really been done" in the trial scene and then invited to "improvise a scene in which a person or a small group have to decide which of two parties in a dispute is in the right."[7] This kind of activity encourages talking back much as my *Merchant of Venice*–Wesker assignment did. To be sure, there are certain hazards associated with such assignments. What does one say to the student who concludes that "Shakespeare's Shylock didn't want the pound of flesh any more than he did in Wesker"? How does one confront a student's effort to resolve her discomfort with

Shakespeare's characters, having, in a sense, drawn attention to it in the first place?

As we continue to adapt our teaching to the technology and culture of the 1990s, we cannot choose whether or not to expose our students to Shakespeare transformations, for they have already made that choice for us. Assign a paper on *Hamlet* and the Hamlet that will come back to you might look remarkably like Mel Gibson in Zeffirelli's film, which takes many more liberties with the text than the BBC films frequently shown in college classrooms. Gibson's Hamlet eavesdrops on Polonius, Ophelia, and Laertes in act 1, scene 3, seems a near-contemporary of his glamorous mother, and occupies a strange intertextual space in the minds of many students with his "Mad Max" and "Lethal Weapon" roles. Classes on *The Taming of the Shrew* still produce conversations about the famous 1986 "Moonlighting" parody, a cultural artifact that has achieved a permanent place in the play's cumulative performance history and may well have done more to alleviate high school students' wariness toward Shakespeare than any other Shakespeare offshoot of recent years.[8] Many of our students, no doubt, are watching the animated twenty-five minute versions of six frequently taught plays that were first aired on HBO in 1993; we will know that they are doing so when the animators' distinctive images make their way into our exam essays and class discussions (for example, in the nunnery scene, Hamlet sees Polonius's and Claudius's feet under the concealing arras).

These "Animated Tales," as they are called by their marketing agents (Knopf and Random House have joined forces to market the videos with accompanying illustrated paperback abridgements), are one more instance of the way the education, publishing, and entertainment industries tap into the "Bardbiz" phenomenon. This venture brought together British actors and Russian animators, a testimony to the cultural authority Shakespeare exerts as a mediator between East and West in a post–Cold War world. The series includes *Hamlet, Macbeth, A Midsummer Night's Dream, Romeo and Juliet, Twelfth Night*, and *The Tempest*; significantly, perhaps, *The Merchant of Venice* is absent. The fifteen-page study guide, distributed free in bookstores (and no doubt to school systems) reveals that at least one current issue among academic Shakespeareans, the postcolonialist critique of *The Tempest*, has filtered down to Shakespeare-for-children. The study guide's questions regarding Caliban are framed by a paragraph about "the problems of colonizing the newly discovered lands" in Shakespeare's time.

> When explorers arrived in places that were new to them, they already had all sorts of ideas about the people who lived there. The different customs, dress,

diets, and religions they encountered did nothing to change their view that Christianity and European culture were to be spread as quickly as possible! . . . When Prospero took the island away from Caliban, he was behaving in a very European way.

Among the questions that accompany this gloss are "Is [Caliban] a person or an animal? Is he a poor savage creature treated badly by Prospero, or someone/something evil to be overpowered? Should we feel disgust or sympathy for him?"[9] Here, as elsewhere in the study guide, Shakespeare is employed for socializing purposes. Miranda, for instance, is "only a teenager" who "really doesn't know what it's like to have lots of people around" while Prospero might be viewed as a mixture of someone trying to be "a good father, an effective Duke, and a safe magician." Students are invited to take part in some talking back exercises, for example: "Ask a member of the class to prepare a defense of Prospero and his actions and act his part in front of the class. Put him in the hot seat!" Similarly, "Imagine you are the nurse looking around the strangely silent and empty house after Juliet's death. Write down your thoughts." Elsewhere, students are asked which of the following statements they agree with and why.

- Juliet belonged to her parents and to their society. She had to die in order to be free of their wishes.
- Juliet was a young girl who created her own life and chose her own death. She belonged to herself.[10]

Although this enterprise is clearly a mainstream project, its tentative move in the direction of using Shakespeare to explore social and cultural differences suggests that classroom teachers are ready for such approaches.

Anticipating the developments of the subsequent five years, Margaret Ferguson, in her 1987 "Afterword" to *Shakespeare Reproduced*, suggested that Shakespeare could be used to "deconstruct" what radical educational theorists call "the hidden curriculum," a curriculum that stresses gender, race, and class differences and reproduces social relationships of domination and subordination. Her call for "historicizing and politicizing the teaching of Shakespeare" through strategies that involve reproduction—such as new editions, for example—may seem quaintly out of date in this era of film and video reproduction. The "Afterword," which comes at the end of a volume designed for Shakespeare scholars, speculates that "it may ultimately be more important, and also more difficult, to effect significant changes in the way Shakespeare is taught than in the way his texts are produced in academic critical writing."[11]

As it turns out, some of the greatest changes in the way Shakespeare's texts are taught will come neither from educational theorists nor from academic critics, but from popular film like Kenneth Branaugh's *Henry V* and *Much Ado* or from the bestseller list. I would not be surprised if *A Thousand Acres* were to begin appearing on school syllabi; just as *Romeo and Juliet* and *West Side Story* are routinely taught together as early as the fifth grade in American classrooms, so an explicitly feminist pedagogy could effectively juxtapose *King Lear* and *A Thousand Acres*. This is more likely to occur first in college-level classrooms, where students can be asked to read two long and complex texts within the space of a few weeks. The problem on the secondary level, of course, is that students read so few texts; the assumption, too, often, is that is will take months to plough through a long, "difficult" play or a 375-page novel (*West Side Story*, by contrast, can be shown on video, so teachers do not have to confront the problem of coaxing students to read it at home). For the teachers and students willing to devote time to the assignment, juxtaposing Smiley and Shakespeare could lead to some very lively conversations about the transferability of plot and characters; the relationship between a work and the values, issues, and prejudices of its age; the differences between poetic drama and first-person narrated fiction; the nature of literary influence; and the kind of textual talking back that happens when an author reworks another's story. Although *A Thousand Acres* could stand on its own as a compelling piece of realistic fiction dealing with topical issues, there is something intensely subversive about it when read in conjunction with *King Lear*. Smiley undermines deeply cherished notions about Shakespeare's "universality" and *Lear*'s "greatness," while implicitly suggesting that it is becoming more and more difficult to read the play the way we are "supposed to" according to traditional assumptions about tragic character and tragic suffering long embedded in that genre's cultural history. Students inclined to protest against Lear's misogynistic language and Shakespeare's negative stereotyping of aggressive, disloyal women as sexual predators and adulterers, might well find their seemingly against-the-grain readings confirmed and validated by the novel. There is always the possibility, of course, that assigning *King Lear* along with *A Thousand Acres* could gradually evolve into replacing *King Lear* with *A Thousand Acres*, a step that would obscure some of the shock value of Smiley's critique and banish Shakespeare from the curriculum. Educators and scholars who set out to redefine the canon for a multicultural society that feels the urgency of the present and future more strongly than the tug of the past might argue that Smiley's powerful novel, with its highly readable diction and vivid depiction of the social and economic conditions in rural America, could and should replace *King Lear* in the curriculum. Would the extraordinary cultural authority invested in Shakespeare be strong enough to resist such a move? My guess is that talking back to Shakespeare, of which Smiley's novel is a wonderful example, needs Shakespeare to talk back to, and that although our notions of canon will continue to change, Shakespeare—an almost infinitely flexible and protean Shakespeare, to be sure—will remain very much with us.

Notes

Introduction

1. R. S. White, "The Year's Contributions to Shakespeare Studies: Critical Studies," *Shakespeare Survey* 43, ed. Stanley Wells (Cambridge: Cambridge University Press, 1991), 220.

2. *The Marowitz Shakespeare* (New York, London: Marion Boyars, 1978), 12–13.

3. Alden and Virginia Vaughan, *Shakespeare's Caliban: A Cultural History* (Cambridge: Cambridge University Press, 1991), 253.

4. Gabriel Josipovici, "A Changeable Report," *Shakespeare Stories*, ed. Giles Gordon (London: Hamish Hamilton, 1982), 65, 66, 69.

5. Paul D'Andrea, "'Thou Starre of Poets': Shakespeare as DNA," *Shakespeare: Aspects of Influence*, ed. G. B. Evans (Cambridge: Harvard University Press), 1976, 163.

6. Jonathan Bate, *Shakespearean Constitutions: Politics, Theatre, Criticism 1730–1830* (Oxford: Clarendon Press, 1989). Other scholars who use this term include Harriet Hawkins and M. M. Mahood.

7. Ruby Cohn, *Modern Shakespeare Offshoots* (Princeton: Princeton University Press, 1976); Michael Scott, *Shakespeare and the Modern Dramatist* (London: Macmillan, 1989), 11. Cohn defines transformations, as distinct from adaptations, as works in which "Shakespearean characters move through a partly or wholly non-Shakespearean plot, sometimes with introduction of non-Shakespearean characters" (4).

8. Marowitz, "Reconstructing Shakespeare or Harlotry in Bardolatry," *Shakespeare Survey* 40 (1988): 6.

9. Alan Sinfield, "Making Space: Appropriation and Confrontation in Recent British Plays," in *The Shakespeare Myth*, ed. Graham Holderness (Manchester: Manchester University Press, 1988), 130. Sinfield emphasizes the political implications of confrontation here and in "Royal Shakespeare: theatre and the making of ideology," in *Political Shakespeare: New Essays in Cultural Materialism* ed. Jonathan Dollimore and Alan Sinfield (Ithaca: Cornell University Press, 1985), where he says that "the cultural and therefore political authority of Shakespeare must be challenged. . . . One way of doing this is to take aspects of the plays and reconstitute them explicitly so that they become vehicles of other values" (178–79).

10. Michael Dobson, *The Making of the National Poet: Shakespeare, Adaptation and Authorship, 1660–1769* (Oxford: Clarendon Press, 1992), 6.

11. David Willbern, "What Is Shakespeare," *Shakespeare's Personality*, ed. Norman W. Holland, Sidney Homan, Bernard J. Paris (Berkeley: University of California Press, 1989), 231.

12. *Orson Welles on Shakespeare*, edited and with an introduction by Richard France (New York: Greenwood Press, 1990), 13–14.

13. Barbara Hodgdon, "Kiss Me Deadly: Or, The Des/Demonized Spectacle," *Othello: New Perspectives*, edited by Virginia M. Vaughan and Kent Cartwright (Rutherford, NJ: Fairleigh Dickinson University Press, 1991), 217.

14. Steven Berkoff, *I Am Hamlet* (London: Faber and Faber, 1989). The book is based on a production that began in Edinburgh in 1979 and continued as a touring production throughout Europe for two years. Berkoff's book, constructed from journals he kept during that period, is thus not a record of a performance, but of a series of evolving performances.

15. Carol Thomas Neely, "Epilogue: Remembering Shakespeare, Revising Ourselves," *Women's Re-Visions of Shakespeare*, ed. Marianne Novy (Urbana: University of Illinois Press, 1990), 243–44. See also Peter Erickson's *Rewriting Shakespeare, Rewriting Ourselves* (Berkeley: University of California Press, 1991) and Novy's *Cross-Cultural Performances: More Women's Re-Visions of Shakespeare* (Urbana: University of Illinois Press, 1993).

16. Susan Bennett, *Theatre Audiences: A Theory of Production and Reception* (London: Routledge, 1990), 61. Bennett gives no further information about these plays.

17. Terence Hawkes, *Meaning by Shakespeare* (London and New York: Routledge, 1992). "Bardbiz" is the title of the final chapter in the book, which originally appeared in *The London Review of Books* and seems to be a review article of several books.

18. Gary Taylor, *Reinventing Shakespeare: A Cultural History, From the Restoration to the Present* (New York: Weidenfeld and Nicolson, 1989), and Michael Bristol, *Shakespeare's America, America's Shakespeare* (London and New York: Routledge, 1990).

19. The essay was also included in Levine's book, *Highbrow/Lowbrow: The Emergence of Cultural Hierarchy in America* (Cambridge: Harvard University Press, 1988).

20. Lawrence Levine, "William Shakespeare and the American People," *American Historical Review* 89:1 (1984): 42, 47–48. Reprinted in *Rethinking Popular Culture: Contemporary Perspectives in Cultural Studies*, ed. Chandra Mukerji and Michael Schudson (Berkeley: University of California Press, 1991).

21. Dympna Callahan, "Buzz Goodbody: Directing for Change," *The Appropriation of Shakespeare: Post-Renaissance Reconstructions of the Works and the Myth*, ed. Jean Marsden (New York: St. Martin's Press, 1992), 164.

22. Hunter Steele, *Lord Hamlet's Castle* (London: Andre Deutsch, 1987), 238. Steele constructs an elaborate plot in which Fortinbras "jolted Claudius into villainy" and planned to marry Gertrude himself, leaving Claudius with a life regency. Claudius mounted a counterplot, and used Fortinbras's threats against Denmark as a lever to persuade Polonius and the Council to sanction his marriage to Gertrude and assumption of the throne (122–23). This novel, in its own way, attempts to 'make sense' of Gertrude's and Claudius' marriage, just as other texts discussed in this book will do.

23. Erica Jong, *Serenissima* (New York: Dell Publishing, 1987). The answer to the question Jong poses is "Let the reader judge!" followed by extensive sex scenes. A decadent, bisexual Southampton and the sonnets also figure large in the novel, which combines

women's fiction conventions regarding motherhood, divorce settlements, and reclaiming control over one's life with time-travel novel strategies that represent Shakespeare as a "very lost and homesick young Englishman" who had not yet written his plays (274).

24. Lee Blessing, *Fortinbras* (New York: Dramatists Play Service, Inc., 1992), 11, 14.

25. Jan Kott, *The Bottom Translation* (Evanston, IL: Northwestern University Press, 1987), 32.

26. David Garrick, "Ode upon Dedicating a Building, and Erecting a Statue, to Shakespeare, at Stratford upon Avon, 1769," reprinted in Samuel Schoenbaum, *Shakespeare: The Globe & the World* (New York: Folger Shakespeare Library and Oxford University Press, 1979), 181.

Chapter 1. Students Talking Back

1. Harry Levin, "The Crisis of Interpretation," *Teaching Literature: What is Needed Now*, ed. James Engell and David Perkins (Cambridge: Harvard University Press, 1988), 35, 43.

2. I am speaking, of course, from a limited sample, consisting of my students at a competitive midsize northeastern public university, where roughly half of the students are from the New York City greater metropolitan area. The student responses I quote from in this book were collected between 1984 and 1992 and do not by any means reflect the full range of readings I have observed in my twenty years of teaching Shakespeare.

3. I. A. Richards, *Practical Criticism* (1929; rpt. New York: Harcourt, Brace & World, 1956), 227, 228, 230.

4. This is Jonathan Culler's argument in *Structuralist Poetics*, as paraphrased by Elizabeth Freund in *The Return of the Reader: Reader-response criticism* (London and New York: Methuen, 1987), 82.

5. Wolfgang Iser, "Indeterminacy and the Reader's Response in Prose Fiction," *Prospecting: From Reader Response to Literary Anthropology* (Baltimore: Johns Hopkins University Press, 1989), 7–8. This essay was first published in 1971 and is reprinted with a brief "Retrospective Note" to critics who were "misled" into thinking that he saw meaning as entirely subjective, not "the result of a guided interaction" (30).

6. Wolfgang Iser, "The Play of the Text," in *Prospecting*. This essay was written in 1989 and is the last in the collection.

7. Alan Sinfield, "Give an account of Shakespeare and Education, Showing Why You Think They Are Effective . . ." in *Political Shakespeare*, 140–41.

8. Maurice Charney, *How to Read Shakespeare* (New York: McGraw Hill, 1971), 84–85.

9. Norman Holland, *5 Readers Reading* (New Haven: Yale University Press, 1975). Holland's approach to readers shares certain assumptions with David Bleich's in *Subjective Criticism* (Baltimore: Johns Hopkins University Press, 1978), which locates the source of meaning exclusively in the reader. As a recent critic has argued, neither Bleich nor Holland is particularly interested in how reader's readings are shaped by social or institutional influences. See Kathleen McCormick, "Theory in the Reader: Bleich, Holland, and Beyond," *College English* 47:8, 836–50.

10. William G. Perry, *Forms of Intellectual and Ethical Development in the College Years: A Scheme* (New York: Holt Rinehart and Winston, 1968), 51–52.

11. David Bartholomae and Anthony Petrosky, *Facts, Artifacts and Counterfacts: Theory and Method for a Reading and Writing Course* (Portsmouth, NH: Boynton/Cook, 1986), 21, 26–27.

12. This and all other quotations from Shakespeare's plays are taken from *The Riverside Shakespeare*, ed. G. Blakemore Evans (Boston: Houghton Mifflin, 1974).

13. Blessing, *Fortinbras,* 62–63.

14. Peter Rabinowitz, *Before Reading: Narrative Conventions and the Politics of Interpretation* (Ithaca: Cornell University Press, 1987), 193–94.

15. It would be interesting to assign the same topic at an institution with a very different student population from that at The University at Albany, where approximately 40% of the incoming freshmen plan to major in business. In fact, far fewer do ultimately major in business, and Albany has a large number of English majors for a university of its size. Can it be that some of these students are using *Hamlet* to articulate their anxieties about their choice of major and their career prospects?

16. Rabinowitz feels that the interpretative technique of applying rules of coherence is taught at school, but that it also reflects an innate psychological need for closure (201). The need to resort to scapegoating may be similarly rooted in the psychological makeup of the student readers.

17. Walter J. Slatoff, *With Respect to Readers: Dimensions of Literary Response* (Ithaca: Cornell University Press, 1970), 19–20.

18. Slatoff, *With Respect*, 86. Slatoff anticipates contemporary poststructuralist theory in his characterization of the experience of literature as "an essentially uncomfortable and disruptive one, a movement not toward order and coherence but away from it" (140), just as he anticipates feminist critics in his remark that "virtually no critic ever admits—in print, at any rate—that his reading of a work may in any way be affected by his own nature, experience, training, temperament, values, biases, or motives for reading" (35).

19. See Sinfield, "Give an account of Shakespeare and Education. . . ," 137, 149. Derek Longhurst has also addressed this issue in "Not for all time, but for an Age: an approach to Shakespeare studies," *Rereading English*, ed. Peter Widdowson (London: Methuen, 1982), 159. In a somewhat related argument, Charles Frey recommends returning to old spelling, acknowledging variants, and offering multiple texts, rather than a melded or "definitive" text, in *Experiencing Shakespeare* (Columbia: University of Missouri Press, 1988), 135–36.

20. Jonathan Culler, *The Pursuit of Signs: Semiotics, Literature, Deconstruction* (Ithaca: Cornell University Press, 1981), 103.

21. Slatoff, *With Respect*, 17.

22. Cathleen M. Bauschatz, "Montaigne's Conception of Reading," *The Reader in the Text: Essays on Audience and Interpretation*, ed. Susan R. Sulieman and Inge Crosman (Princeton: Princeton University Press, 1980), 289.

23. Richard Levin, "Shakespearean Defects and Shakespeareans' Defenses," *"Bad" Shakespeare*, ed. Maurice Charney (Rutherford, NJ: Fairleigh Dickinson University Press, 1988), 26.

24. Judith Fetterley, *The Resisting Reader: A Feminist Approach to American Fiction* (Bloomington: Indiana University Press, 1978), 21.

25. Many of these responses reflect attitudes very similar to those of some feminist Shakespeare critics who, although they employ a somewhat different vocabulary, are talk-

184NOTES

ing back in comparable ways. I suspect that readings of *Othello* by women students a generation ago would contain fewer judgments and complaints of this sort.

26. I encountered a very similar response to *A Winter's Tale* in another class. Speaking of Leontes' jealousy, a first reader remarked: "Everything [would have] worked out if they took the time out to trust in each other. They needed to discuss their problems and everything would have worked out."

27. James L. Calderwood, "Speech and Self in Othello," *Shakespeare Quarterly* 38:3 (Autumn, 1987): 301.

28. Calderwood, 302.

29. A high school teacher reported to me that in her class a recurring response to *Othello* was "I felt angry." As one sixteen-year old first reader put it, "I was mad at Othello for believing Iago so much and murdering Desdemona. I'm glad he died too." Although more naively expressed, this response is similar to that of some of my first readers.

30. This response was described in similar terms by a male student in an upper-level Shakespeare course: "We want to get up and shout at the character to make him/her change their ways," and feel a sense of anguish because we cannot alter a tragic sequence of events.

31. Susan Sulieman, in her introduction to *The Reader in the Text: Essays on Audience and Interpretation* (Princeton: Princeton University Press, 1980), discusses Wayne Booth's concept of the "implied reader" in connection with Iser's "contemporary reader" or "participant" versus the "later reader" or "observer" (22, 26). The teaching of Shakespeare requires particular attention, I would suggest, to the differences between these two kinds of readers. If, as Iser says, the text has the function of recreating the original social and cultural context for the later reader, what happens if that reader disregards or reinterprets this context in ways that produce what Iser calls "idiosyncratic realizations" of the text? How, as teachers, not only of individual students (which we are when we read papers) but of students in groups (which we are when we preside over class discussions) do we respond to such readings?

32. In *The Act of Reading: A Theory of Aesthetic Response* (Baltimore and London: Johns Hopkins University Press, 1978) Wolfgang Iser observes that readers attempt to reduce the complexity of the text, by creating a "black-white" structure in a process he calls "consistency-building." The reader selects (and thus omits) based on what seems familiar; but while doing so, he/she is "bombarded" by "alien associations" which modify the formulated *gestalt*, or "consistent-interpretation" (125–26, 132).

33. Eleanor Rowe, *Hamlet: A Window on Russia* (New York: New York University Press, 1976), 179.

Chapter 2. Shakespeare Transformed:
The Merchant of Venice

1. Frank E. Halliday, *The Cult of Shakespeare* (London: Gerald Duckworth and Co., Ltd., 1957).

2. Grace Ioppolo, *Revising Shakespeare* (Cambridge: Harvard University Press, 1991), 4.

3. Sinfield, "Making space," 130.

4. Charles Marowitz, "Shakespeare Recycled," *Shakespeare Quarterly* 38:4 (Winter, 1987): 477–78.

5. Marowitz, *The Marowitz Hamlet* (London: The Penguin Press, 1968), 35–37.

6. St. John G. Ervine, *The Lady of Belmont* (New York: Macmillan, 1924), 77. Subsequent references will be included parenthetically in the text.

7. For discussions of other *Merchant of Venice* transformations, see Toby Lelyveld, *Shylock on the Stage* (Cleveland: Western Reserve University Press, 1960), especially chapter VII, and Thomas Wheeler, *The Merchant of Venice: An Annotated Bibliography* (New York: Garland Publishing Inc., 1985).

8. Marowitz, "Reconstructing Shakespeare," 10.

9. Arnold Wesker, Simon Trussler, and Glenda Leeming, "A Sense of What Should Follow," *Theatre Quarterly* 7 (Winter 1977–78): 21.

10. Arnold Wesker, Preface, *The Merchant*, with commentary and notes by Glenda Leeming (London: Methuen Student Editions, 1983), lii. References to the text of the play will be included parenthetically in the text.

11. Wesker, Trussler, and Leeming, "A Sense of What Should Follow," 21–22.

12. Ann-Mari Hedbáck, "The Scheme of Things in Arnold Wesker's *The Merchant, Studia Neophilologia* 51:2 (1979): 235.

13. Wesker, *The Merchant*, xx.

14. cf. Shakespeare, William, *The Merchant of Venice*, John Russell Brown, ed. (1955; rpt. London: Methuen, 1985), 141.

15. Jonathan Dollimore, "Shakespeare, Cultural Materialism, Feminism and Marxist Humanism," *New Literary History* 21:3 (Spring 1990): 482.

16. Efraim Sicher, "The Jewing of Shylock: Wesker's *The Merchant*," *Modern Language Studies*, 21:2 (Spring 1991): 60.

17. Hedbáck, "The Scheme of Things," 236.

18. Wesker identifies his Rebecca da Mendes as the daughter of the late Francisco Mendes, banker of Lisbon. Gracia Mendes was actually the widow of Francisco Mendes, the senior partner in an important banking and trading firm. She arrived in Ferrara in 1550, after being forced to leave Portugal and then Antwerp; there, she openly professed her Jewish faith and became the patroness of a circle of Jewish scholars, poets and printers. Among these was Abraham Usque, whose famous translation of the the Bible, printed in 1553, was dedicated to her. His kinsman, Samuel Usque, later dedicated his Portuguese chronicle about "the tribulations of Israel" to Gracia Mendes. Cecil Roth, *The Jews in the Renaissance* (Philadelphia: The Jewish Publication Society of America, 1959), 55; and Hermann Sinsheimer, *Shylock: The History of a Character* (New York: Benjamin Blom, 1947), 54–55.

19. Sicher observes that "Wesker is also honoring a tradition of the Yiddish theatre which adapts Shakespeare and other world classics to the Jewish stage from the angle of intermarriage and the disaffection of Jewish youth" (66). See also Ellen Schiff, *From Stereotype to Metaphor: The Jew in Contemporary Drama* (Albany: State University of New York Press, 1982).

20. Clive Barnes, no longer the reviewer for the *New York Times*, said on a radio show that *The Merchant* was Wesker's "finest play, the most deeply felt theatrically, the most beautifully written" (Glenda Leeming, *Wesker the Playwright* [London: Methuen, 1983], 136), Other critics were less positive, although the first night audience, Wesker and others felt, gave it a wonderful reception.

21. Jeanne Addison Roberts, "Shakespeare in Washington D.C. *The Merchant,*" *Shakespeare Quarterly* 29:2 (Summer, 1978): 238.

22. Sinfield, "Making Space," 128–29.

23. *The Merchant,* l.

24. Sinfield, "Making Space," 139–40. Michael Scott also discusses *The Merchant* as part of the "textual and intertextual history" of *The Merchant of Venice.* He feels, however, that Wesker is "deconstructing *The Merchant of Venice* only to reconstruct it in a sincere but necessarily reductive manner" and proposes instead that "we may need to demythologize Shylock" by "throw[ing] out the intertextual tradition of the Shylock performance" (58).

25. *The Merchant,* xlix.

26. John E. Stout, in *The Development of High-School Curricula in the North Central States from 1860 to 1918* (Chicago: University of Chicago Press, 1921), reports that *The Merchant of Venice* was the most frequently assigned literary text in more than twenty-five per cent of the schools in the North Central region between 1886 and 1900. The play had first appeared on the reading lists in 1874, and was still among the top ten most popular texts in 1907. This information appears in Arthur N. Applebee, *Tradition and Reform in the Teaching of English: A History* (New York: NCTE, 1974), 32, 50.

27. I am indebted to Janet Hayes Walker, producing director of The York Theatre Company, for lending me an unpublished libretto of Ed Dixon's *Shylock.* Quotations are from pages 41 and 35, and references to Dixon's intentions are taken from the playbill.

28. Lelyveld, *Shylock on the Stage,* 51–52; M. M. Mahood, Introduction, *The New Cambridge "Merchant of Venice"* (Cambridge: Cambridge University Press, 1987), 44, 47.

29. Lelyveld, *Shylock on the Stage,* 91–93.

30. Gershon Shaked, "The Play: Gateway to Cultural Dialogue," *The Play Out of Context: Transferring Plays from Culture to Culture,* ed. Hanna Scolnicov and Peter Holland (Cambridge: Cambridge University Press, 1989), 21–22.

31. Lelyveld, *Shylock on the Stage,* 97.

32. Werner Habicht, "Shakespeare and Theatre Politics in the Third Reich," *The Play Out of Context,* 116.

33. Bernard Grebanier, *The Truth About Shylock* (New York: Random House, 1962), 34.

34. Sinsheimer, *Shylock,* 107, 109.

35. Jacob Lopes Cardozo, *The Contemporary Jew in the Elizabethan Drama* (reprint New York: Burt Franklin, n.d.), 327–28.

36. Cardozo theorizes that *Il Pecarone* was derived from the twelfth century Latin prose romance *Dolopathos,* rather than from the versions of the Flesh Bond tale that appeared in the *Gesta Romanorum* (265). It is perhaps worth noting that neither Cardozo nor Sinsheimer nor Grebanier appears in the index of the best known full-length study of *The Merchant of Venice,* Lawrence Danson's *The Harmonies of The Merchant of Venice* (New Haven: Yale University Press, 1978). By the 1970s the historical approach, discredited perhaps by the kind of naive critical assumptions about Shakespeare's "greatness" writers like Sinsheimer and Grebanier resort to, was no longer in fashion.

37. Walter Cohen, "*The Merchant of Venice* and the possibilities of historical criticism," *ELH* 49 (1982): 771.

38. Laura Stevenson, *Praise and Paradox: Merchants and Craftsmen in Elizabethan*

Popular Literature (Cambridge: Cambridge University Press, 1984), 103–4. Arthur Bivens Stonex's "The Usurer in Elizabethan Drama" (*PMLA*, 31 [1916]) counted some sixty usurers on the Elizabethan and Jacobean stage, many of them not identified as Jews.

39. Julia Briggs, *A Woman of Passion: The Life of E. Nesbit 1858–1924* (London: Hutchinson, 1987), 457, 460. The British publishing house Raphael Tuck & Son, which published many of Nesbit's works, was known for its distinctive illustrations.

40. Edith Nesbit, *Twenty Beautiful Stories from Shakespeare* ("Official Text for Members of The National Junior Shakespeare Club") ed. and arranged by E. T. Roe (Chicago: D. E. Cunningham & Co., n.d.), 184–85, 192.

41. Seymour Lainoff, *Ludwig Lewisohn* (Boston: Twayne, 1982), 56.

42. Ludwig Lewisohn, *Up Stream: An American Chronicle* (New York: Boni and Liveright, 1922), 51, 73, 199, 247. *Up Stream* went through seventeen printings between 1922 and 1926.

43. Lainoff, *Ludwig Lewisohn*, 107, 122.

44. Grebanier, *The Truth,* 346.

45. Cecil Roth, *History of the Jews in Venice* (1930; rpt., New York: Schocken Books, 1975), 75ff. Ludwig Lewisohn, *The Last Days of Shylock* (New York: Harper & Bros., 1931), 29ff. Subsequent references will be included parenthetically in the text.

46. Cf. Roth, *History*, 82–86. Roth says that the Mendes family had not yet taken "the drastic step of returning to Judaism" when they arrived in Venice; Lewisohn presents them as secretly observant Jews.

47. *The Last Days of Shylock*, 186ff. See also Roth, *History*, 87. Lewisohn ends his story before the Battle of Lepanto in 1571, in which the Turks were overrun by a Christian alliance.

48. Joseph Shatzmiller, *Shylock Reconsidered: Jews, Moneylending, and Medieval Society* (Berkeley: University of California Press, 1990), 1.

49. Shatzmiller, *Shylock Reconsidered,* 3, 71, 91.

50. For more narrowly focused instances of talking back, prompted by the legal aspects of the trial scene, see H. H. Furness's 1888 New Variorum *The Merchant of Venice* (rpt. New York: American Scholar Publications, 1965). Furness includes "A Dramatic Reverie" published in 1838 in *The Monthly Chronicle* and inspired by an earlier article entitled "A Lawyer's Criticism on Shakespeare." The author, Richard H. Horne, adds to the trial scene by giving Shylock a speech which "confounds" the Christians after Portia warns Shylock not to shed one drop of Christian blood. He argues that "blood is liquid flesh" and that "each includes the other" (400–401). The court remains silent and perplexed for some time; then Portia seizes upon the ploy of prohibiting Shylock from cutting neither more nor less than a pound. Horne does not change the way the scene ends, but he does intensify the reader's uneasy sense that the law has been twisted to suit the Christians. In a subsequent discussion of "Law in the Trial Scene," Furness cites a number of other legal defenses of Shylock, including a mock decision of the Supreme Court of New York which appeared in *The Albany Law Journal* in 1872. The decision rules that the original conclusion in favor of the plaintiff was "utterly absurd" and goes on, in great detail, to explain why (405–8).

51. *The Marowitz Shakespeare*, 21–22. References to the text of the play will be included parenthetically in the text.

52. Charles Marowitz, "Giving Them Hell," *Plays and Players* 24:10 (July 1977): 16.

53. *The Jew of Malta* 2.3.123–33 in the New Mermaid Edition, ed. T. W. Craik (1966; rpt. New York: W. W. Norton, 1988).

54. John Gross, *Shylock: A Legend and Its Legacy* (New York: Simon and Schuster, 1992), 204, 344.

55. Gross, *Shylock,* 348.

Chapter 3. American Hamletology: Two Texts

1. Geoffrey Bullough, *Narrative and Dramatic Sources of Shakespeare*, 8 Vols. (London: Routledge and Kegan Paul; New York: Columbia University Press, 1973), 7:5ff. Bullough reviews the various theories about the saga's origins, and I will use the 1894 translation by Charles Elton in his collection. For a more recent translation and extensive commentary on Saxo, see William Hansen, *Saxo Grammaticus and the Life of Hamlet* (Lincoln: University of Nebraska Press, 1983).

2. Bullough, *Narrative and Dramatic Sources* , 7:11.

3. Bullough, *Narrative and Dramatic Sources* , 7:72–73.

4. Bullough, *Narrative and Dramatic Sources* , 7:79.

5. Belleforest's text was finally translated into English as *The Hystorie of Hamblet* in 1608. The English version of the closet scene indicates the influence of performances of the play, with its reference to the "arras" (Bullough, 7:94).

6. Bullough, *Narrative and Dramatic Sources,* 7:98.

7. Laura Bohannan, "Miching Mallecho: That Means Witchcraft," *From the Third Programme: A Ten-Years' Anthology*, ed. John Morris (London: Nonesuch Press, 1956), 178, 174. I discovered this essay through a reference to it in Bill Overton's *The Winter's Tale: The Critics Debate*, a handbook for students on critical method in a series edited by Michael Scott (Atlantic Highlands, NJ: Humanities Press International, 1989). Overton uses Laura Bohannan's story in his introduction to illustrate the concept that no interpretation is ever definitive, and that *Hamlet* is a part of Western, not "universal," culture (9).

8. P. Ramamoorthi, "Hamlet in Tamil," *Shakespeare Worldwide: Translation and Adaptation XI* (Tokyo: Ushodo Shoten, Ltd., 1986), 44. This annual was begun at the 1971 World Shakespeare Congress.

9. Lillie Buffum Chace Wyman, *Gertrude of Denmark: An Interpretive Romance* (Boston: Marshall Jones Company, 1924), 1–2. Subsequent references to the text will be included parenthetically in the text.

10. Ann Douglas, *The Feminization of American Culture* (1977; rpt. New York: Avon, 1978), 89. Douglas devotes considerable attention to Henry Ward Beecher, "who, like all his siblings, made his dead mother the rationale and center for a feminized theology, [and] told his hearers that a mother's love is 'a revelation of the love of God'" (130–31).

11. Jane Tompkins, *Sensational Designs: The Cultural Work of American Fiction 1790–1860* (New York: Oxford University Press, 1985), 124–25.

12. Douglas, *Feminization,* 87.

13. Tompkins, *Sensational Designs,* 144–45.

14. Hugh Grady, *The Modernist Shakespeare: Critical Texts in a Material World* (Oxford: The Clarendon Press, 1991), 35. Grady cites L. M. Griffiths's 1889 handbook of instructions on setting up Shakespeare societies as evidence of an egalitarian system of

study independent of academic institutions designed to lead to "self-cultivation." Hundreds of these Shakespeare societies existed in late nineteenth-century America (41).

15. C. L. Barber and Richard Wheeler, *The Whole Journey* (Berkeley: University of California Press, 1986), 272.

16. Lillie Buffum Chace Wyman and Arthur Crawford Wyman, *Elizabeth Buffum Chace: Her Life and Its Environment*, 2 vols. (Boston: W. B. Clarke Co., 1914), 1:33. Subsequent references will be included parenthetically in the text.

17. In *Elizabeth Buffum Chace*, Lillie remarks that her mother "did not invite the little girls I met at Mrs. Greene's school to visit me. She did not try to get me chances to visit their homes. She did not seem to know their parents" (1:126).

18. Lillie Buffum Chace Wyman, *American Chivalry* (Boston: W. B. Clarke Co., 1913), 132–33.

19. In her appendix to *Gertrude of Denmark* Wyman refers approvingly to Mrs. Jameson's explanation of Ophelia's songs (244).

20. Anna Jameson, *Characteristics of Women, Moral, Poetical, and Historical* (New York: Wiley and Putnam, 1847). The book was variously published under the titles *Shakespeare's Heroines* and *Characteristics of Women* . . . . (111; 328; 332–33; 269–70; 271).

21. Christy Desmet, "Intercepting the Dewdrop: Female Readers and Readings in Anna Jameson's Shakespearean Criticism," *Women's Re-Visions of Shakespeare*, ed. Marianne Novy (Urbana: University of Illinois Press, 1990), 44.

22. Mary Cowden Clarke, *The Girlhood of Shakespeare's Heroines*, 3 Vols. (1851; rpt. AMS Press, 1974). Subsequent references will be included parenthetically in the text. Mary Cowden Clarke was married to the distinguished Shakespeare scholar Arthur Cowden Clarke, with whom she labored for sixteen years on a *Concordance of Shakespeare* (1844–45). It is one of the peculiarities of literary history that Wyman's book was published seventy years after Cowden Clarke's but only fifty or so years before Stoppard's *Rosencrantz and Guildenstern are Dead*.

23. Nina Auerbach, *The Woman and the Demon: The Life of a Victorian Myth* (Cambridge: Harvard University Press, 1982), 212.

24. Auerbach, *The Woman and the Demon*, 212–13.

25. Helena Faucit, *On Some of Shakespeare's Female Characters* (New York: Scribner and Welford, 1888), 19, 26, 39–41.

26. There is a fourth text written by a group of nineteenth-century women that ought to be mentioned here. Wyman's biography of her mother includes four letters from Elizabeth Cady Stanton, written over a period of thirty years. Stanton evidently knew Lillie as well: in a letter dated November 12, 1879, Stanton asked Chace if she or her daughters would write a chapter on Rhode Island for a proposed history of women's suffrage. It is therefore quite likely that Wyman knew Stanton's *Woman's Bible*, written collectively by a committee of distinguished British and American women (reprinted as *The Original Feminist Attack on the Bible*, intro. Barbara Welter (1895, 1898; rpt. New York: Arno Press, 1974). More a commentary than a rewriting, Stanton's work challenged an acknowledged canonized text to such an extent that it offended one branch of the suffrage movement, which voted to repudiate the book. As Wyman does here in her portrayal of Gertrude, Stanton expands upon Exodus 4:18–25 to draw attention to the "quick intuition and natural courage" shown by Zipporah, when she saved the life of her husband by quickly circumcising her son (75).

27. It is also a literary formula familiar to readers of nineteenth-century novels: the heroine's first love or husband is a conventionally, perhaps superficially attractive man, whom she chooses over the less charming but far more intelligent and truly devoted rival. The rival finally wins her hand through persistence and unflagging devotion, once she is sufficiently mature to recognize his worth. Jo's experience in Alcott's *Little Women* and *Little Men* is an example Wyman would have been familiar with.

28. A. C. Bradley, *Shakespearean Tragedy* (rpt. New York: Fawcett, 1965), 140.

29. Jameson, *Characteristics of Women* 115; 117–18.

30. Agnes Mure MacKenzie, *The Women in Shakespeare's Plays: A Critical Study from the Dramatic and Psychological Points of View* (Garden City, NY: Doubleday, 1924), 200, 224, 225.

31. *Book Review Digest* (1924), 648.

32. Carolyn Heilbrun, "The Character of Hamlet's Mother," *Hamlet's Mother and Other Women* (New York, Columbia University Press, 1990), 10, 11, 15–17. Baldwin Maxwell's 1964 essay entitled "Hamlet's Mother" seems to take issue with Heilbrun's theory, offering instead John Draper's argument that Gertrude is "no slave to lust." Like Wyman, he wonders about the accuracy of the Ghost's characterization of Gertrude. For Maxwell, Gertrude's first gesture of independence comes when she defies Claudius's order not to drink the poisoned cup. Her moment of recognition comes immediately afterwards: only in this last speech does she recognize or admit to herself the villainy of her second husband. *Shakespeare Quarterly* 15:2 (1964): 235. The quote from Draper is from *The Hamlet of Shakespeare's Audience* (Durham, NC: Duke University Press, 1938), 126.

33. Rebecca Smith, "A Heart Cleft in Twain: The Dilemma of Shakespeare's Gertrude," *The Woman's Part: Feminine Criticism of Shakespeare*, ed. Carolyn Ruth Smith Lenz, Gayle Greene, and Carol Thomas Neely (Urbana: University of Illinois Press, 1980), 201, 207. Smith's notes indicate that she read the Appendix of *Gertrude of Denmark*, which she quotes in connection with Henry's marriage to Catherine of Aragon.

34. Northrop Frye, *Anatomy of Criticism* (Princeton: Princeton University Press, 1957), 313 and *passim*). Frye uses the term "encyclopedic form" not only for such epic works as *The Faerie Queene, Paradise Lost, The Divine Comedy, Ulysses* but also the prophecies of Blake and the mythological poems of Keats and Shelley.

35. Cohn, *Modern Shakespeare Offshoots*, 186.

36. "Percy MacKaye's Plays on *Hamlet*," *Shakespeare Association Bulletin*, XXIV (April, 1949): 85–86.

37. Percy MacKaye, *Epoch: The Life of Steele MacKaye, Genius of the Theatre: In Relation to His Times and Contemporaries*, 2 Vols. (New York: Boni and Liveright, 1927; rpt. Scholarly Press, 1969), 1:198, 197. Subsequent references will be included parenthetically in the text.

38. Percy MacKaye, *The Playhouse and the Play and Other Addresses* (MacMillan, 1909; rpt. New York: Greenwood Press, 1968), 116.

39. MacKaye, *Epoch*, 2:481; from a letter to Percy MacKaye on his fiftieth birthday.

40. Mel Gordon, "Masque of Caliban (1915)," *Tulane Drama Review*, 20:2, 93.

41. Gordon, "Masque," 99.

42. Gordon, "Masque," 107.

43. Gordon, "Masque," 95.

44. MacKaye, *The Mystery of Hamlet, King of Denmark, or, What We Will* (New

York: Bond, Wheelwright Co., 1950), 655. Reissued by Adonis Press. Subsequent references will be included parenthetically in the text.

45. Aeschylus, *The Oresteia*, trans. Robert Fagles, intro. W. B. Stanford (New York: Bantam, 1977), 240.

Chapter 4. Shakespeare in the Sixties

1. Jan Kott, *Shakespeare Our Contemporary*, trans. Boleslaw Taborski (New York: W. W. Norton, 1964), 5.

2. John Elsom, ed., *Is Shakespeare Still Our Contemporary?* (London: Routledge, 1989), 12, 15.

3. Kott, *Shakespeare Our Contemporary*, vii.

4. Kott, *Shakespeare Our Contemporary*, 341, xv. Elsom observes in his introduction that Kott was perceived in the 1980s as "an old-fashioned pessimist" who saw Shakespeare as our contemporary because "human nature could not change or progress," a man "too subversive for his own, or anybody else's, good" (6). This, I suspect, is a misreading of Kott, by readers who never got as far as the last page.

5. See Fredric Jameson, "Periodizing the 60s," *The 60s without Apology*, ed. Sohnya Sayres, Anders Stephanson, Stanley Aronowitz, Fredric Jameson (Minneapolis: University of Minnesota Press, 1984), 205, 208.

6. Donald Reid, "1968 and All That," *Radical History Review* 45 (1989), 155. Reid reviews five recent books on the sixties.

7. Ronald Hayman, *Theatre and Anti-Theatre: New Movements since Beckett* (London: Secker & Warburg, 1979), 180. Hayman says that one of Brook's conditions for becoming a director of the Royal Shakespeare Theatre was that the company should subsidize experimental work; the first twelve weeks of this experimental work were directed by Brook and Marowitz.

8. Kott, *Shakespeare Our Contemporary*, 17, 45–47.

9. Kott, *Shakespeare Our Contemporary*, 48.

10. Orson Welles, *Chimes at Midnight*, ed. and intro. by Bridget Gellert Lyons (New Brunswick, NJ: Rutgers University Press, 1988), 14, 175, 179. References to Shakespeare's text are from act 5, scene 4.

11. Kott, *Shakespeare Our Contemporary*, 70–73.

12. Marowitz, Introduction, *The Marowitz Hamlet*, 12, 24.

13. Marowitz, Introduction, *The Marowitz Shakespeare* (London: Marion Boyars, 1978), 13.

14. Marowitz, *The Marowitz Shakespeare*, 29–32. References to the text of Marowitz's *Hamlet* will be taken from this edition and included parenthetically in the text.

15. Introduction, *The Marowitz Hamlet*, 22–23.

16. Introduction, *The Marowitz Hamlet*, 22–23, Kott, *Shakespeare Our Contemporary*, 64.

17. Tom Stoppard, *Rosencrantz and Guildenstern Are Dead* (New York: Grove Press, 1967), 39–41. Subsequent references will be included parenthetically in the text.

18. Irving Wardle remarks that: "Their blankness is the whole point. They exist only

to be occasionally involved in great events." But Stoppard arranges for them to "emerge from the shadows of nonentity for a single moment." Quoted in Joseph M. McCrindle, ed. *Behind the Scenes: Theatre and Film Interviews from the Transatlantic Review* (New York: Holt, Rinehart and Winston, 1971), 77.

19. Ronald Hayman, *Tom Stoppard* (London: Heinemann, 1977), 33–34.

20. Kott, *Shakespeare Our Contemporary*, 62.

21. Elizabeth Joyce, "From Prince to Punk: Student Reception and the English Hamlet of the Mid-Century," *New Comparison* 2 (Autumn 1986). Joyce is quoting Alan Brien in the *Sunday Telegraph* (34). Joyce goes on to describe other politicized, "teenager" Hamlets, including Alan Bates's 1970 Hamlet, Ian McKellen's 1971 Hamlet, and a Kott-influenced 1975 Hamlet with a "cynically opportunist Fortinbras and Claudius [as] industrial trouble shooter." The "unprincely Hamlet" had become the "new orthodoxy" by 1980, when Michael Pennington, in John Barton's Stratford production, "restored to Hamlet the physical presence of a Renaissance prince" (34–37).

22. "Ambushes for the Audience," a 1974 interview in *Theatre Quarterly* (May–June 1974), as excerpted in *File on Stoppard*, compiled by Malcolm Page (London: Methuen, 1986), 14.

23. Hayman, *Tom Stoppard*, 40.

24. Martin Esslin, in *The Theatre of the Absurd*, suggests that "the Theatre of the Absurd is facing up to a deeper layer of absurdity—the absurdity of of the human condition itself in a world where the decline of religious belief has deprived man of certainties. When it is no longer possible to accept complete closed systems of values and revelations of divine purpose, life must be faced in its ultimate, stark reality." He concludes that "like ancient Greek tragedy and the medieval mystery plays and baroque allegories, the Theatre of the Absurd is intent on making its audience aware of man's precarious and mysterious position in the universe." (rev. ed. Garden City, NY: Doubleday Anchor, 1969), 352–53.

25. Michael Billington, *Stoppard: The Playwright* (London: Methuen, 1987), 39. Quoted from an interview with Janet Watts in 1973 in the *Guardian*.

26. Joseph Papp, with Ted Cornell, *William Shakespeare's 'Naked' Hamlet: A Production Handbook* (London: Macmillan, 1969), 25–26. Subsequent references will be included parenthetically in the text.

27. Except for this instance and that of Claudius's death Papp doesn't develop the idea that Shakespeare's text is present and exerts a kind of "authority" over the play. Were the play to be produced again in the nineties, this "bit" would undoubtedly get much more play.

28. Hal Hester and Danny Apolinar, *Your Own Thing*, intro and notes by Stewart H. Benedict (New York: Dell, 1970), 11.

29. Barbara Garson, *Macbird* (New York: Grove Press, 1967), 3. Subsequent references will be included parenthetically in the text.

30. Helene Wickham Koon, *How Shakespeare Won the West: Players and Performances in America's Gold Rush—1849–65* (Jefferson, NC: McFarland, 1989), 10–15.

31. Terry Eagleton, *William Shakespeare* (Oxford: Basil Blackwell, 1986), 2–3.

32. Hester and Apolinar, *Your Own Thing*, 14–15. Subsequent references will be included parenthetically in the text.

33. The rock group Apocalypse consists of four singers nicknamed Death, War, Disease and Famine, in jarring contrast to the cheery and celebratory sentiments of their songs.

34. Esslin, *The Theatre of the Absurd* 45. Esslin points out that *Waiting for Godot* was one of the greatest successes of the postwar drama. Five years after its first performance in January 1953, it had been seen by over one million spectators in more than twenty different languages (20–21). Stoppard was thus commenting simultaneously on two cultural icons and their popularity.

35. Marowitz, *A Macbeth, The Marowitz Shakespeare*, 85. Subsequent references will be included parenthetically in the text.

36. Cohn, *Modern Shakespeare Offshoots,* 87. The interview Cohn quotes from was with John L. Hess in the *New York Times* (January 18, 1972).

37. Eugène Ionesco, *Exit the King, The Killer,* and *Macbett*, trans. Charles Marowitz and Donald Watson (New York: Grove Press, 1985), 3 (each play is paginated separately). Subsequent references will be included parenthetically in the text.

38. Cohn, *Modern Shakespeare Offshoots,* 101.

39. Jameson, "Periodizing the 60s,"180–81.

40. Trevor R. Griffiths, "'This Island's Mine': Caliban and Colonialism," *The Yearbook of English Studies: Colonial and Imperial Themes Special Number*, 13 (1983). Griffiths cites *English Plays of the Nineteenth Century*, ed. Michael R. Booth (Oxford and London, 1969–76) for the text of *The Enchanted Isle.*

41. Cohn, *Modern Shakespeare Offshoots,* 274.

42. Ernest Renan, *Caliban*, trans. Eleanor Grant Vickery (New York: The Shakespeare Press, 1971), 19, 64. My discussion of Renan's *Caliban* is indebted to Jane Rose's unpublished paper, "The Tempest: Its Sources and Adaptations."

43. Annabel Patterson, *Shakespeare and the Popular Voice* (Cambridge: Basil Blackwell, 1989), 158.

44. Cohn, *Modern Shakespeare Offshoots,* 274–76. Cohn's chapter on *The Tempest* also includes discussion of Robert Browning's 1864 poem "Caliban upon Setebos" and W. H. Auden's "The Sea and the Mirror," 1944, subtitled "A Commentary on Shakespeare's Work." (268ff; 280ff).

45. Griffiths, "This Island's Mine," 165. Griffiths discusses several other nineteenth-century works which use Caliban's name, as well as productions of the play by Beerbohm Tree and others.

46. Charlotte H. Bruner, "The Meaning of Caliban in Black Literature Today," *Comparative Literature Studies* 13:3 (1976). Barnes' book and other African uses of the name 'Caliban' are discussed on 241–42.

47. These and other texts are discussed at length by Alden and Virginia Vaughan in the "Colonial Metaphors" chapter of *Shakespeare's Caliban.*

48. Rob Nixon, "Caribbean and African Appropriations of *The Tempest*," *Critical Inquiry* 13 (Spring 1987): 562–64.

49. Chantel Zabus, "A Calibanic Tempest in Anglophone & Francophone New World Writing," *Canadian Literature* 104 (Spring 1985): 37.

50. Zabus, "A Calibanic Tempest," 37–38.

51. Bruner, "The Meaning of Caliban," 244.

52. Vaughan and Vaughan, *Shakespeare's Caliban*, 258–59.

53. Cohn, *Modern Shakespeare Offshoots,* 297.

54. Aimé Césaire, *A Tempest*, trans Richard Miller (Ubu Repertory Theatre Publications, 1985), 53. Subsequent references will be included parenthetically in the text.

55. This production used stark white half-masks for all of the European characters except for Prospero, who wore a molded rubber skin-toned half-mask. This, too, seems to have been a statement about the kinship among the European visitors to the island and Miranda (whose mask was identical to Ferdinand's) in contrast to the more "naturalized" Prospero, who occupied a middle ground between them and the unmasked inhabitants of the island—Caliban, Ariel, and four lively singing and dancing goddesses and male spirits, who contributed much of the production's festive aspects. *A Tempest* was directed by Robbie McCauley, and based on the Richard Miller translation, Ubu Repertory Theater, 1991, October 9–27.

56. This appeared in translation in the Winter/Spring 1974 issue of *Massachusetts Review*.

57. Nixon, "Caribbean and African Appropriations," 576. Nixon cites Marta E. Sánchez, "Caliban: The New Latin-American Protagonist of *The Tempest*" in *Diacritics* 6 (Spring 1976), in connnection with this idea.

58. Nixon, "Caribbean and African Appropriations," 574–76.

59. Zabus, "A Calibanic Tempest," 46, 48, 42–43.

60. Zabus, "A Calibanic Tempest," 41. This poem can be found in *African Poetry for Schools and Colleges*, ed. O. R. Dathorne (London, MacMillan, 1969).

61. Zabus, "A Calibanic Tempest," 42.

62. Cohn, *Modern Shakespeare Offshoots,* 255. Quoted from an interview that appeared in *Gambit*, 17:24.

63. Cohn, *Modern Shakespeare Offshoots,* 263.

64. Guido Almansi, "The Thumb-Screwers and the Tongue-Twisters: On Shakespearian Avatars," *Poetics Today* 3:3 (1982), 90. The "tongue-twisters," by contrast, are "much less violent and severe, and insist on the element of 'theatre within the theatre' already present in Shakespeare himself." He places Stoppard and Marowitz in this group, although one could argue that Marowitz is closer to Bond in his anger.

65. Cohn, *Modern Shakespeare Offshoots,* 263.

Chapter 5. What Happy Endings?

1. Carol Rutter, with Sinead Cusack, Paola Dionisotti, Fiona Shaw, Juliet Stevenson and Harriet Walter, *Clamorous Voices: Shakespeare's Women Today*, ed. Faith Evans (New York: Routledge/Theatre Arts Books, 1989), xxvii.

2. Papp, *"Naked" Hamlet*, 23–24.

3. Rutter et al., *Clamorous Voices*, xxvii, 52.

4. George Bernard Shaw, *Complete Plays and Prefaces*, 7 Vols. (New York: Dodd, Mead and Company, 1962), 4:784, 786. Subsequent references will be included parenthetically in the text.

5. As quoted in Ann Thompson, "Cymbeline's Other Endings," *The Appropriation of Shakespeare*, ed. Jean Marsden (New York: St. Martin's Press, 1992), 212. Thompson observes that Faucit's speculations about the characters' psyches are not completely remote from the readings of contemporary psychoanalytic critics, and indeed from the practices of performers trying to discover a character's "inner life" (215).

6. Rutter et al., *Clamorous Voices* xv, 91.

7. In this modern dress production placed in an urban setting characterized by a graffiti-covered back wall and prison guards carrying clipboards, Isabella waits until the stage has emptied, then walks purposefully up to the middle-aged businessman Duke (still in his friar's habit) and kisses him assertively. The image is wholly unprepared for—although the audience has seen earlier signs of the Duke's growing attraction to Isabella, there is nothing to suggest that she regards him with anything other than the youthful trust of a novice toward an older friar.

8. The University at Albany, Theatre Department, October 1988.

9. This rather pessimistic feminist interpretation of the ending of *Measure for Measure* contrasts sharply with Marcia Reifer's feminist analysis of the play. Reifer draws on a number of recent readings that defend Isabella and are critical of the Duke (whom Reifer views as "villainous") and concludes that the silent Iasabella has suffered a "tragic loss of voice" at the end, comparable to Lavinia's in *Titus Andronicus*. "The Constriction of Female Power in *Measure for Measure*," *Shakespeare Quarterly* 35:2 (Summer,1984): 160, 167.

10. Cowden Clarke, *Girlhood,* II:42, 45. Subsequent references will be included parenthetically in the text.

11. Rutter et al., *Clamorous Voices,* 41.

12. Marowitz, *Measure for Measure, The Marowitz Shakespeare*, 213. Subsequent references will be included parenthetically in the text.

13. David Margolies, "Teaching the handsaw to fly: Shakespeare as a hegemonic instrument," *The Shakespeare Myth*, ed. Graham Holderness (Manchester: Manchester University Press, 1988), 48, 43, 49.

14. Wilhelm Hortmann, "Changing Modes in *Hamlet* Production: Rediscovering Shakespeare after the Iconoclasts," *Images of Shakespeare* (Proceedings of the International Shakespeare Congress), ed. Werner Habicht, D. J. Palmer, Roger Pringle (Newark: University of Delaware Press, 1986), 222.

15. *Roundheads and Peakheads*, in Bertolt Brecht, *Jungle of Cities and other plays* (New York: Grove Press, 1966), 177. Subsequent references will be included parenthetically in the text.

16. Martin Esslin discusses some of Brecht's other plays as "counterplays" that assimilate the work of another playwright as a way of replying to or refuting its premises. He reports that Brecht was planning a counterplay to Beckett's *Waiting for Godot* at the time of his death. *Brecht: The Man and His Work* (New York: W. W. Norton, 1959), 122–23.

17. Frederic Ewen, *Bertolt Brecht: His Life, His Art and His Times* (New York: Citadel, 1967), 307.

18. J. L. Styan, *All's Well That Ends Well* (Shakespeare in Performance series) (Manchester: Manchester University Press, 1984), 1. After 1852, the play went unperformed in both England and America until 1916; it was written off by *The Observer* as "very nearly the worst play its distinguished author ever wrote" in 1921, and was still seldom read or performed as late as 1959 (2–3).

19. Rutter et al., *Clamorous Voices,* 80–81.

20. Howard Cole views Helena as a "self-deceiving deceiver, intriguing as shrewdly as the ruthless Vincentio, while honestly seeing herself as a benevolent Prospero" in *The All's Well Story from Boccaccio to Shakespeare* (Urbana: University of Illinois Press, 1981), 131.

21. Susan Snyder, *"All's Well That Ends Well* and Shakespeare's Helens: Text and Subtext, Subject and Object," *ELR: Women in the Renaissance II* 18:1 (Winter, 1988): 70.

22. Susan Snyder, "Naming Names in *All's Well That Ends Well*," *Shakespeare Quarterly* 43:3 (Fall, 1992): 272.

23. Cole, *The All's Well Story,* 91.

24. Cole, *The All's Well Story,* 96–98.

25. Rutter et al., *Clamorous Voices,* 84–85.

26. Janet Adelman, "Bed Tricks: On Marriage as the End of Comedy in *All's Well That Ends Well* and *Measure for Measure*," *Shakespeare's Personality*, ed. Norman N. Holland, Sidney Homan, and Bernard J. Paris (Berkeley: University of California Press, 1989), 156. Adelman's psychoanalytic reading argues that Bertram recoils from a marriage that seems incestuous, because Helena is "virtually his sister," and because of "the close association of her with [his] mother" and his "surrogate father." "Marriage to her would thus be a sign of his bondage to the older generation rather than of his growing independence" (155).

27. Susan J. Wolfson, "Explaining to Her Sisters: Mary Lamb's *Tales from Shakespeare*," *Women's Re-Visions of Shakespeare*, ed. Marianne Novy (Urbana: University of Illinois Press, 1990), 16, 22. Wolfson argues that Lamb "attempts a sympathetic portrait of a woman who persists in her aims against the conventional constraints of feminine propriety and passivity" in her *All's Well* and that Helena becomes a study of "female ambition in a world of social restriction," a model of what young ladies "can accomplish with wit, intelligence, and commitment" (30).

28. Styan, *All's Well,* 3.

29. Charles and Mary Lamb, *Lambs' Tales from Shakespeare* (London: Cathay Books, 1985), 140.

30. Wolfson, "Explaining to Her Sisters," 35.

31. Lamb and Lamb, *Tales,* 143.

32. Nesbit, *Stories from Shakespeare,* 277. Subsequent references will be included parenthetically in the text.

33. Shaw and Nesbit became lovers in 1886; he boasted that she wanted to leave her husband, Hubert Bland, to run away with him. They continued to see one another as friends, and Shaw paid for the Blands' son John to go to Cambridge after Hubert's death (Briggs, *A Woman of Passion,* 104–5). When approached in 1931 about helping with a biography of Nesbit, Shaw "politely refused on the grounds that . . . Edith was an unconventional lady and Hubert an exceedingly unfaithful husband . . ." (86).

34. Styan, *All's Well,* 12.

35. Snyder, *"All's Well That Ends Well* and Shakespeare's Helens," 67.

36. Bernard Miles, *Favorite Tales from Shakespeare* (Chicago: Rand McNally, 1976).

37. Kenneth Rothwell, "The Shakespeare Plays: *Hamlet* and the Five Plays of Season Three," *Shakespeare Quarterly* 32 (Autumn, 1981), reprinted in *Shakespeare on Television: An Anthology of Essays and Reviews*, ed. J. C. Bulman and H. R. Coursen (Hanover, NH: University Press of New England, 1988), 273–74. Students in my classes have always commented, often quite indignantly, about the mixed signals produced by the erotic kiss.

38. Paul Galloway, "Blondie Bumstead, Career Woman," *The Albany Times Union*, August 30, 1991, C1.

39. Snyder, "*All's Well That Ends Well* and Shakespeare's Helens," 77.

40. Cole, *The All's Well Story,* 133.

41. Marowitz, "Reconstructing Shakespeare," 9.

42. Ann-Marie MacDonald, *Goodnight Desdemona (Good Morning Juliet)* (Toronto; Coach House Press, 1990), 20. This play had its American debut in Pittsburgh in the summer of 1991 and was produced in New York by the Classic Stage Repertory Company in the autumn of 1992. Subsequent references will be included parenthetically in the text.

43. Howard Barker, *Seven Lears: The Pursuit of the Good and Golgo: Sermons on Pain and Privilege* (London: John Calder; New York: Riverrun, 1990), n.p. Feminist and psychoanalytic critics are also interested in the absent mother in *King Lear*. Cf. Coppelia Kahn, "The Absent Mother in *King Lear*," *Rewriting the Renaissance: The Discourses of Sexual Difference in Early Modern Europe*, ed. Margaret W. Ferguson, Maureen Quilligan, and Nancy J. Vickers (Chicago: University of Chicago Press, 1986).

44. Smiley, *A Thousand Acres* (New York: Alfred Knopf, 1991), 19. Subsequent references will be included parenthetically in the text.

Teaching Shakespeare in the Nineties: An Epilogue

1. Arthur N. Applebee, *A Study of Book-Length Works Taught in High School English Courses* (Albany, NY: Center for the Learning and Teaching of Literature, 1989). Applebee's table for the three most popular titles at each public school grade level has *Romeo and Juliet* in first place for grade 9, *Julius Caesar* in first place for grade 10, and *Macbeth* and *Hamlet* in first and second places for grade 12 (8). Comparisons with similar data from 1963 indicate very little change; the same four plays were taught in large percentages of schools, although *Romeo and Juliet* is now taught much more frequently, compared with the other three (13). As I will be suggesting later in this epilogue, the reasons can be traced, I believe, to the availability of the Zeffirelli film and and the film of *West Side Story*.

2. Samuel Crowl, "Introduction: Where the Wild Things Are: Shakespeare in the American Landscape," *Teaching Shakespeare Today: Practical Approaches and Productive Strategies*, ed. James E. Davis and Ronald E. Salomone (Urbana: NCTE, 1993), xiii–xvii.

3. Harriet Hawkins, *Classics and Trash: Traditions and Taboos in High Literature and Popular Modern Genres* (Toronto: University of Toronto Press, 1990), 107.

4. Crowl, "Where the Wild Things Are," xix. The catalogue referred to is *Shakespeare on Screen* by Kenneth S. Rothwell and Annabelle Melzer (New York: Neal-Shulman, 1990).

5. Simon Shepherd, "Acting against bardom: some utopian thoughts on workshops," *Shakespeare in the Changing Curriculum*, edited by Lesley Aers and Nigel Wheale (London and New York: Routledge, 1991), 91.

6. Shepherd, "Acting against bardom," 93.

7. *The Merchant of Venice*, ed. Gamini and Fenella Salgado (London: Longman Group Limited, 1989), 272–75.

8. The "Moonlighting" episode has even begun to turn up in scholarly journals. Cf.

Barbara Hodgdon, "Katherina Bound; or, Play(K)ating the Strictures of Everyday Life," *PMLA* 107:3 (May, 1992).

9. "Shakespeare: The Animated Tales: Study Assignments for Students," (Westminster, MD: Knopf Books for Young Readers/ Random House Home Video, 1993), 12.

10. "Shakespeare: The Animated Tales," 12, 10.

11. Margaret Ferguson, "Afterword," *Shakespeare Reproduced: The text in history and ideology*, ed. Jean E. Howard, and Marion F. O'Connor (New York and London: Methuen, 1987), 279, 274.

Bibliography

Adelman, Janet. "Bed Tricks: On Marriage as the End of Comedy in *All's Well That Ends Well* and *Measure for Measure*." In *Shakespeare's Personality*, edited by Norman N. Holland, Sidney Homan, and Bernard J. Paris. Berkeley: University of California Press, 1989.

Aeschylus. *The Oresteia*. Translated by Robert Fagles, with an introduction by W. B. Stanford. New York: Bantam, 1977.

Almansi, Guido. "The Thumb-Screwers and the Tongue-Twisters: On Shakespearian Avatars." *Poetics Today* 3:3 (1982): 87–100.

Applebee, Arthur N. *A Study of Book-Length Works Taught in High School English Courses*. Albany, NY: Center for the Learning and Teaching of Literature, 1989.

———. *Tradition and Reform in the Teaching of English: A History*. New York: NCTE, 1974.

Auerbach, Nina. *The Woman and the Demon: The Life of a Victorian Myth*. Cambridge: Harvard University Press, 1982.

Barber, C. L., and Richard Wheeler. *The Whole Journey*. Berkeley: University of California Press, 1986.

Barker, Howard. *Seven Lears; The Pursuit of the Good and Golgo; Sermons on Pain and Privilege*. London: John Calder; New York: Riverrun, 1990.

Bartholomae, David, and Anthony Petrosky. *Facts, Artifacts and Counterfacts: Theory and Method for a Reading and Writing Course*. Portsmouth, NH: Boynton/Cook, 1986.

Bate, Jonathan. *Shakespearean Constitutions: Politics, Theatre, Criticism 1730–1830*. Oxford: Clarendon Press, 1989.

Bauschatz, Cathleen M. "Montaigne's Conception of Reading." In *The Reader in the Text: Essays on Audience and Interpretation*, edited by Susan R. Sulieman and Inge Crosman. Princeton: Princeton University Press, 1980.

Bennett, Susan. *Theatre Audiences: A Theory of Production and Reception*. London: Routledge, 1990.

Berkoff, Steven. *I Am Hamlet*. London: Faber and Faber, 1989.

Billington, Michael. *Stoppard: The Playwright*. London: Methuen, 1987.

Bleich, David. *Subjective Criticism*. Baltimore: Johns Hopkins University Press, 1978.

Blessing, Lee. *Fortinbras*. New York: Dramatists Play Service, Inc., 1992.

Bohannan, Laura. "Miching Mallecho: That Means Witchcraft." In *From the Third Programme: A Ten-Years' Anthology*, edited by John Morris. London: Nonesuch Press, 1956.

Bradley, A. C. *Shakespearean Tragedy*. 1904. Reprint. New York: Fawcett, 1965.

Brecht, Bertold. *Roundheads and Peakheads*. In *Jungle of Cities and other plays*. New York: Grove Press, 1966.

Briggs, Julia. *A Woman of Passion: The Life of E. Nesbit 1858–1924*. London: Hutchinson, 1987.

Bristol, Michael. *Shakespeare's America, America's Shakespeare*. London and New York: Routledge, 1990.

Bruner, Charlotte H. "The Meaning of Caliban in Black Literature Today." *Comparative Literature Studies* 13:3 (1976): 241–53.

Bullough, Geoffrey. *Narrative and Dramatic Sources of Shakespeare*. 8 Vols. London: Routledge and Kegan Paul; New York: Columbia University Press, 1973.

Bulman, J. C., and H. R. Coursen, eds. *Shakespeare on Television: An Anthology of Essays and Reviews*. Hanover, NH: University Press of New England, 1988.

Calderwood, James L. "Speech and Self in *Othello*." *Shakespeare Quarterly* 38:3 (Autumn, 1987): 293–303.

Callahan, Dympna. "Buzz Goodbody: Directing for Change." In *The Appropriation of Shakespeare: Post-Renaissance Reconstructions of the Works and the Myth*, edited by Jean Marsden. New York: St. Martin's Press, 1992.

Cardozo, Jacob Lopes. *The Contemporary Jew in the Elizabethan Drama*. 1925. Reprint. New York: Burt Franklin, n.d.

Césaire, Aimé. *A Tempest*. Translated by Richard Miller. Ubu Repertory Theatre Publications, 1985.

Charney, Maurice. *How to Read Shakespeare*. New York: McGraw Hill, 1971.

Cohen, Walter. "*The Merchant of Venice* and the possibilities of historical criticism." *ELH* 49 (1982): 265–89.

Cohn, Ruby. *Modern Shakespeare Offshoots*. Princeton: Princeton University Press, 1976.

Cole, Howard. *The All's Well Story from Boccaccio to Shakespeare*. Urbana: University of Illinois Press, 1981.

Cowden Clarke, Mary. *The Girlhood of Shakespeare's Heroines*. 3 vols. 1851. Reprint. AMS Press, 1974.

Crowl, Samuel. "Introduction: Where the Wild Things Are: Shakespeare in the American Landscape," In *Teaching Shakespeare Today: Practical Approaches and Productive Strategies*, edited by James E. Davis and Ronald E. Salomone. Urbana: NCTE, 1993.

Culler, Jonathan. *The Pursuit of Signs: Semiotics, Literature, Deconstruction*. Ithaca: Cornell University Press, 1981.

D'Andrea, Paul. "'Thou Starre of Poets': Shakespeare as DNA." In *Shakespeare: Aspects of Influence*, edited by G. B. Evans. Cambridge: Harvard University Press, 1976.

Danson, Lawrence. *The Harmonies of The Merchant of Venice*. New Haven: Yale University Press, 1978.

Dixon, Ed. *Shylock*. Typescript and Playbill.

Desmet, Christy. "Intercepting the Dewdrop: Female Readers and Readings in Anna Jameson's Shakespearean Criticism." In *Women's Re-Visions of Shakespeare*, edited by Marianne Novy. Urbana: University of Illinois Press, 1990.

Dobson, Michael. *The Making of the National Poet: Shakespeare, Adaptation and Authorship, 1660–1769*. Oxford: Clarendon Press, 1992.

Dollimore, Jonathan. "Shakespeare, Cultural Materialism, Feminism and Marxist Humanism." *New Literary History* 21:3 (Spring 1990): 471–93.

Dollimore, Jonathan, and Alan Sinfield, eds. *Political Shakespeare: New Essays in Cultural Materialism*. Ithaca: Cornell University Press, 1985.

Douglas, Ann. *The Feminization of American Culture*. 1977. Reprint. New York: Avon, 1978.

Eagleton, Terry. *William Shakespeare*. Oxford: Basil Blackwell, 1986.

Elsom, John, ed. *Is Shakespeare Still Our Contemporary?* London: Routledge, 1989.

Erickson, Peter. *Rewriting Shakespeare, Rewriting Ourselves*. Berkeley: University of California Press, 1991.

Ervine, St. John G. *The Lady of Belmont*. New York: Macmillan, 1924.

Esslin, Martin. *Brecht: The Man and His Work*. New York: W. W. Norton, 1959.

———. *The Theatre of the Absurd*. Revised edition. Garden City, NY: Doubleday Anchor, 1969.

Ewen, Frederic. *Bertolt Brecht: His Life, His Art and His Times*. New York: Citadel, 1967.

Faucit, Helena. *On Some of Shakespeare's Female Characters*. New York: Scribner and Welford, 1888.

Ferguson, Margaret. "Afterword." In *Shakespeare Reproduced: The text in history and ideology*, edited by Jean E. Howard, and Marion F. O'Connor. New York and London: Methuen, 1987.

Fetterley, Judith. *The Resisting Reader: A Feminist Approach to American Fiction*. Bloomington: Indiana University Press, 1978.

Frey, Charles. *Experiencing Shakespeare*. Columbia: University of Missouri Press, 1988.

Freund, Elizabeth. *The Return of the Reader: Reader-response criticism*. London and New York: Methuen, 1987.

Frye, Northrop. *Anatomy of Criticism*. Princeton: Princeton University Press, 1957.

Garson, Barbara. *Macbird*. New York: Grove Press, 1967.

Gordon, Mel. "Masque of *Caliban* (1915)." *Tulane Drama Review* 20:2: 93–107.

Grady, Hugh. *The Modernist Shakespeare: Critical Texts in a Material World*. Oxford: The Clarendon Press, 1991.

Grebanier, Bernard. *The Truth About Shylock*. New York: Random House, 1962.

Griffiths, Trevor R. "'This Island's Mine'" Caliban and Colonialism." *The Yearbook of English Studies: Colonial and Imperial Themes Special Number* 13 (1983): 159–80.

Gross, John. *Shylock: A Legend and Its Legacy.* New York: Simon and Schuster, 1992.

Habicht, Werner. "Shakespeare and theatre politics in the Third Reich." In *The Play out of Context: Transferring Plays from Culture to Culture,* edited by Hanna Scolnicov and Peter Holland. Cambridge: Cambridge University Press, 1989.

Halliday, Frank E. *The Cult of Shakespeare.* London: Gerald Duckworth and Co., Ltd., 1957.

Hansen, William. *Saxo Grammaticus and the Life of Hamlet.* Lincoln: University of Nebraska Press, 1983.

Hawkes, Terence. *Meaning by Shakespeare.* London and New York: Routledge, 1992.

Hawkins, Harriet. *Classics and Trash: Traditions and Taboos in High Literature and Popular Modern Genres.* Toronto: University of Toronto Press, 1990.

Hayman, Ronald. *Theatre and Anti-Theatre: New Movements Since Beckett.* London: Secker & Warburg, 1979.

———. *Tom Stoppard.* London: Heinemann, 1977.

Hedbáck, Ann-Mari. "The Scheme of Things in Arnold Wesker's *The Merchant. Studia Neophilologia* 51:2 (1979): 233–44.

Heilbrun, Carolyn. "The Character of Hamlet's Mother." In *Hamlet's Mother and Other Women.* New York: Columbia University Press, 1990.

Hester, Hal, and Danny Apolinar. *Your Own Thing.* Introduction and notes by Stewart H. Benedict. New York: Dell, 1970.

Hodgdon, Barbara. "Katherina Bound; or, Play(K)ating the Strictures of Everyday Life." *PMLA* 107:3 (May, 1992): 538–53.

———. "Kiss Me Deadly: or, The Des/Demonized Spectacle." In *Othello: New Perspectives,* edited by Virginia M. Vaughan and Kent Cartwright. Rutherford, NJ: Fairleigh Dickinson University Press, 1991.

Holderness, Graham, ed. *The Shakespeare Myth.* Manchester: Manchester University Press, 1988.

Holland, Norman. *5 Readers Reading.* New Haven: Yale University Press, 1975.

Hortmann, Wilhelm. "Changing Modes in *Hamlet* Production: Rediscovering Shakespeare after the Iconoclasts." In *Images of Shakespeare* (Proceedings of the International Shakespeare Congress), edited by Werner Habicht, D. J. Palmer, Roger Pringle. Newark: University of Delaware Press, 1986.

Ionesco, Eugène. *Exit the King, The Killer, and Macbett.* Trans. Charles Marowitz and Donald Watson. New York: Grove Press, 1985.

Ioppolo, Grace. *Revising Shakespeare.* Cambridge: Harvard University Press, 1991.

Iser, Wolfgang. *The Act of Reading: A Theory of Aesthetic Response.* Baltimore and London: The Johns Hopkins University Press, 1978.

———. *Prospecting: From Reader Response to Literary Anthropology.* Baltimore: The Johns Hopkins University Press, 1989.

Jameson, Anna. *Characteristics of Women, Moral, Poetical, and Historical.* New York: Wiley and Putnam, 1847.

Jameson, Fredric. "Periodizing the 60s." In *The 60s Without Apology*, edited by Sohnya Sayres, Anders Stephanson, Stanley Aronowitz, Fredric Jameson. Minneapolis: University of Minnesota Press, 1984.

Jong, Erica. *Serenissima.* New York: Dell Publishing, 1987.

Josipovici, Gabriel. "A Changeable Report." In *Shakespeare Stories*, edited by Giles Gordon. London: Hamish Hamilton, 1982.

Joyce, Elizabeth. "From Prince to Punk: Student Reception and the English Hamlet of the Mid-Century." *New Comparison* 2 (Autumn, 1986): 31–41.

Kahn, Coppelia. "The Absent Mother in *King Lear*." In *Rewriting the Renaissance: The Discourses of Sexual Difference in Early Modern Europe*, edited by Margaret W. Ferguson, Maureen Quilligan, and Nancy J. Vickers. Chicago: University of Chicago Press, 1986.

Koon, Helene Wickham. *How Shakespeare Won the West: Players and Performances in America's Gold Rush—1849–65.* Jefferson, NC: McFarland, 1989.

Kott, Jan. *The Bottom Translation.* Evanston, IL: Northwestern University Press, 1987.

———. *Shakespeare Our Contemporary.* Translated by Boleslaw Taborski. New York: W. W. Norton, 1964.

Lainoff, Seymour. *Ludwig Lewisohn.* Boston: Twayne, 1982.

Lamb, Charles and Mary Lamb. *Lambs' Tales from Shakespeare.* London: Cathay Books, 1985.

Leeming, Glenda. *Wesker the Playwright.* London: Methuen, 1983.

Lelyveld, Toby. *Shylock on the Stage.* Cleveland: Western Reserve University Press, 1960.

Lenz, Carolyn Ruth Smith, Gayle Greene, and Carol Thomas Neely, eds. *The Woman's Part: Feminine Criticism of Shakespeare.* Urbana: University of Illinois Press, 1980.

Levin, Harry. "The Crisis of Interpretation." In *Teaching Literature: What is Needed Now*, edited by James Engell and David Perkins. Cambridge: Harvard University Press, 1988.

Levin, Richard. "Shakespearean Defects and Shakespeareans' Defenses." In *"Bad" Shakespeare*, edited by Maurice Charney. Rutherford, NJ: Fairleigh Dickinson University Press, 1988.

Levine, Lawrence. "William Shakespeare and the American People." *American Historical Review* 89:1 (1984): 34–66.

Lewisohn, Ludwig. *The Last Days of Shylock.* New York: Harper & Bros., 1931.

———. *Up Stream: An American Chronicle.* New York: Boni and Liveright, 1922.

Longhurst, Derek. "Not for all time, but for an Age: an approach to Shakespeare studies." In *Rereading English*, edited by Peter Widdowson. London: Methuen, 1982.

McCormick, Kathleen. "Theory in the Reader: Bleich, Holland, and Beyond." *College English* 47:8: 836–50.

McCrindle, Joseph M., ed. *Behind the Scenes: Theatre and Film Interviews from the Transatlantic Review.* New York: Holt, Rinehart and Winston, 1971.

MacDonald, Ann-Marie. *Goodnight Desdemona (Good Morning Juliet).* Toronto: Coach House Press, 1990.

MacKaye, Percy. *Epoch: The Life of Steele MacKaye, Genius of the Theatre: In Relation to His Times and Contemporaries.* 2 Vols. New York: Boni and Liveright, 1927. Reprint. Scholarly Press, 1969.

———. *The Mystery of Hamlet, King of Denmark, or, What We Will.* New York: Bond, Wheelwright Co., 1950.

———. *The Playhouse and the Play and Other Addresses.* 1909. Reprint. New York: Greenwood Press, 1968.

MacKenzie, Agnes Mure. *The Women in Shakespeare's Plays: A Critical Study from the Dramatic and Psychological Points of View.* Garden City, NY: Doubleday, 1924.

Mahood, M. M. "Introduction." In *The New Cambridge "Merchant of Venice."* Cambridge: Cambridge University Press, 1987.

Margolies, David. "Teaching the handsaw to fly: Shakespeare as a hegemonic instrument." In *The Shakespeare Myth*, edited by Graham Holderness. Manchester: Manchester University Press, 1988.

Marowitz, Charles. "Giving them hell." *Plays and Players* 24:10 (July 1977): 15–17.

———. *The Marowitz Hamlet.* London: The Penguin Press, 1968.

———. *The Marowitz Shakespeare.* New York, London: Marion Boyars, 1978.

———. "Reconstructing Shakespeare or Harlotry in Bardolatry." In *Shakespeare Survey* 40, edited by Stanley Wells. Cambridge: Cambridge University Press, 1988.

———. "Shakespeare Recycled." *Shakespeare Quarterly* 38:4 (Winter, 1987): 467–68.

Marsden, Jean. *The Appropriation of Shakespeare: Post-Renaissance Reconstructions of the Works and the Myth.* New York: St. Martin's Press, 1992.

Maxwell, Baldwin. "Hamlet's Mother." *Shakespeare Quarterly* 15:2 (1964): 235–46.

Miles, Bernard. *Favorite Tales from Shakespeare.* Chicago: Rand McNally, 1976.

Mukerji, Chandra, and Michael Schudson, ed. *Rethinking Popular Culture: Contemporary Perspectives in Cultural Studies.* Berkeley: University of California Press, 1991.

Neely, Carol Thomas. "Epilogue: Remembering Shakespeare, Revising Ourselves." In *Women's Re-Visions of Shakespeare*, edited by Marianne Novy. Urbana: University of Illinois Press, 1990.

Nesbit, Edith. *Twenty Beautiful Stories from Shakespeare* ("Official Text for Members of the The National Junior Shakespeare Club"). Edited and arranged by E. T. Roe. Chicago: D. E. Cunningham & Co. n.d.

Nixon, Rob. "Caribbean and African Appropriations of *The Tempest*." *Critical Inquiry* 13 (Spring, 1987): 557–78.

Novy, Marianne, ed. *Cross-Cultural Performances: More Women's Re-Visions of Shakespeare.* Urbana: University of Illinois Press, 1993.

Overton, Bill. *The Winter's Tale: The Critics Debate.* Atlantic Highlands, NJ: Humanities Press International, 1989.

Page, Malcolm, ed. *File on Stoppard.* London: Methuen, 1986.

Papp, Joseph, with Ted Cornell. *William Shakespeare's 'Naked' Hamlet: A Production Handbook.* London: Macmillan, 1969.

Patterson, Annabel. *Shakespeare and the Popular Voice.* Cambridge: Basil Blackwell, 1989.

Perry, William G. *Forms of Intellectual and Ethical Development in the College Years: A Scheme.* New York: Holt Rinehart and Winston, 1968.

Rabinowitz, Peter. *Before Reading: Narrative Conventions and the Politics of Interpretation.* Ithaca: Cornell University Press, 1987.

Ramamoorthi, P. "Hamlet in Tamil." In *Shakespeare Worldwide: Translation and Adaptation* XI. Tokyo: Ushodo Shoten, Ltd, 1986.

Reid, Donald. "1968 and All That." *Radical History Review* 45 (1989): 145–56.

Reifer, Marcia. "The Constriction of Female Power in *Measure for Measure.*" *Shakespeare Quarterly* 35:2 (Summer, 1984): 157–69.

Renan, Ernest. *Caliban.* Translated by Eleanor Grant Vickery. New York: The Shakespeare Press, 1971.

Richards, I. A. *Practical Criticism.* 1929. Reprint. New York: Harcourt, Brace & World, 1956.

Roberts, Jeanne Addison. "Shakespeare in Washington, DC." *Shakespeare Quarterly* 29:2 (Summer, 1978): 234–38.

Rose, Jane. "*The Tempest:* Its Sources and Adaptations." Typescript.

Roth, Cecil. *History of the Jews in Venice.* 1930. Reprint. New York: Schocken Books, 1975.

———. *The Jews in the Renaissance.* Philadelphia: The Jewish Publication Society of America, 1959.

Rothwell, Kenneth S. and Annabelle Melzer. *Shakespeare on Screen.* New York: Neal-Shulman, 1990.

Rowe, Eleanor. *Hamlet: A Window on Russia.* New York: New York University Press, 1976.

Rutter, Carol, with Sinead Cusack, Paola Dionisotti, Fiona Shaw, Juliet Stevenson and Harriet Walter. *Clamorous Voices: Shakespeare's Women Today.* Edited by Faith Evans. New York: Routledge/Theatre Arts Books, 1989.

Sánchez, Marta E. "Caliban: The New Latin-American Protagonist of *The Tempest.*" *Diacritics* 6 (Spring 1976): 54–61.

Schiff, Ellen. *From Stereotype to Metaphor: The Jew in Contemporary Drama.* Albany: State University of New York Press, 1982.

Schoenbaum, Samuel. *Shakespeare: The Globe & the World.* New York: Folger Shakespeare Library and Oxford University Press, 1979.

Scolnicov, Hanna, and Peter Holland, eds. *The Play out of Context: Transferring Plays from Culture to Culture.* Cambridge: Cambridge University Press, 1989.

Scott, Michael. *Shakespeare and the Modern Dramatist.* London: Macmillan, 1989.

Shaked, Gershon. "The Play: Gateway To Cultural Dialogue." In *The Play out of Context: Transferring Plays from Culture to Culture*, edited by Hanna Scolnicov and Peter Holland. Cambridge: Cambridge University Press, 1989.

"Shakespeare: The Animated Tales: Study Assignments for Students." Westminster, MD: Knopf Books for Young Readers/ Random House Home Video, 1993.

Shakespeare, William. *The Merchant of Venice.* Edited by John Russell Brown. 1955. Reprint. London: Methuen, 1985.

————. New Variorum *The Merchant of Venice*. Edited by H. H. Furness. 1888. Reprint. New York: American Scholar Publ., 1965.

————. *The Merchant of Venice*. Edited by Gamini and Fenella Salgado. London: Longman Group Limited, 1989.

————. *The Riverside Shakespeare*. Edited by G. Blakemore Evans. Boston: Houghton Mifflin, 1974.

Shatzmiller, Joseph. *Shylock Reconsidered: Jews, Moneylending, and Medieval Society*. Berkeley: University of California Press, 1990.

Shaw, George Bernard. *Complete Plays and Prefaces*. 7 vols. New York: Dodd, Mead and Company, 1962.

Shepherd, Simon. "Acting against bardom: some utopian thoughts on workshops." In *Shakespeare in the Changing Curriculum*, edited by Lesley Aers and Nigel Wheale. London and New York: Routledge, 1991.

Sicher, Efraim. "The Jewing of Shylock: Wesker's *The Merchant*." *Modern Language Studies*, 21:2 (Spring 1991): 57–69.

Sinfield, Alan. "Making space: appropriation and confrontation in recent British plays." In *The Shakespeare Myth*, edited by Graham Holderness. Manchester: Manchester University Press, 1988.

————. "Give an account of Shakespeare and Education, showing why you think they are effective. . . ." In *Political Shakespeare: New Essays in Cultural Materialism*, edited by Jonathan Dollimore and Alan Sinfield. Ithaca: Cornell University Press, 1985.

————. "Royal Shakespeare: theatre and the making of ideology." In *Political Shakespeare: New Essays in Cultural Materialism*, edited by Jonathan Dollimore and Alan Sinfield. Ithaca: Cornell University Press, 1985.

Sinsheimer, Hermann. *Shylock: The History of a Character*. New York: Benjamin Blom, 1947.

Slatoff, Walter J. *With Respect to Readers: Dimensions of Literary Response*. Ithaca: Cornell University Press, 1970.

Smiley, Jane. *A Thousand Acres*. New York: Alfred Knopf, 1991.

Smith, Rebecca. "A Heart Cleft in Twain: The Dilemma of Shakespeare's Gertrude." In *The Woman's Part: Feminine Criticism of Shakespeare*, edited by Carolyn Ruth Smith Lenz, Gayle Greene, and Carol Thomas Neely. Urbana: University of Illinois Press, 1980.

Snyder, Susan. "*All's Well That Ends Well* and Shakespeare's Helens: Text and Subtext, Subject and Object." *ELR: Women in the Renaissance II* 18:1 (Winter, 1988): 66–77.

————. "Naming Names in *All's Well That Ends Well*." *Shakespeare Quarterly* 43:3 (Fall, 1992): 265–79.

Stanton, Elizabeth Cady, et al. *The Original Feminist Attack of the Bible*. Intro. by Barbara Welter. 1895, 1898. Reprint. New York: Arno Press, 1974.

Steele, Hunter. *Lord Hamlet's Castle*. London: Andre Deutsch, 1987.

Stevenson, Laura. *Praise and Paradox: Merchants and Craftsmen in Elizabethan Popular Literature*. Cambridge: Cambridge University Press, 1984.

Stonex, Arthur Blivens. "The Usurer in Elizabethan Drama." *PMLA* 31 (1916): 190–210.

Stoppard, Tom. *Rosencrantz and Guildenstern Are Dead.* New York: Grove Press, 1967.

Styan, J. J. *All's Well That Ends Well.* Shakespeare in Performance series. Manchester: Manchester University Press, 1984.

Sulieman, Susan, ed. *The Reader in the Text: Essays on Audience and Interpretation.* Princeton: Princeton University Press, 1980.

Taylor, Gary. *Reinventing Shakespeare: A Cutural History, From the Restoration to the Present.* New York: Weidenfeld and Nicolson, 1989.

Thompson, Ann. "Cymbeline's Other Endings." In *The Appropriation of Shakespeare*, edited by Jean Marsden. New York: St. Martin's Press, 1992.

Tompkins, Jane. *Sensational Designs: The Cultural Work of American Fiction 1790–1860.* New York: Oxford University Press, 1985.

Vaughan, Alden, and Virginia M. Vaughan. *Shakespeare's Caliban: A Cultural History.* Cambridge: Cambridge University Press, 1991.

Vaughan, Virginia M., and Kent Cartwright, eds. *Othello: New Perspectives.* Rutherford, NJ: Fairleigh Dickinson University Press, 1991.

Welles, Orson. *Chimes at Midnight.* Rutgers Films in Print Series. Edited and intro. by Bridget Gellert Lyons. New Brunswick, NJ: Rutgers University Press, 1988.

———. *Orson Welles on Shakespeare.* Edited and intro. by Richard France. New York: Greenwood Press, 1990.

Wells, Henry. "Percy MacKaye's Plays on *Hamlet.*" *Shakespeare Association Bulletin* XXIV (April 1949): 85–90.

Wesker, Arnold. *The Merchant.* Commentary and notes by Glenda Leeming. London: Methuen Student Editions, 1983. Reissued as *Shylock* in *The Journalists/The Wedding Feast/Shylock* (Harmondsworth: Penguin, 1990).

Wesker, Arnold, Simon Trussler, and Glenda Leeming, "A Sense of What Should Follow." *Theatre Quarterly* 7 (Winter 1977–78): 5–24.

Wheeler, Thomas. *The Merchant of Venice: An Annotated Bibliography.* New York: Garland Publishing Inc., 1985.

White, R. S. "The Year's Contributions to Shakespeare Studies: Critical Studies." In *Shakespeare Survey* 43, edited by Stanley Wells. Cambridge: Cambridge University Press, 1991.

Willbern, David. "What is Shakespeare?" In *Shakespeare's Personality*, edited by Norman W. Holland, Sidney Homan, and Bernard J. Paris. Berkeley: University of California Press, 1989.

Wolfson, Susan J. "Explaining to Her Sisters: Mary Lamb's *Tales from Shakespear.*" In *Women's Re-Visions of Shakespeare*, edited by Marianne Novy. Urbana: University of Illinois Press, 1990.

Wyman, Lillie Buffum Chace. *American Chivalry.* Boston: W. B. Clarke Co., 1913.

———. *Gertrude of Denmark: An Interpretive Romance.* Boston: Marshall Jones Company, 1924.

Wyman, Lillie Buffum Chace, and Arthur Crawford Wyman. *Elizabeth Buffum Chace: Her Life and Its Environment.* 2 vols. Boston: W. B. Clarke Co, 1914.

Zabus, Chantel. "A Calibanic Tempest in Anglophone & Francophone New World Writing." *Canadian Literature* 104 (Spring 1985): 35–70.

Index